THE BOSS SITUATION

THE BILLIONAIRE SITUATION SERIES
LYRA PARISH

Copyright © 2025 Lyra Parish
www.lyraparish.com

The Boss Situation
Billionaire Situation Series, #3

Editor: Jovana Shirley
Unforeseen Editing
unforeseenediting.com

Proofreader: Marla Esposito
proofingstyle.com

Cover Design: Bookinit! Designs
bookinitdesigns.com

All rights reserved. No parts of the book may be used or reproduced in any manner without written permission from the author, except for the inclusion of brief quotations in a review. This book is a work of fiction created without the use of AI technology. This book may not be used to train AI models. Names, characters, establishments, organizations, and incidents are either products of the author's imagination or are used fictitiously to give a sense of authenticity. Any resemblance to actual persons, living or dead, events, or locales is entirely coincidental. No part of this book may be used to create, feed, or refine artificial intelligence models for any purpose without written permission from the author.

CONTENT WARNING

While this book is considered a romantic comedy with a dash of suspense, it does include adult content and language not suitable for minors.

For a complete content warning list, please visit: https://lyraparish.com/pages/boss-contentwarning

OFFICIAL PLAYLIST

HUMBLE. - Kendrick Lamar
Toxic - Britney Spears
Look What You Made Me Do - Taylor Swift
BOYTOY - Halle Abadi
Castle - Halsey
Run Me Like a River - Chloe Crimson
Aphrodite - Sam Short
So It Goes… - Taylor Swift
Dirty - KSI
Can't Help Falling in Love - The Chillest
We Go Down Together - Dove Cameron, Khalid
Fade Into You - Mazzy Star
The Only Exception - Paramore
How Does It Feel To Be Forgotten - Selena Gomez, benny blanco
Better Together - Jack Johnson

LISTEN TO THIS PLAYLIST:
https://bit.ly/boss-playlist

This is for phoenixes, the ones who were set on fire by those they once trusted, but managed to rise from the ashes anyway...

Asher Banks is waiting for you, bad girl.

*You know I'm not a bad girl,
but I do bad things with you*

-Taylor Swift, So it Goes

1
ASHER

"Asher," Lauren, my assistant, says from the doorway.

"No good morning or hello?" I blink up at her.

"Why waste time on pleasantries when I don't care?" she replies, entering.

I've known her since I was a kid because she first worked as an executive assistant at my father's financial corporation. When I expanded this marketing firm, I offered Lauren a higher salary, more paid vacation, and a yearly bonus to join me. She put in her two-week notice and dropped my dad without hesitation. After her twenty years of loyal service, no one blamed her, not even my father.

I tell myself I didn't hire her to be nice. She's a bulldog, and no one gets past her, which I need more than a daily ass-kissing. I get that *everywhere* I go.

Lauren is proof that no one gives a shit about my feelings and that the world is cruel. Her sharp tongue serves as a reminder that I have to be tough.

She clears her throat. "I wanted to remind you about your appointment at Bellamore. Seven sharp."

"I haven't forgotten."

This meeting has been on my mind since Harper Alexander, one of the partners at Bellamore, set up an emergency one-on-one meeting with me.

I lean back in my chair, wishing I could fast-forward to Saturday. That night, I'm attending an award ceremony, where I've been nominated for the Cityscape Award. It's prestigious and one of the greatest honors a CEO can receive.

I refocus on the blinking cursor.

To Whom It May Concern:

"You have twenty minutes," Lauren urges. "Ms. Calloway already wants you dead. Arrive late, and you will be."

I remove my fingers from the keys, knowing everyone is aware that Billie Calloway and I have *always* been at each other's throat. Our college rivalry started at eighteen and lasted throughout our entire twenties. Now we're in our thirties, and the dislike is the *only* constant between us.

I breathe out and return my glare to Lauren. "Bellamore is directly across the street. If I finish this email in the next three minutes, I can be in the ice queen's office with ten minutes to spare."

"Remember who used to change your diapers when your father was too busy," she reminds me. "Also, helping them is your *personal* choice. Bellamore isn't on your agenda this year. And let me remind you, *little boy*, you don't have time for anything *extra*. Your schedule is already too full. You are only one person, and you'll burn out if you keep this up. Having no work-life balance destroyed your parents' marriage."

"Luckily, I'm not married," I state. "And just know that I'd rather swallow my fucking tongue than speak to Billie Calloway this morning, but my hands are tied. I have no choice. Understood?"

She nods.

"Now, anything else?" I pick up my cup of coffee and take a sip.

"That's all," she says, moving toward the door.

A second later, it clicks closed, and I watch her cross in front of the glass-windowed wall that separates my office from the pit—the area of cubicles that houses many high-level PR reps and illustrators.

I close my blinds so my employees cannot see me. Gone are the days when I could be alone at the office early. Since Bellamore moved into this building two years ago, someone is always here. It's why security stays on-site around the clock.

Lauren is right about one thing: I am on the verge of burnout, and it fucking sucks. There is no stopping now because when the ball drops, only I can catch it. The success of this business is on my shoulders, and I can't let it fail. I won't. It's my sister's legacy.

I pace several steps behind my desk and stop in front of the wall of windows. The sun has barely risen, and the city is still waking. Directly in front of me is the ice queen's office. Hers faces mine, and it's one of the few reasons I purchased this building. Twenty-six months have passed since I moved the headquarters here, and I've never once witnessed her glance my way.

I might as well be invisible. It's for the absolute best.

Right now, Billie is standing at her desk, wearing her favorite color—soulless black. She's using her hands as she speaks, but her jet-black bob remains in place.

Her fashion company, Bellamore—the one she dreamed up while we were in college together—is located in the building most known as the Crystal Palace. It's nicknamed that because of its clear blue windows and castle-like architecture. The inside looks like it fell from a fairy tale. Bellamore really exploded a year ago, and neither Billie nor Harper, her business partner and best friend, are experienced enough to handle it. They need me. However, Billie is too stubborn to accept my help, solely because it's me.

If Bellamore files for bankruptcy, I'll buy the building and move my firm there. Knowing how much Billie will despise that makes me so fucking happy.

I'll even choose her office as my own since it's twice the size of my current one and she has a fancy conference room tucked in the corner. A devilish smile spreads across my face as I think about it, and I return to my keyboard.

I quickly write and send the unavoidable email I've tried to put together for almost a month.

After locking my screen, I grab my phone and leave the security my office provides.

"Please let me know when you return," Lauren says as I pass the reception desk. "You have a conference call at eight with a high-profile client that I did not reschedule, per your instructions."

"Don't worry. This won't last longer than ten minutes."

She gives me a pointed look.

I hold up my hand. "Trust me, the ice queen's enormous Calloway ego won't handle me being the only person who can save her ass. So, we'll play games until she's so utterly desperate that she'll crawl and beg for my help."

Lauren isn't amused. "This isn't a game."

"I wonder how long it'll take her." I smirk, thinking about it. "Billie will complicate this. It's her MO with everything she does. She's intelligent but an overthinker and overanalyzer. It gets her into trouble and creates executive dysfunction."

"If I didn't know better, I'd say you have a crush," Lauren says, narrowing her eyes at me.

"On the Wednesday Addams of the fashion world? Fuck no. We're just basically the same person. It's how I can predict her moves." Sarcastic laughter escapes me, and I'm offended she'd assume something so ridiculous. "Also, you know I don't date bitches. Especially ones who don't know how to smile."

"Oh, you only hire them then?" Lauren lifts a brow and playfully smiles.

"Good one," I tell her as I enter the elevator with a chuckle. "Bitches get things done and rule the world. Don't get it twisted; I've got mad respect."

"You don't know what you're missing," she says.

I do know what I'm missing—constant attitude and brat behavior. I've known Billie Calloway for over a decade, and I've never seen her genuinely smile. When we met in college, I learned that the valedictorian—the real-life Hermione Granger—must be the most intelligent person in the room, or she'd lose it. I get it; I've lived in the shadows of my highly successful siblings, too, but she overcompensates, to the point of annoyance.

Billie was so used to receiving praise for her brains and beauty that she expected everyone to bow down to her, the diamond princess. When we met, she received zero free passes from me. I knew she was an ice queen the first time we crashed into one another, and I looked into her light-blue eyes.

Ruthless. Intelligent. Bitch.

The female version of Weston and Easton Calloway, all wrapped into one. They were my heroes, and she was unlike any woman I'd ever fucking met, even to this day. So, I pushed her to her limit, and she pushed me to mine. Purposely.

Now we hate each other, and she avoids me like the plague, which is great. I prefer not to be around her. It's better if she keeps her distance.

As soon as I enter Bellamore, I'm greeted by security and given credentials. The building is stunning; the bottom floor is an atrium with beautiful trees that stretch up to forty feet high. A botanical garden and waterfall flow as sunlight streams through the clear windows. Classical music drifts throughout the space where the boutique is located. Shoppers can buy directly from the showroom floor; some pieces are thousands of dollars. Taking a picture in front of the window has become a viral phenomenon. One thing Billie is great at is building community without trying.

It's heaven down here. Hell and Satan are located on the forty-second floor.

I suck in a deep breath, knowing I thrive in the uncomfortable. I settle into it, make peace with it. I become friends with my demons and rule them instead of the other way around. Nothing scares or intimidates me. I laugh at most challenges. But this woman makes me feel it all and stirs something deeply primal inside of me.

Billie is aware of what many call me—the Boogeyman of Business. I can give success and take it away with one marketing campaign. She doesn't care. Nothing impresses her.

I take the elevator, and as soon as I step off, I'm greeted by a cute woman sitting at a moon-shaped desk. The phone rings, and she answers. As I move closer, her brown eyes travel from my head down to my toes. After she finishes eye-fucking me, she grins.

"Good morning," she purrs, covering the mouthpiece.

"Morning. Still determining if it's good or not." I glance at the nameplate sitting on the edge of her desk. "Hannah, I have an appointment with Ms. Alexander and Ms. Calloway at seven."

"Are you *the* Asher Banks?" She blushes.

I nod, realizing my reputation may precede me.

"The pics don't do you justice, Mr. Banks."

"Uh, thanks."

Wonder if Billie and Harper know their secretary is five seconds from asking for my number.

Hannah finishes the phone call, then stands and sashays to Billie's office. She knocks on the door and then cracks it open.

"Your seven o'clock meeting has arrived," Hannah says.

Everything in this waiting area is a distraction and a complete waste of money, from the two-hundred-thousand-dollar pristine white sofa with claw feet to the gaudy chandelier hanging from the ceiling. It might be made from diamonds, considering she's the heiress of Calloway Diamonds. In the center of the room are oddly shaped vases on museum-like tables with lights pointing down on them.

I roll my eyes, knowing I couldn't be friends with someone who decorates their office like this. She's a perfect example of the type of woman I avoid—one who flaunts her wealth because she can.

"Send them in," Billie harshly commands.

She must wake up rude.

I remind myself that I cannot go back and forth with her today, even if she tries to pull me into an argument.

It never fails; our conversation always grows heated, and then, somehow, we're full-blown pissed at one another. The two of us are never on the same page. If I say the sky is blue, she'll say it's purple, even if she knows she's wrong, just to aggravate me more. It's like she gets off on being under my skin, rotting away my flesh. She's like bacteria, and I want to rid myself of *wanting* her. She's a curse to all men. None have ever survived her.

Hannah returns to me and escorts me inside. Billie's light-blue eyes pierce through me, and her signature grimace remains firmly in place.

A smirk touches my lips as she silently rages. I see the fire behind her eyes as the blood boils in her veins. I shouldn't love having this power over her, but I do. It's a reaction that's so personal. It's one of her tells, and it shows me that I'm buried deep under her skin too—just a single glance from me sets her off. That must be the real reason she hates me so much; she can't seem to control herself around me. It's why I hate her.

"Are you fucking kidding me?" she hisses under her breath, as if she can read my thoughts. The words barely escape her lips, but I hear them loud and clear. "No. No way. Hell will have to freeze over."

I want to tell her it has—that's why I'm here—but I'm trying my best to be cordial and professional. It's what my sister, Eden, would have wanted me to do.

"Harper," I say, nodding. "Billie." Her name slips from my mouth like a curse.

A low growl escapes her throat. It's *hot*.

I glare at Harper, knowing this meeting is already over. "Harper, can I speak with you outside?"

My jaw clenches tightly. She promised me Billie would be open to having this discussion. I should've known better. I don't wait for her to stand before I move toward the door.

"Give me one minute," Harper says to Billie.

"Harp"—frustration seeps through Billie's tone—"this is low."

Ah, she's really mad. Good. I'm glad I could ruin her day, like she's currently ruining mine. When she's out of sight, it's easy for me to forget she exists. It's why I've forced myself to be around her lately. It's my own personal hell—a shock therapy of sorts. Eventually, I'll be immune, and *she* won't be able to frustrate me any longer.

I wait in the hallway for Harper, and a few seconds later, she joins me. Harper blinks up at me with kind blue eyes. Her hair is pulled half up, and she looks so much like her older brother, Zane, that it's uncanny.

"You said she'd be aware," I say, lowering my voice.

"I had no other choice. I apologize," Harper states, her voice urgent and tinged with desperation.

"I should go." I glance at the elevator.

"Please, Asher. I know you two don't like each other—"

"It's not about that, Harper. You should never blindside someone if it can be prevented, especially given the dire situation. You're right; I don't like her. She's stubborn and cocky, and she deserves to fail so she can be humbled. However, if my business partner did to me what you did to her, I'd be furious. This is not how progress is made, and she will never be open to a corporate intervention if you continue to approach your issues like this. Communication is key. Do you understand what I'm saying?"

"Yes, but you and I both know she would never agree to see you."

"Why?" I ask.

"You tell me," she says. "I don't know what happened between you two. No one does."

"She doesn't like that I won't kiss her ass," I tell her.

Harper exhales. "And she won't kiss yours. So, we're at a

standstill. Please reconsider. I will owe you big time," she whispers. "Billie will never ask for your help, but it's not beneath me to beg. I know you're the best—there's no doubt about that—and we need you, Ash. Pretty please. It honestly makes you the bigger person for offering."

"I will not waste my time, so know that when she pushes me out that door again, it will be much harder to ever have me return," I state matter-of-factly. "I'm very busy."

"I respect that. Thank you," Harper says, meeting my eyes. "Thank you so much. I promise it will be worth your while in the end."

"Damn. You owe me big, Harp," I say, and I can already predict how this meeting will continue. I can foresee Billie's moves—moves she doesn't even know she'll make.

I glance down at my watch, taking note of the time.

"You're going to earn all the good karma points for this," Harper says, much happier than she should be.

We enter, and I sit in front of Billie.

Over her shoulder is a direct view of my office. The screen saver jumps around on my computer screen. I smirk, knowing it must annoy her, having me as her shadow while she's working. Like at Stanford, I'm always close, watching everything she does.

I meet Billie's gaze, and the tension thickens. She narrows her eyes, and her nostrils flare.

"Why are you still here?" she barks.

"Because you need me," I say, cocky as hell, ready to challenge her. I've been waiting all week for this very moment, knowing exactly what I'll say to her next.

"I need you?" She scoffs, rolling her eyes.

"Badly," I confirm, checking my watch. Two minutes have passed since I arrived. "And I won't help until you ask me."

"You can leave." She points toward the door.

I think the scowl might be permanently etched on her pretty face.

Of course, she refuses the easy option, as I knew she would. I stare at the ice queen, fully aware of how badly she needs me. If she wants to play, we'll go to the extreme. I love strategy games, and she's my favorite one.

"Perfect." I grin widely. "You'll have to beg for my help next time."

This gets under her skin because Billie Calloway begs for no one. However, she will beg for me.

"We can find someone else." She glances at Harper, as if searching for reassurance.

There is no one else but me. I'm the corporate grim reaper. When I help one business, it usually destroys another. With death comes new life and a fresh start.

I lean back slightly in my chair, licking my lips, knowing this is option three. "You'll beg on your knees."

Sarcastic laughter—that I've heard on many occasions—escapes her pouty red lips. "Goodbye, Banks."

With brows raised, I stand and adjust my tie. "I'll have the last laugh, Calloway."

"Asher," Harper whispers urgently, but I don't wait for her this time.

I shut the door and head straight to the elevator. It's too early for the chaos Billie Calloway creates.

When I arrive at the firm, Lauren's brows lift when she sees me. "You're already back?"

"Told you so. It went exactly how I'd predicted."

"What's your next move?" she asks.

I tap my fingers on top of her desk. "Can you have someone deliver one of those thick rolls of paper we use for mapping quarterly marketing strategies?"

"The banner-sized paper?" she asks.

"That's right, and a lot of black markers."

"I'll get right on it." She picks up the phone. "What are you up to?"

"You'll see." I enter my office, moving to my windows to see what the ice queen is up to.

As I approach, I notice Billie staring back at me. I'm shocked, considering this is the first time we've ever acknowledged one another this way. The silent conversation flows between us, and I know she's cursing me under her breath.

What will it be, Ice Queen? What's your next move?

I give her a wave, twinkling my fingers. I see the real her, and she doesn't like that. She flips me off and storms out of her office, her hips swinging.

I can only imagine what's racing through her mind.

If the roles were reversed and she were the only person on the planet who could save my company, would I accept her help? I would because I'd do anything for the success of my firm and my employees.

Billie Calloway will beg, or she'll go bankrupt. Right now, she has everything to lose.

2

BILLIE

I wish I could blame my current bad luck on a curse I picked up from an antique, a planet being in retrograde, or even a broken mirror. I've not crossed paths with a black cat, walked under a ladder, or opened an umbrella indoors. However, my life—personal and professional—sucks. That's putting it lightly.

Unfortunately, I have nothing to blame for my current misfortunes other than myself.

Every action has a consequence. Choose wisely.

It's something my father drilled into me when I was a kid, living in the shadows of my genius brothers. They're nine years older than me. My father was the CEO of Calloway Diamonds for nearly four decades before he retired six months ago.

The Calloway children were educated and raised to run a multibillion-dollar company. When I turned eighteen, I was offered a position working beside my dad with a guaranteed path that would lead me straight to the top. I declined and chose to carve my path forward in the fashion world.

Basically, if I don't solve my company's financial problems immediately, I'll be forced to ask a man for help. The fun part is choosing *which* man.

Eye roll.

There are my identical twin brothers—Easton or Weston.

They're the most powerful men in the world. Easton is the CEO, and Weston is the COO of Calloway Diamonds. Throughout my life, they've always saved their baby sister. I can't allow them to do that this time. I'll be thirty-one soon, and I need to learn how to solve things like this without their help.

Next up is my father.

He *never* wanted me to create Bellamore and hated the idea, because fashion was my mother's passion. I genuinely believe he's always resented my decision to do what I love instead of giving myself to the Calloway crown. Running to him with my tail between my legs would only prove him right, and I cannot give him that satisfaction.

Then there's my mortal enemy—Asher Banks.

Total asshole. Annoying billionaire, trust-fund fuckboy. He's ridiculously attractive with honey-colored brown eyes and dark hair. High cheekbones and a chiseled jaw that's lined with scruff. The man is a sculpture, pure art, and he ruins it anytime he opens his gorgeous mouth. Not to mention, he comes from an extremely influential family. Some believe they're a part of a shadow government because in the financial world, the Banks are pure royalty. Oh, and he's one of the smartest men I've ever regretfully been introduced to.

Hate at first sight. It's the only way to describe how our first meeting went. I stare off into the distance as my vision blurs.

Stanford is magical in the fall when the leaves begin to change. I've always loved the ber *months, and they're upon us now that we're suddenly at the end of August. With my book bag tossed over my shoulder, I turn the hallway's corner and crash into brick. Strong hands grab and steady me, and I look up into light-brown eyes. Kind eyes.*

"Um, hi," he says, smiling. It's the perfect smile too.

"Hi," I tell him, and time feels like it stands still. "You can let go of me now."

"Oh, right. I'm Asher Banks." He moves his hands from my arms, still smiling.

"Ah. I'm Billie Calloway," I say, and his brows rise.

"The diamond princess. You're Weston and Easton's little sister?" he asks.

I nod.

"Great," he mutters.

"Great? You said it like it's not your greatest honor," I tell him.

He scoffs, leaning in. "What they say about you is true."

"Yeah? And what do they say?" I ask, not liking the way my heart races as he challenges me.

"That you're a little miss know-it-all who demands the peasants bow down to her," he says.

"That's utter bullshit," I tell him, growing offended. "You don't know me."

He blinks down at me. "I do though. Stay away from me."

I storm away from him with a groan.

"What the fuck?" I whisper, and immediately pull my phone from my backpack.

BILLIE
You'll never guess who I finally just met.

HARPER
Who?

BILLIE
Asher Banks.

HARPER
Banks? Wow. Royalty, just like the Calloways. And is he as hot as they say he is?

BILLIE
If by hot, you mean asshole, yes. He told me to stay away from him. Why?

The Boss Situation

HARPER

Probably scared of your brothers. They put a target on anyone who dates you.

BILLIE

Too bad I can't divorce them.

HARPER

Too bad I can't marry them. Both of them. Mmm. Twins.

BILLIE

GROSS!!! Anyway, I gotta go. Class is starting soon. Have a great first day.

HARPER

You too! Try to be nice. Smile some. Okay?

BILLIE

I'm good. I need the next four years to fly by so we can start our company!

HARPER

It will! Love ya, bestie! Try not to fall in love with Asher Banks.

BILLIE

Please STFU.

I find a seat in the middle of the room in my Economics class. Just after the professor walks in, Asher enters, and his eyes slide to mine. Our gazes lock, and I don't look away when it grows uncomfortable. He moves down the aisle, taking the seat directly beside me. I smell his cologne—a mixture of mint and cedar.

"Billie," *he whispers.*

"Don't talk to me," *I tell him as my body temperature rises.* "It's best if you pretend I don't exist."

"Cold," *he whispers.* "A fucking ice queen."

I glance over at him, and our eyes meet again. "Don't call me that."

He smirks. "Okay ... Ice Queen."

. . .

If there were a word worse than *hate*, I'd use it to describe how I feel about him, how I've always felt about him.

Unfortunately for me, he owns the *best* marketing firm in the world and is incredible at what he does. The man is strategic and innovative and consistently delivers fresh *go to hell* looks and fuck-offs when we're in the same room. Being around him is infuriating, and don't even get me started on how fucking good he smells—a scent that has always been distinctly him. It's a guilty pleasure, and I'm sure I could find him by smell while blindfolded in a crowd. And I hate that about myself.

Now that Banks is uber-successful, he's become *more* insufferable than he was thirteen years ago, when we attended Stanford together. I didn't think his ego could grow any larger, but I was wrong.

I think I'd rather go bankrupt before I ever dropped to my knees and *begged* for his help. He'd enjoy it too much and not let me live it down for the rest of his miserable existence. Guaranteed.

Oh, and there is one other desperate option—the most desperate of them all—find a temporary fill-in husband and cash in my inheritance. I have billions locked away that I can't access until I'm married. Harper's is locked away until she turns thirty-five. Bellamore, in its current state, won't survive that long.

Right now, my choices are to beg Asher Banks on my knees or find a husband.

After Banks cockily strolled into my office, I'm five hundred miles past *staying positive*.

"Double espresso for Billie," the barista calls out, pulling me from my thoughts.

My heels click on the tiled floor as I go to grab my drink and offer a small smile.

"Good luck, Ms. Calloway," Ellis, the barista, tells me.

He's cute, but he's also a twenty-two-year-old film student. If his age doesn't start with a three, no thanks. I'm not made to be a sugar mama to fuckboys, even if they're sexy.

"Thanks. I could use a lot of luck," I say.

"See you tomorrow, *Ms. Calloway*." Ellis shoots me a flirtatious wink. It's routine for him—something he does each morning.

"Tomorrow," I repeat.

I stop by Roosters Café every day before work and grab a double espresso. I've done this since I purchased the Crystal Palace and moved my headquarters into the glass building that looks like a castle.

I'm married to my job, and I wonder if that's why it's failing. Maybe I'm smothering it. I've always sucked at relationships, especially long-term ones. Let's be honest—short-term ones too. I'm beginning to believe that I'm difficult to be with. I'm the common denominator, and I recognize that.

I'll know when I've finally met my person because they'll want to spend time with me, doing absolutely nothing. They'll challenge me. They'll truly love me for exactly who I am and not expect me to change.

Does Prince Charming exist? *Hell no.*

I remove the lid from my tiny cup and step outside, breathing in fresh air. The sun beams against the sidewalk, lighting the path like it's a yellow brick road. Spring is upon us, which means Harper and I have to nail down the fall fashion line within the next month. Afterward, we'll pitch to merchandisers and make our order for production. We need to triple our baseline orders to survive until next year.

Harper and I can turn the shit show around, can't we?

If she called Banks and somehow convinced him to meet with *me*, knowing how we feel about one another, then she believes our problem is beyond our control. That's the hard reality I'm trying to swallow.

The espresso doesn't help force it down.

Has my best friend given up hope?

Two blocks later, I approach the Crystal Palace. Right across the street is his company: Banks Advertising and Marketing Firm. The gold letters reflect sunlight, making it shine.

I shake my head. He purchased that building as soon as it was posted for sale. It was on the market for less than a day. I'm convinced he did it so I'd see his stupid fucking name in gold every day. It's like he wanted me to have a front-row seat to watch him climb to the top of the business world. Yes, he's *that* petty, and he always has been.

Even at Stanford, he was like my shadow lurking close by. He even changed his schedule several times to match my classes. I had to see his stupid face for four torturous years. It didn't help that he was one of the most liked men on campus. Athletic. He even played soccer on the university team. Then there was me, the girl who spent her weekends studying and designing outfits for Fashion Week and the Met. While he was having fun, fucking random women at frat parties, I was busy building Bellamore in my dorm.

After graduation, I officially asked Harper to partner with me to make our dream legitimate. Our dreams were endless, and now they're ending. It hurts so much.

Our entire lives, we were never given the proper credit for our accomplishments because of who we were. It's why Harper and I created Bellamore. We *are* more than our names or our looks. This company represents our hearts, and it means everything to me. But still, failure looms on the horizon. This is personal for me.

I take the elevator to my office, and as I move down the hallway, no one speaks to me, which I prefer.

I'm an introvert, like my brother Easton, and prefer silence. While Easton and I have a lot in common, I'm closer with Weston. He's the comedic relief, my fun, extroverted brother who always brings out the best in me. Weston is pure sunshine, just like Harper.

The rumor is, I'm unapproachable, and sometimes, it's easier to let people believe whatever they want. And when they finally get the balls to approach me, they realize how wrong they were. I can hold a conversation, and I'm kind to those who deserve my kindness. I might not always smile or go out of my way to be friendly, but it doesn't mean I'm not. Why would I randomly approach someone if I don't want to be approached?

The nicknames are endless too. Last year, an article coined me as the Wednesday Addams of Fashion, and it stuck.

Every picture they captured of me for the next year, I made sure I was wearing black. The styles changed with the season, but the color never did. I leaned so heavily into it that I became an icon. It's been said that I'm the only woman who can make black look great in the spring. The world wanted Miranda from *The Devil Wears Prada*, so I gave it to them.

The badass-bitch persona saves me a lot of headaches. One look, and most people just stop talking. Most sentences need to end a few words earlier anyway.

Before I enter my office, my assistant, Hannah, meets my eyes. "Your eight o'clock is confirmed."

"Thank you," I tell her, closing the door behind me.

When I approach my desk, I look toward Banks's office. Across the glass is a sign taped to his window. I step forward to read it.

<u>**YOU WILL BEG**</u>!!

My mouth falls open. He even underlined it.

I scream at the top of my lungs, unable to control the rage that soars through me. There's nothing I can do about what's in his office. I will have to look at *that* for who knows how long.

"I cannot do this," I mutter, shaking my head.

I pick up the phone and call Harper. Her office is on the opposite side of the building, so I know she hasn't seen it yet.

"Good morning," she singsongs, and I can hear Taylor Swift playing in the background.

"You're listening to *Reputation*?" I ask.

"It's my fight-song album. It motivates me," she says, and I can tell she's smiling. "Anyway, what's up?"

"Can you pretty please come to my office?" I try to stay calm.

"Give me five."

The call ends, and I slam my phone on the base and sit at my desk.

Harper walks in and glances at the window. She immediately tries to hold back laughter. She keeps it in for five seconds before it bursts out of her. She nearly folds over, gasping for air. "He's hilarious."

"It's not funny! I'm *pissed*," I growl out with frustration. "I have a meeting at eight. I cannot have Benjamin Gibson, the editor of *Fashion News*, witnessing that. We need that fall feature." I point back at Banks's office. "This message will have everyone talking."

"No problem," she says, sitting. "Have you reconsidered him? He *could* actually save us."

"I won't beg him," I tell her.

"What if you just tried asking? Nicely?"

"He won't accept anything else, Harp. Not with me. He's trying to humiliate me, like he always does."

She huffs. "This vendetta you two have has to end."

"Impossible," I say between gritted teeth.

"Why? I don't understand it. You can't even tell me why you hate him."

My heart races. "I hate him because he's a dickhead and he treats me like shit. He's humiliated and embarrassed me countless times. He purposely does things to poke at me and drive me insane. He bought that building. Now he has a thirty-foot sign stretched across his office. He claims he's so fucking busy, but he has plenty of time to write a message and hang it. He's an inconsiderate jerk. Do you want me to keep going? Egomaniac. Man-whore. One-upper. He probably kicks puppies for fun and laughs afterward."

Harper laughs. "He's not that bad."

"I know exactly who he is and the mask he wears."

"The one he wears or the one you put on him?"

I glare at her. "When did you become a Banks apologist?"

"Your brothers wouldn't be friends with him if he were awful. They're very careful about who they get close to, Billie. I find it hard to believe he's horrible if he has Easton's and Weston's friendship."

"I'm convinced it's all strategic," I tell her. "My brothers keep the right people around just in case they need them."

"Weston proposed to his current wife at Asher's house." She blinks at me, not buying it. "No way your brother would've felt comfortable doing something like *that* just anywhere. Not to mention, they hang out all the time. They were together twice last week."

My face contorts. "How do you know that?"

"Weston told me. He was the one who suggested I contact Asher. You think no one knows we're struggling, but everyone does. We needed help three months ago, and right now, we're losing time. Don't forget, Lustre approached Asher, and Josh won't stop until you're nothing. He hates you more than Asher ever could. Choose your poison."

Lustre is our number one competitor. They play dirty. Not to mention, the CEO, Josh Lustre, is my ex.

Fuck him too. My shit list is written on a scroll, and it's full of men.

I'm convinced Lustre has access to our designs. What he's launched is slightly different, so I can't sue them, but the color schemes are exact. Lustre produces the clothing faster, releases their line close to ours, and sells it to customers at a cheaper price point. By the time we launch, we look like copycats. He's nothing more than a cheap Bellamore knock-off.

We haven't discovered how he's gaining access. Josh—because it's always a fucking Josh—was a dream at first. He very quickly became a nightmare. With Lustre copying our designs and undercutting us, our market share has dropped significantly this past quarter.

This competition began after I dumped his ass because I'd finally snapped and had enough.

"I will not work with Asher Banks. We can hire someone else to help us with this. Who's number two in the world?"

"If Asher signs with us first, he won't work with Josh. It's a safe move," she says. "Together, they will become supervillains, Billie. We will lose. Asher will not half-ass it. He knows our weaknesses. He will exploit them and ruin us while wearing a smirk."

I place my head on my desk. "I hate them. Knowing they'd work together to destroy me ... I'm fucking *livid*! What choice does this give me? Work with one devil to obliterate another?"

"It's the only option," she says. "I'd love to see Josh get what he has coming. Asher will go *all in* without backing down. Even you know that. Sure, he's a total asshole, but he's also unafraid." Her face softens, and she smiles. "I'd rather have him work for us than against us. He single-handedly raised handfuls of companies from the bottom to the very top."

I turn in my chair and focus on the sign. "We can't afford him."

"We can't afford to lose him to Lustre. A classic example of keeping your friends close and your enemies closer." She stands. "Asher will be at the CEO ball on Saturday. You should make an appearance. Talk to him there."

I glare at her. "I *never* attend."

She grows serious. "You were nominated for the Cityscape Award. It's an honor after everything we've been through. Skipping this year isn't an option. I must be at another event the same night, and Bellamore must be seen. Show Josh we're not backing down and not selling to him."

"Selling to him?" I ask.

Harper comes around my side of the desk and slides the keyboard close to her. She opens a web browser and loads Fashion Network—a site that posts industry news. Front and center is Josh's face. Underneath, it says, *Inside the mind of fashion's hottest trendsetting designer.*

I groan. "Trendsetting designer, my ass. He stole *our* shit."

"I know. It gets worse," she tells me, clicking on the article and scrolling to the bottom. She highlights a direct quote, where he was asked about competition.

"Bellamore is no longer fresh. I know it's not for sale, but I dream of purchasing it and merging it with Lustre. We'd become a superpower then. Considering their designs are so eerily similar, it only makes sense for it to be a sister company. Not to mention, they're struggling. Billie, if you're reading, babe, let's join forces. I miss you and still love you."

I can hear my racing heart pounding in my ears. It's too early to be this upset.

"*I miss you? Still love you?* Fuck him! I cannot believe this is happening," I state, my nostrils flaring. "After everything he did to me? How about *I'm sorry?*"

Harper sits on the edge of my desk, inhaling with her arms crossed over her chest. "That's why we need Asher."

"This is an actual nightmare." I breathe, the weight of despair heavy on my shoulders.

My gaze locks on to her crystal-blue eyes that are almost gray, and I can feel my body tensing, muscle by muscle.

"How long do I have to decide?" I ask, each word laced with urgency as the air around us nearly suffocates me.

"Two weeks, maybe less," she tells me, hopping off my desk. "Basically, the sooner, the better."

3
ASHER

THE NEXT DAY

When I leave my mid-month investor meeting, it's dark outside. I move into my office, and the overhead lights automatically turn on. As I stare across the way, I see Billie in her office, pacing back and forth with her headset attached. Her hands are flailing. I assume whoever she's speaking to is getting the ass-chewing of their life; then again, she has a mad case of resting bitch face, even when she's happy. Billie RBF Calloway—pretty sure it's her middle name.

I cross my arms over my chest, hating how fucking cocky she is in her high-as-heaven heels. Even though she wears black no matter what time of year, the skirts and blouses get shorter the higher the temperatures are.

Just as I'm about to sit at my desk, she turns and stares at me. I point up at the sign.

She clearly mouths, *Go to hell*, before turning around.

Laughter escapes me as I sit at my desk. "Already there, Ice Queen."

Although I cleared my email directly after lunch, over four

hundred wait for me now. I'm too exhausted to reply, so I log off. It's something I'll deal with tomorrow.

I grab my shoulder bag, pack a few files and my laptop, and leave. As I shut my door, I catch a final glimpse of Billie. I thought I was married to my job, but then I moved to this building and saw how hard she works. It's a pity she's failing. She's proof that the number of hours put in each day doesn't always end with results.

On the way out, I say goodbye to security. My driver meets me at the front, and we zoom across the city, avoiding most traffic. Considering it's nearly eight, we travel quickly. When the weather is nice, I walk to work. When I'm mentally exhausted, like right now, I'll have a car drop me off or pick me up.

Relief floods me as the SUV slows in front of my townhouse. I offer a thank you and get out.

Once I'm inside, I drop my laptop in the living room. I go upstairs and change into something more comfortable before heading to Johnny Be Good—the bar on the corner that I frequent. It was one of my sister's favorite places too. We used to have drinks here once a week, and I've kept the tradition going without her.

I sit at the same stool I had the last time Eden and I were together. I drink the same drink too. It's a tradition to have a bourbon on the rocks. The owner, Johnny, stopped asking me for my order a few years ago.

Baseball plays on the TV in the corner, and I'm lost in my head, not thinking about anything. The anniversary of losing my sister is coming up soon—a day I dread. She's been gone for four years, passing at the age of thirty-two. Sometimes, it feels like the accident happened just yesterday; other times, it seems like a lifetime has passed. She left the firm to me in her will, and my only goal has been to build it up to where Eden always envisioned it going—to the very top.

"How's life?" Johnny asks, pulling me from my thoughts. He leans across the bar. His mustache is curled at the ends. The guy is in his late thirties, bought the place from his uncle, and made it a dive bar.

I love it in here. It's everything I'm not.

"Busy," I tell him with a smile, lifting the glass.

A blonde sits on the stool next to me, giving me a smile. "Hi."

"Hi," I say.

"I'm Mel," she says sweetly. "Short for Melody."

"Hello, Mel. I'm Asher."

"Asher," she repeats. "It's very nice to meet you. Can I buy you a drink?" she asks.

Flirty. Attractive. Confident. This woman knows exactly who she is without apology.

"Unfortunately, no. I insist on buying you one. I'm a gentleman."

She grins widely. Perfect teeth. Plump lips. "I won't say no."

Mel orders a cosmo with a wink. "What do you do?"

"Survive," I tell her.

"Oh, you're one of those types—an intellectual. Let me guess. A software bro? Or do you own a start-up?"

"Nope," I admit.

"Are you a struggling artist who's always sad and in his feelings?"

I chuckle. "Do I give off those vibes?"

"It's the scruff."

Laughter spills out. "I didn't realize I signed up to be roasted by a stranger."

"A stranger. For now. Asher, I think I'd like to get to know you."

I turn toward her. "Why?"

"It's your confidence and style. It's sexy."

I shoot down my drink and order another round. "You flatter me."

"I don't waste time. Tell me about yourself," she says.

I take another shot of bourbon. Johnny's pouring extra.

"I'm boring. A total dickhead." I give her a smile, keeping details out of our conversation.

"You're in luck because I actually enjoy dickheads. But I dunno about the boring part. Hmm."

I laugh. "Do you live close by?"

"My sister does. I'm visiting for the next few weeks before I return to Europe. Wanted to welcome spring in the city."

"Spring in New York is an experience. Especially in the park."

"Reading in Central Park is on my to-do list while I'm here."

"What do you do?" I ask.

"Guess," she says.

I create space between us. My eyes slide over her clothing and her style.

"You're an artist. A photographer."

"Close." She laughs. "I'm a tattoo artist."

"You're a tattoo artist? That's cool," I say. "Do you have ink?"

"Yes. But I'd have to privately show you," she says, giving me a wink.

We continue making small talk, never discussing anything too deep.

Too many shots later, and we're drunk.

She leans in. "Take me home with you."

"Really?" I ask, not remembering the last time I had a one-night stand.

We stumble the two blocks to my place, laughing and kissing on our way inside. She pushes me back on the couch. Her lips are on mine, and she straddles me. I'm lost in her touch, in her mouth, growing hard beneath her.

"Who's Billie?" she asks between kisses.

"Excuse me?" I blink up at her, knowing I'm too intoxicated for this. Am I being pranked?

"You called me Billie," she whispers against my lips.

My eyes bolt open, and I pull away from her. "I did?"

"It's okay. Call me whatever you want. I don't care." She shakes her head, unbuttoning my shirt. Her eyes light up as she sees the tattoos splashed across my chest. Seconds later, her mouth returns to mine.

I try to get lost in her taste, in her touch, but I can't.

"I'm sorry. I can't. I can't do this," I say with a sigh.

She sits back on the cushions. "It's fine. So you've got a thing for this guy—no big deal."

I chuckle. "Not a guy."

"Okay," she says. "If you want to have fun later, call me. I'll be in the city for a few more weeks. I'll rock your world, Asher."

"Mel, I'm so sorry." I sigh, frustrated with myself.

"Nah, don't worry about it. I get it. I know what it's like to be in love with someone but trying to forget them."

"That's not what this is," I try to explain as I follow her to the door.

"You're so damn cute," she says, gently kissing me on the cheek.

"Please, let me call you a car," I offer.

She shakes her head. "Nah. I'm just around the corner."

"Okay." I give her a nod.

"I hope to see you around," she says as she walks down the stoop.

I lean against the doorjamb, watching her walk away. Then I see the photographer across the street, snapping photos of me.

"Fuck," I groan, moving back to the couch with a raging hard-on. Now I'm frustrated as fuck with myself and *sick* of Billie Calloway.

The Calloway Curse is true. She's ruining everything!

I walk into work the next morning, whistling, but I'm in a shit mood. I'm trying to use reverse psychology on myself. Can't believe I denied having incredible sex with a cute little blonde. I can't believe Billie's name fell out of my mouth. I'm going insane—I have to be.

After I grab a cup of coffee from the break room, I enter my office.

Seconds later, Nicolas—my brother and partner—enters. He's six years older than me, and he's actually my half-brother, but I didn't know what that meant, growing up. Nicolas Banks is my dad's love child from an affair he had on my mother. It used to bother Nick when we were younger, but now he doesn't give a shit.

"Good morning," he says, his dress shirt sleeves rolled to his elbows. It's barely past seven, and he looks like he's put in a full day of work. "How is it that everything magically works out in your favor? I swear you have a genie in a bottle or something. I was just catching up on the meeting notes from yesterday."

"My intuition about a company is never wrong," I state, smirking, excited about how successful the next quarter will be for the firm.

"I *wish* I had that skill," he admits. "Might save me some heartache."

"Oh, it doesn't work with women. My superpower only extends to businesses that make over six figures."

"Lame," he tells me, glancing at the sign plastered thirty feet across my window. He points at it. "So, about *that*."

"Ah, you noticed." I turn and look at it proudly. "Isn't it great? A twenty-four-hour troll. I honestly should've thought of it sooner."

"Bellamore isn't on our quarterly agenda," Nick says, repeating what Lauren said yesterday. "My stepsister says things didn't go well during your meeting."

"It's gross when you call Harper your stepsister like that. You're nearly forty."

He laughs. "Her dad literally married my mom six months ago; she's my stepsister. What happened when you spoke?"

"Billie doesn't want my help," I say. "That was to be expected.

Why is everyone concerned that I might help Bellamore? Is there something more I should know about her company?"

"No. Bellamore is solid." He meets my eyes. "It's just that the board grows uncomfortable when *you* go off script. You can only handle so much."

"Luckily, I don't need the board's approval when volunteering my time."

"You'd give Billie Calloway a golden ticket to you?" He blinks at me like I'm an idiot. Maybe I am. "If you work with her, even on a volunteer basis, we can't accept Lustre's contract. We'd lose a three-billion-dollar contract, Ash. Have you lost your mind?"

"Don't make me remind you again that this has never been about the money."

He gives me a small smile. "I know. I apologize. Eden would be so damn proud of what you've built. This is what she always wanted, and you made her dream come true."

"Thank you."

Just hearing my older sister's name makes me miss her so fucking much. She was four years older than me, and we were close. The only reason this firm exists is because of her.

"For the record, if I don't work with Lustre, it won't be because of the ice queen. I just haven't fully decided if I can trust Josh yet. I'm having drinks with him soon. If it goes well, then I'll move forward." I point to the sign over my head. "And I'll help him destroy her out of spite."

"You say that without remorse."

"Maybe it's time I give her a real reason to hate me." I pick up my lucky baseball, which I keep on the corner of my desk, and toss it in the air a few times.

"I look forward to watching this play out. One of them will be sacrificed. Which one do you like more?" He stretches his hand, catching it.

Nick tosses it a few times before giving it back.

"You're asking me to compare two different-sized turds. They're both pieces of shit. They're both horrible options. I'd rather not work with either. However, it's a good opportunity for the firm. It could bridge a gap between fashion and advertising in a way that's never been done before. I have some ideas, and whoever I choose will benefit the most," I explain.

He chuckles. "Tonight, I'm meeting Dyson for drinks. Would you like to join us?"

Dyson is our older brother; he's forty-one and the CEO of our family's company, Banks Finance. When my father retired, Dyson took over so the company wouldn't be controlled by someone who wasn't family. It was always supposed to be me, but I decided to continue forward with my sister's legacy and took over her firm. It only took me two years before we were at the top, changing the lives of so many. Thankfully, all the traveling I did in my twenties paid off. I found investors, expanded the business, and used my contacts to forge connections between various industries.

"We'll be at the bar by his house around eight," Nick says.

"I appreciate the invite, but I can't. I have tons of work to catch up on before the end of next week. I'm working from home because of it."

He gives me a pointed look. "Will you ever forgive him?"

"I don't know," I state.

He dated a woman I thought I was in love with. I wasn't. However, it hurt to know that Dyson didn't respect my boundaries. I lost trust in him the day he asked Emma out.

"Do you think we're cursed?" I ask Nick.

"What do you mean?"

"Do you think we're incapable of being in a relationship, just like our father? Look at Dyson. You. Me. The three of us are in the same boat with our relationships. Maybe it's bred into us," I say, throwing the ball into the air.

The conversation isn't that serious; Nick knows how I've felt about this for months. I need more time.

"Look, I've done some shitty things in relationships. Ruined my best friend's soon-to-be wedding. But I'm not a bad person. He isn't either. I think the problem we each have is that we fall hard and fast, and when that happens, we lose our logic. Dad was the same way. Otherwise, I wouldn't be sitting here right now."

I smile. "I'm glad he fucked your mom."

"I'm glad he decided to re-fuck your mom," he tells me with a laugh. "I think it would've been lonely, being an only child."

Nick also has an older half-sister, but she was never around. It was always just us. He was the cool older brother who snowboarded competitively and played hockey professionally. It's how he became best friends with Zane Alexander. Years later, he ruined that brotherhood. To make things even more awkward, they are now officially stepbrothers. He's currently trying to repair their friendship, which is hanging by a thread.

"Just to play devil's advocate, you and Emma had been over for three months when Dyson asked her out," Nick says. "And you weren't supposed to be at that party."

"Hmm. Maybe your stepsister shouldn't have invited me," I tell him. "He knew how I felt about Emma. We'd talked about it in depth. He knew I would've married her."

"I get it." Nick sighs. "But I don't think you were in love. The two of you were much better friends."

I smile. "Maybe I wasn't, but I could see myself falling in love with her. And it felt like a betrayal. He never apologized."

He nods. "That's why you should come tonight. Give him an opportunity."

"Maybe some other time," I say.

"I just don't want you to regret something," Nick tells me.

"He can make the effort if he cares. Now, can we talk about something else?"

Nick's brows crease as he looks behind me. Then he suddenly bursts into laughter. I turn in my seat to see Billie directing someone on a ladder as a sign is hung. It says **ASSHOLE** in big letters with several exclamation points behind it.

I smile, interlocking my fingers together. "Oh, she wants to play."

Billie glances at me, and I wave. She glares and then returns to her desk.

"Little Calloway has spirit. Gotta give her that." His phone buzzes. "Shit, I'm supposed to be in a meeting. I'll catch you later."

"Sure." I give him a nod, turning back to my desktop, trying to push thoughts of her out of my head.

"You think she'll cave?" he asks, moving toward the door.

"Eventually," I tell him. "She loves Bellamore. She'll do whatever it takes to save it."

"Even work with you?"

"Abso-fucking-lutely," I say confidently. "Or I'll make her regret it."

4
BILLIE

TWO DAYS LATER

"Hey, sis," Weston says, pulling me into a side hug outside the restaurant.

"Gucci," I say, running my hand across the lapel of the three-piece suit, feeling the smooth silk on the inside. "Looks very nice."

"Thanks. *You* picked it out," he tells me.

He had a meeting at the office—yes, even on a Saturday—and offered to meet me for lunch so we could catch up.

"Proof I have good taste. I assume Easton is dressed the same?"

He laughs. "Yep. Now that Lexi, Easton's lovely and pregnant wife, is in on the prank, he's *very* confused."

Weston likes to wear the same thing as Easton to drive him nuts. Even though they're forty, Weston enjoys a nice twin joke. Easton, not so much.

I snicker. "That's so wrong."

"Lexi gives me a heads-up if he randomly changes his mind to throw me off. Easton thinks I have sensors hidden in his closet or on his hangers."

"Sometimes, the simplest answer is the best," I tell him. "But Easton will complicate anything."

"Kinda like you," he says, leading the way to our regular table at our favorite Italian restaurant.

Our grandfather—may he rest in peace—loved this place. He said it was the only Italian food that tasted exactly how it had in Italy the first time he visited. This is also where Weston and Easton decided to go their separate ways for college. I was barely nine when they moved away, but they visited me often. They're the best big brothers a girl could have.

Gretchen—one of the servers who's worked here since I was a kid—approaches us with a smile as she sets breadsticks and glasses of ice water before us. "Your usual?" She glances between us.

"Yes, please," Weston and I say in unison.

"Of course," she says before walking away.

"How's being married this time around?" I ask Weston, ripping the paper from my straw and blowing it toward him. It darts into his cheek, and he laughs it off.

He's been on top of the world since he married his secret best friend, Carlee.

My head is still spinning from the revelations I learned about their past. I'm thrilled for him and only a tad jealous that he found the love of his life so quickly after his dirty divorce. Even Easton, who I thought would *never* get married, found his queen. And then there's me, single and still trying to bury my breakup with Josh Lustre.

I ended things with him nearly fifteen months ago. In the fashion world, we were the equivalent of Selena Gomez and Justin Bieber. Everyone said we were a fairy-tale couple, and many still won't accept that Josh and I are over. Forever. We will *never* get back together.

"Part of me never believed life could be like this," Weston admits, pulling me from my thoughts. "Love *actually* exists. Who would've fucking known?"

I give him a smirk. "I'll take your word for it."

There was a time when I believed in love, but not anymore. I trusted Josh. I would've married him. Still, to this day, I don't know how I could've been so stupid when the signs were there. He *never* loved me. He *used* me. He's still using me.

"At your age, I was an unbeliever too. But when you meet *the one*, you'll immediately know. When I looked at Carlee for the very first time, I felt an awakening. Still, to this day, she stirs every emotion inside me, and she's all I can think about. Even right now, she is front and center in my mind. I didn't know what it was like until I had it. Forty-year-old me realizes I've never really experienced love until now. Finally," he whispers, lost in his thoughts, grinning ear to ear.

"Insightful." I give him an exaggerated yawn.

He chuckles. "Don't be a hater."

"Sorry. It's hard for me to feel anything because I'm so anti-relationship right now. I'm scared I might be this way forever. Stunted by heartbreak."

"You'll fall again."

"Actually, I'm good," I tell him. "Thanks though."

"Fine. How's work?" He abruptly changes the subject to another one I'd prefer to avoid.

Usually, when my brothers ask me this question, I play it off as if everything were great. Weston has seen through the facade I built around Bellamore for months. I can't hide it anymore. I'm in over my head—that much I can admit.

Weston watches me as he takes a sip of water.

I suck in a deep breath. "Bellamore's sales have dropped by half. I'm trying to stay calm."

"Do you have a cash flow issue?" he questions. Weston's a genius with numbers.

My heart races. "It's Josh. He's still ripping off our designs and changing his launch dates to cross with ours."

"How is he getting this information?" Weston lowers his voice.

"Not sure. Our designs are created in-house by some of the best illustrators in the world, who have signed exclusivity contracts with us. I hired a private IT firm to audit our computers to ensure we weren't hacked. We weren't. I'm at a loss. I don't know how this keeps happening."

"When did it start?"

"I think it was happening when we were together, but I only noticed it after I left him," I state, shaking my head. "I've heard he still talks about me at parties. He tells everyone he's still in love with me. I'm sick over this."

"Fuck him." Weston seethes. "This is psychological warfare."

I nod. "I know. I don't need you to do anything, Weston. Please do not get involved. I just need your advice because you're obligated to give it to me as my super-intelligent big brother. What would you do?"

"You forgot to mention handsome," he says, interlocking his fingers in front of him. "Hmm, what would I do if I were in your position?"

I brace myself for the bomb he'll drop.

He waits a single beat. "I'd hire Banks."

I glare at him. "Not an option."

Weston shrugs. "Did you know Josh offered Asher a three-billion-dollar contract? Josh knows what Asher is capable of. Do you?"

"I'm not afraid of him," I say between clenched teeth.

"And that will be your downfall, little sis." Weston tilts his head. "You should be very afraid of Asher. He's the Boogeyman of Business. If Josh's goal is to buy Bellamore—"

"For the last fucking time, it's not for sale."

My brother gives me a devilish smirk. "I'm aware. But some assholes in this world believe everything has a price tag. Josh is one of them. So is Asher. So am I. Together, they will ensure you sell before they bankrupt you. When you're desperate, they'll swoop in and buy you out ninety percent below market value, then become the saviors who rescued your failing company, even if they were the ones who had forced you to drown. You're not cutthroat enough for this, Billie. Asher is, especially when he believes in something. Your hatred for each other is more than enough to fuel him. He'd get satisfaction from your downfall, and that alone makes me scared for you and Bellamore."

Our spaghetti and meatballs slide before us, and suddenly, I don't feel hungry. Gretchen sets a stack of napkins on the table's edge and leaves us to our conversation.

I return my attention to Weston. "I don't know why you're friends with someone like Banks."

Weston twirls spaghetti around his fork. "He's a great friend. Trustworthy. Generous. Doesn't have a greedy bone in his body. Asher cares about other people and the environment. He always puts himself last and would give anyone the shirt off his back if they asked. Well, everyone except you. I think he'd let you rot. Plus, he's really fucking fun at parties and to travel with."

"Ugh." I pick up my fork. "I'm sure he is."

The noodles and sauce are steaming hot. I mix them around so they'll cool faster.

"He won't help me unless I beg." I take a small bite. "I refuse to humiliate myself for his entertainment."

My brother bursts into laughter. "He did mention that. Didn't realize he was serious."

"You've got to be kidding me. He's telling people this?"

"Before you get pissed, it was just us and Nick. Last week, I confronted him about the Lustre deal and asked what it'd take for him to work with you instead."

"Please tell me you didn't," I whisper.

"I did, and he knew I hadn't asked on your behalf, but because I was genuinely concerned. Anyway, he said you'd have to beg, and I told him he was being a facetious asshole. I think he knows you'd never do that."

My jaw clenches tightly. "Good. But it hasn't stopped him from posting a thirty-foot sign across his office."

Weston shrugs. "The two of you are so much alike; it's disgusting. Except he's nicer. Laughs more. Enjoys a joke."

I glare at him. "Don't make me add your name to my shit list. There are only a few more available spots."

"Between the two—Asher or Josh—who's listed first?"

I take a sip of water, as my throat feels dry. "Right now, they're sharing the number one spot. Knowing two people I can't stand might join forces feels like a nightmare. Am I the supervillain, or are they?"

"Sometimes, I think it might be you," he says, winking. "Also, Asher shouldn't be beside Josh on your shit list," Weston says between bites. "What happened between you and Josh was personal."

"Banks has been a terror in my life for thirteen years—a decade before Josh and I officially met. He made my life at Stanford hell, and it's never stopped. Trust me when I say, he's more than earned his place at the very top. You know what? Let's forget I mentioned any of this. Thanks for the suggestion." I roll my eyes.

"When you decide you'd like a lesson at Petty University, you know where Easton and I are. We're the masters of petty." He gives me an evil grin.

"I might," I tell him. "Do you think I have a chance at beating them?"

He smiles. "I don't know. We will help you strategize. The three of us are smarter than the two of them, even with Banks's connections."

"And not a tad modest either."

"Why should I be? It's the truth," he says, studying me. "You need a vacation."

I chuckle. "I'd love a vacation. However, there is no rest for the wicked."

Honestly, I'm thankful for the subject change. I'm tired of

having Banks at the center of my conversations this week, and it's primarily because of Josh. He wanted my attention, and now he's got it. They both do.

"Apparently, the house in the Hamptons is ready for guests," Weston says.

"Dad didn't tell me." It used to be my tradition to go up there and escape for a weekend once every quarter.

"Because you haven't been since you broke it off with Josh. Why?"

"I don't want to have this conversation," I say.

"Okay," he says.

While we eat, Weston discusses a surprise art show he's hosting over the summer, featuring Carlee's favorite artists. She won't know until the day it launches, which I find adorable. He's painting special pieces that will be revealed on opening night as a gift to her. Their love is what most of us dream of finding.

"I heard Louis contacted you." Weston changes the subject again. "You cannot afford to get caught up with him, dear sister."

"It's Prince Louis." I glare at my brother, knowing I'm going to murder Harper, considering she's the only person who knows.

"You cannot date him," Weston whispers. "He's a man-whore."

"I can date whoever I want, whenever I want, so drop the scary big-brother shit. That man will one day rule an entire country. He's more than capable of ruling my body. I'd probably have a fiancé by now if it weren't for you. It's getting old, and so am I. I'm almost thirty-one."

"No one will ever be good enough for my baby sister." He wipes his mouth with a napkin, growing annoyed with me. "You deserve only the best. Someone who can match you intellectually."

"It's bad timing for a long-distance relationship, and I explained as much to His Royal Highness. However, he doesn't like to take no for an answer."

"I wonder why. He's spoiled." Weston rolls his eyes. "But when it comes to love, remember, the wrong time is sometimes right." It's what's inscribed on the bottom of my grandfather's watch that Weston wears daily. "Except for when it comes to Josh. Fuck him. It was the wrong time for him."

I chuckle. "Spare me the *I told you so*."

Weston decided he hated Josh within the first five minutes of meeting him. In the end, my brother was right. Weston's great at reading people and their intentions, and he never once trusted Josh, even when I begged him to. It's why whoever I end up with has to have my brothers' blessings, or it's a no-go. They see red flags in people before I do, and will not surround themselves with those who are problems.

After we've eaten too much pasta, we ask for to-go containers. Weston pays, and we stand.

"Did you get the laptop?" I ask, pulling him into a side hug.

"Yes." He squeezes me tighter. "Thank you."

"You're not mad?"

"No," he says with a smile and pulls away. He leads the way toward the exit. "Work with Asher. What he can do for you is worth begging for. Still attending the CEO ball tonight?"

"Yep, after I go home and take a nap," I admit.

"Great. Showing your face publicly is enough to send a message to everyone watching. It tells them you're not backing down or afraid. When someone wants you to disappear, the only option is to shine like a diamond. You're a Calloway. Act like it," he says, smiling as paparazzi snap photos of us leaving the restaurant.

"I'll make you proud," I whisper.

"You already have," he admits.

The flashes continue, and I cover my face, wishing we still had our privacy. "I'll never get used to this."

"You will," he says, squeezing my shoulder. "It's just a matter of time."

"Do not put that curse on me," I snap back.

"See you tonight," he yells over his shoulder, laughing as he walks away.

My driver arrives, and I escape into the back seat of the SUV, thankful to be alone.

Easton and Weston were raised in the limelight, and cameras were constantly shoved in their faces. My parents were more careful with me, and I was barely in the public eye because I was always over sexualized.

I look like my supermodel mother, with the same height and features, and teen magazines took notice of my style. I became the elusive diamond princess and was treated like royalty. My outfits were picked apart, fan clubs were formed, and accounts on social media started doing breakdown hauls of my clothes so others could copy my look. I became a teen icon without trying, which also put a lot of unnecessary scrutiny on me at a young age.

I was quickly given media training and a publicist, even if I wasn't allowed to have social media accounts. I was isolated and lost myself in romance books, academics, and fashion. Harper was my only real friend growing up.

I'd dream about the clothes the princesses and princes wore and started drawing at a young age. My mother wanted me to model, just like her. After a few shows during my teenage years, I knew I wanted to design the clothes, not showcase them. Watching my mother and her beautiful friends walk the runway in glittery dresses only inspired me to create them.

While I was kept in a boarding school away from the world, my brothers—mostly Weston—were splashed across every tabloid worldwide. Walking in the shadows of the diamond princes has always been difficult, but I've managed it gracefully. I was trained to.

Fifteen minutes later, the SUV slows in front of my penthouse. While I have several properties in the city, this is my escape, and it feels most like home. It's full of things I love—from the vintage furniture to the pastel walls and high ceilings. It's not Billionaires' Row or the Park Towers, but I avoid that area as much as possible. I prefer to surround myself with artists and fashionistas who see beauty in things that are often overlooked. Luxury doesn't impress me. Authenticity does.

When I enter, I immediately strip out of my clothes and shower. I stand under the water, washing away the day and the dread creeping up.

I'll be dateless tonight. The tabloids will discuss it tomorrow, especially if Josh has a twenty-something hanging on his arm. My relationship never mattered to anyone until I was with Josh Lustre, and now everyone's concerned about who I'll end up with next.

It'll be a miracle if I don't skip tonight.

5

BILLIE

My hairstylist, April, and celebrity makeup artist, Oliver, arrived ten minutes early. It's known that I'm a stickler for time, especially with people that I pay. Even though they work for me and travel during press tours, I consider them my friends. They're my fairy godmothers and have me fully glammed in less than two hours.

Though my hair is usually styled in a straight bob, April does loose beach waves.

"Girl, you're sexy as hell," Oliver says as he finishes up with a setting spray.

He gently adjusts the tiara on my head. It's one my father gave me on my twenty-first birthday, constructed from the diamonds of one of my grandmother's necklaces.

"Stunning," April says, her hot-pink glasses and matching hair making quite the statement. "The smoky eyes will have men falling in love with you tonight."

"Oh, please do not say that. Love is the *last* thing I need. I'm ready to skip straight to marriage these days," I tell her with a laugh as I guide them toward the door.

They laugh, but I'm not joking. A marriage would give me

access to my inheritance, and then Bellamore would be unstoppable.

"Good luck tonight, sweetie. Hope you win," she says.

"Thanks. Appreciate it." I close the door with a smile, then take one last look at myself in the mirror.

I'm wearing an iconic, vintage black Chanel Haute Couture from the early '90s that fits me perfectly. Anyone who follows and appreciates fashion will drool over this fit. I won it at an auction a few months ago and couldn't find an occasion for it until now. Knowing my mother wore it on the runway in her early twenties made the purchase more special. The fact that I can fit in it is a miracle. The dress is a statement of timeless elegance and craftsmanship that people like Josh Lustre are destroying.

Tonight, my outfit screams *don't fuck with me*. It's a message to whoever needs to hear it, especially Josh and Banks.

My phone dings, letting me know my driver has arrived. I go downstairs and slide inside the limo, cracking open the champagne I requested. It takes me nearly forty-five minutes to arrive at the venue, and I quickly get two glasses in. I'm more relaxed than I was, but I'm still on edge.

Eventually, the car falls in line with the rest of those arriving. Classical music plays as I'm let out of the limo and led onto the red carpet while media outlets take countless photos. The constant flashing causes my heart to race, and I feel myself slowly unraveling.

"Wow," I hear from behind me.

I glance over my shoulder to see Banks staring directly at me.

"You look like you're going to a funeral."

"I hoped it was yours," I state, climbing the stairs that lead inside. My right hand slightly shakes—something that happens when my anxiety increases—and I curl it into a fist.

He catches up, meets my eyes, and glances at my hand. "Everything okay?"

He shouldn't have noticed that.

"Please don't act like you give a shit about me," I say with furrowed brows and keep walking.

As I enter the building, someone calls his name. Thankfully, he stops and chats, leaving me alone.

In public settings, I bury my emotions and dissociate, as my publicist taught me. It was the only way to protect myself from the people's unhealthy obsession with me, and I still use those tactics. I give the general public the Billie Calloway character they created—the ice queen, the Wednesday Addams of fashion, and the diamond princess, all wrapped into one bitchy character who's perfect in every way. Though my hand might shake and my anxiety spikes, the shield of confidence I wear is impenetrable. It's one of my greatest superpowers. My parents and brothers are responsible for that.

After a deep breath, I lock my jaw and raise my chin.

It's showtime.

I enter the foyer and pull my phone from the tiny satchel hanging over my shoulder. I take a photo, not smiling, and send it to Harper.

The room is full of the who's who of business, and no one speaks to me. I prefer it.

Most attendees are rarely self-made. The keys to success were handed to them or purchased, but only a tiny percentage of companies were built from the ground up. This is one reason why I'm highly respected. The same goes for Banks, who inherited his sister's company and turned it from six figures the first year to eight figures the next.

Josh took over his family brand and knows nothing about colors, textures, or patterns. Josh is a puppet who has to steal to make a profit.

HARPER
Wow, you look really HOT.

The Boss Situation

> BILLIE
> My plan is to drink champagne until my alter ego comes out to play. Drunk Billie can handle Banks better.

> HARPER
> Leave Drunk Billie at home. DB is too much!

> BILLIE
> Talking to that man is a job for her. Sober me cannot handle him without raging. Plus, my anxiety has already peaked.

> HARPER
> I'm so sorry. You don't have to do this. We'll think of something else.

> BILLIE
> I have to try.

Before I can type another message, I'm handed a glass of champagne. I snap a picture of myself with it and send it to Harper.

> BILLIE
> I finished a bottle in the limo.

> HARPER
> This won't end well.

> BILLIE
> Have some faith, bestie. Me and my old pal, the bubbly, will solve this.

As my eyes slide across the room, I spot my brothers standing at a high-top table, laughing about something. Weston waves me toward them. I lift my bubbly and smile. I need two more glasses of this before I join the conversation.

"How long will the portal to hell be open?" Banks asks from beside me in a low, gruff voice.

I turn, and my eyes meet his honey-browns. I expect them to be cold and calculating, but somehow, they aren't.

"Why are you talking to me?"

He smirks. "You came here for me."

I scoff. "Please don't flatter yourself. I'm receiving an award."

Banks laughs, grabbing a few quiches from a server walking around with a platter of them. He pops one into his mouth. "You were only nominated. That award is mine. Between you, me, and Josh, I earned it. You're both lazy as fuck, waiting for someone else to save your asses."

"Excuse me?" I grow irritated as my eyes slide from his mouth down to his shoes. Designer. All of it. He has style, and I *hate* him for it. "Don't you have a prostitute to entertain tonight?"

"I heard *you* weren't available. All booked up or something," he says sarcastically.

"Leave me alone, Banks." I gulp down the rest of my champagne and grab another glass, chugging it.

"No," he says. "You don't rule the world, Ice Queen. I do whatever the fuck I want."

"Stop calling me that," I hiss.

"You'd have to cut out my tongue."

"That would be lovely, actually," I tell him as my eyes land on Josh.

He's chatting with Phillip, whose family owns one of the largest cattle ranches in the country. He's known as the playboy cowboy.

Josh's gaze locks on me, and a smirk touches his lips. I turn my back, only to realize I'm facing Banks.

"Ahh, ex-lovers. Some called you the perfect couple—Jo-illie," Banks mocks, nodding at Josh standing thirty feet behind me. "His model girlfriend of the night is cute. Do you find it odd that every woman he's dated after you looks nothing like you?"

My jaw clenches, but he doesn't stop.

"Don't get it twisted. You're drop-dead fucking gorgeous in comparison. Having a twenty-five-year-old wannabe model on his arm after getting dumped by the ice queen is not a flex for him. You were the best he'll ever fucking get. The echelon."

Somehow, Drunk Billie holds it together.

"However, I can't believe you fucked him or kissed that dirty mouth. I always knew you were disgusting, but wow. Low, even for you, Ice Queen." Banks shakes the thought away, then downs a glass of champagne before grabbing another one.

I want to be mad at his words, but I can't. The truth might hurt, but it doesn't make it less true.

"I agree," I tell him, raising my glass and tossing it back.

"Oh, it looks like Joshie is getting *really* fucking jealous that I'm chatting with you. Mmm. That's a surprise actually," Banks says.

"Josh knows exactly how I've always felt about you, trust me," I explain.

"Nah, he's threatened. Wow! I think he may still have it bad for you." His brows crease before he glances back at me. "You must have one of those magical kitties." Banks takes a step forward, removing more space between us. "You think I'm making it up. Go ahead. Take a peek, princess. It's fine to gloat about it. He's the one who fucked up. Not you."

I slowly glance over my shoulder, fake searching for my brothers. Weston meets my eyes, and I wave at him again, and then I see Josh. He's livid, with his jaw clenched tight and nostrils flared. He's glaring at Banks like he wants to fight him, ignoring the woman on his arm. I turn my back to him again.

"You weren't lying," I say, looking up into Banks's light-brown eyes. "I don't understand that reaction."

"You do," he says.

I glare at him. "Josh knows you're the last man on this planet I'd ever be with, along with every single person in this room."

"Ouch," he says, focusing back on Josh. "But you're lying. Your tell always gives you away."

"I do *not* have a tell."

"Ah, you do. You always have. I noticed it within five minutes of meeting you. Wait." He laughs sarcastically. "No one has told you? It's so obvious."

"You're lying," I say. "Have you forgotten who I am?"

"I don't give a shit about that, little Calloway. You *do* have a tell." He glares at me. "Not knowing your weakness is dangerous, Billie. It disrupts the power of negotiation. How have you survived in your industry this long? By being a good person? Unbelievable." He rolls his eyes like he's mocking me.

"This conversation is a perfect example of why I can't fucking stand you. I grow exhausted by the mental gymnastics. And the reason Josh is probably pissed is that he wants to pay you billions and you're busy eye-fucking his competition like you're putting me in a to-go box to have for later."

He bursts into laughter. "I don't eat another man's leftovers, princess. I'm going to pass on Josh Lustre's sloppy as fuck seconds."

"Notice you didn't refute the eye-fucking. You're scared of me," I say, blinking up at him. "You and Josh both are."

He tilts his head and narrows his eyes. "Sweetie, you're acting too cocky, considering you've already hit the iceberg. Right now, you're taking on gallons of water, and you don't realize how much. You're going down with the ship like a stubborn captain. In the end, I hope you keep your dignity. If I take that, I might feel guilty."

"You're not taking me down," I say. My heart doesn't even race when I say it, because I truly believe it. I'm silently thanking the champagne for the confidence boost.

"When carrying that big fat *L* on your back, I'd like you to remember that you ultimately forced me to do this. If it feels personal to you, it's because it fucking is. I hope you lie awake every night and thoughts of me coming for Bellamore haunt you." He gives me his boyish smile, and it's wicked, considering the topic. "The thought of that brings me joy."

"You're an asshole." I glare at him. "You probably already signed the contract."

"Not yet. I was giving you a chance to humble yourself," Banks says, leaning in, twisting a piece of my hair in his fingers, causing my breath to hitch. His voice lowers an entire octave. "I won't work with him if you drop to your knees for me. You have the power to stop this."

My blood pumps faster as the smell of him encapsulates me. I take a step away from him and meet his eyes, lost in him. We're surrounded by crowds of people, but every single one of them fades away when our eyes lock.

I'm almost at a loss for words, but I quickly snap out of it and find them. "The next time you get that close to me again, I will bring *you* to *your* knees. Do you understand? I'm not fucking kidding."

"Wait, are you trashed?" he asks, searching my face. "You actually brought Drunk Billie to the party. She's a *menace*."

"You know what? Kiss my ass," I say, grabbing another glass of champagne. I've lost count of how many I've had now. Whatever number it is, it's not enough to deal with this man.

"Is that what you fantasize about? Having my lips all over you?" he asks under his breath. "A projection?"

"I'd *never* consent to that," I say, pushing the visual out of my head. "Neither would Drunk Billie. Now, kindly return to pretending I don't exist, like before, when you were busy dating my best friends."

He scoffs. "You were jealous."

"Jealous? No," I say. "Why were you jealous when I was with Josh? That a projection?"

His face cracks into a smile. "Your ex is a creep. Are you color blind? Red flags everywhere."

"I seriously can't stand you."

"Great, because once I start working with Josh, you'll see a lot more of me," he warns.

I glance around, not meeting his eyes. "Did someone hear something? Hmm. Pesky breeze."

He smiles. "You should get that tell looked at."

I take a step forward, nostrils flared. "I really can't stand you."

We glare at one another.

"Keep it that way, Ice Queen. Makes my job easier," he states, cockily drinking his champagne.

To anyone watching us from the outside, his sarcastic laughter, smiles, and winks make it seem like we're having a flirty conversation. It's anything but that.

"I'd say it was a pleasure, but ..." My gaze slides from his eyes to his mouth. "It was torture, per usual."

As I walk away, I glance at Banks over my shoulder. His eyes are locked on me, but I can't read the expression on his face as he lifts his glass toward me. I feel like I just won a mini battle. As I glance over, I notice Josh is watching me too. Our eyes meet briefly before I lift my head high and hold back a smile. I cannot deal with the testosterone and mixed signals.

I huff as I meet up with my brothers.

Easton gives me a side hug. "You and Banks looked friendly. Making up?"

"I threatened to kick him in the balls if he ever entered my personal space again."

Weston chuckles just as Carlee and Lexi approach, both with mini quiches in their hands.

"Valentino was made for you," I tell Carlee as she spins for me.

She's wearing an A-line skirt with a studded, fitted bodice that reflects the light. Even though my brothers weren't nominated for any awards tonight, it was vital for them to be present and offer support.

"How are you surviving after the triplet news?" I ask Lexi with a grin.

Two weeks ago, she and Easton held a surprise baby reveal party—a day none of us will forget anytime soon. We learned they were expecting three babies instead of just one, and the shock on their faces was priceless.

"Well, for some reason, I want chocolate cake for *every* meal.

Every single meal. Five layers with fudge icing. I've also been having recurring nightmares, where I'm the next Octomom and reality TV cameras follow me around at home. Each time I wake up, I'm relieved it's a trio instead of eight and that I only get photographed in public." She chuckles, lowering her voice. "And I want to have tons of sex. Like, even right now. How are things with you?"

I burst into laughter. "Sounds like it's going well. As long as you're getting the cake and the sex."

"Shh," Easton says, glaring at me.

I wave him away as Weston steals his attention.

Carlee and Lexi listen to the CliffsNotes version of what's happening with Bellamore, Banks, and Lustre. Their expressions go from happy to confused to angry. The most basic details are given, but they're married to my brothers, so they understand the code.

When I'm finished, they look at me, concerned.

"Do you have a picture of this sign?" Lexi asks.

"Sadly, no. But I'm sure you can search it online. Someone has posted it. Anyone in the surrounding buildings can see it."

"What will you do?" Carlee asks.

"Survive," I tell her. "Just as all the other women who came before me in fashion did. It may be full of pretty dresses, but this is a man's world. I'm just determined to rule it."

Carlee nods. "Wow. I might have to quote you on that when I write the article about how Bellamore took down Lustre and outsmarted Banks's firm. You're going to be a hero."

"Don't flatter me," I say. "But if I outsmart them, you have my permission. The devil's in the details though."

"I've got you," Carlee whispers and grows giddy.

She runs a gossip website called LuxLeaks and is the writer behind it. She is LadyLux. I only discovered it a few weeks ago, when I took her laptop to push her and my brother together. To my surprise, I learned they'd done the same to Lexi and Easton. If fashion isn't the industry for me, maybe I'll go into matchmaking with the two of them.

As I drink my champagne, I realize it no longer has a taste. Drunk Billie has officially arrived. The lights slowly lower and rise—an indicator that the ceremony will begin soon. It's being televised, which makes me more nervous. However, I have a prepared speech, just in case I win, and enough champagne in my body to keep me toasted until the morning.

"Let's get together soon," Lexi offers.

"Can I join you?" Carlee asks.

"The three of us. And Harper," I add with a grin. "I'll plan something."

We hug before going our separate ways. I find my seat in the auditorium, unsure of who will be on either side of me.

Moments later, I smell him. Asher fucking Banks. I turn my head, and our eyes meet as he sits beside me.

"You're kidding me," I mutter, shaking my head.

"Wonder who I pissed off to be sat here," he mutters under his breath just as the lights dim and fade to black.

Everyone focuses on the stage as the opening speech is given. We sit through different skits and performances between awards.

Banks laughs at every dumb joke and is having the time of his life. I'd rather be at home in my bed, watching D-rated slasher films as I reply to the hundreds of emails I haven't read yet.

"And now it's time to present the Cityscape Award," the announcer says. "This is one of the greatest honors any CEO can be given. It's dedicated to someone innovative who continues to move the world forward by focusing on people instead of profits. The nominees are Asher Banks, with Banks's Advertising and Marketing Firm. Asher Banks brought the company from the bottom to the top and is known for discovering the next hottest companies and giving them a chance to succeed."

The camera zooms in on his face.

"Josh Lustre, with Lustre Fashion. Established in 1905 and still the industry leader in fashion."

I look at the screen and hate that he still looks that good. I sigh.

"Billie Calloway, with Bellamore. A corporation that worked its way from the bottom to billions and changed a manufacturing process that helps lessen the environmental impact that fast fashion creates on the world."

I nod at the camera, not smiling.

The woman unfolds the envelope and smiles. "And the Cityscape Award goes to ... Asher Banks."

"Told you so," he leans in and whispers in my ear as the camera zooms in on him and me.

"Fuck off," I cover my mouth and whisper as applause fills the room.

I give him a slow clap, and he shoots me a wink.

The music plays, and Asher makes his way to the front. He *has* worked hard this past year. No one in this room can deny that. Many stop to shake his hand as he moves toward the stage. Eventually, he makes it to the front as the fanfare for him continues.

I'm disappointed I didn't win, but I'm happy Josh isn't the one accepting the award. Between Asher and Josh—as much as it pains me to say this—I'll choose Asher any day of the goddamn week.

6

ASHER

I make my way to the front of the beautiful auditorium. Everyone rises to their feet, offering me a standing ovation as the award is handed over. I'm overwhelmed with emotion as I adjust the microphone. Right now, I'm aware that I'm surrounded by the most successful entrepreneurs on the planet.

"Wow, I'm at a loss for words," I say, choking up, knowing I've crossed an item off my sister's dream-goal list.

The golden-plated cityscape is heavy in my hands. I hold it, and it glimmers in the light.

"It's truly an honor to stand before some of the greatest. Many of you know I don't do this for recognition or money, but to honor my sister, Eden. The firm wouldn't exist today without her vision. She desperately dreamed of helping those who made a positive difference in the world. Eden was the embodiment of *people over profits*. That's now my mission. And I will honor her with everything I do, even if many of you don't understand it at first. Eventually, you will. I've learned to trust the process and enjoy the journey because this might be all we have—this very moment in time."

I meet Billie's eyes across the room, and our gazes lock. I clear my throat, almost losing my train of thought as I glance around the room at my peers.

"Each of us can make a positive impact, even just a small one. Being your Cityscape CEO of the year is something I will forever cherish, but we have more work to do. What imprint will *you* leave when you're gone? What's your legacy? This is your moment of truth. We only get one chance at this, so make it count without regrets. If you want it, be willing to fight for it. Be willing to clap for yourself when no one else will. Work the long hours that no one recognizes but you. In the end, you are all you've ever needed. I believe in you."

The music starts playing, and I know I've used up my time, but I continue, "I'd like to end this with one of my sister's favorite quotes. 'Be yourself; everyone else is already taken.' Thank you all." I hold the award in the air. I place my fingers on my lips, kiss them, then point up. "This is for you, sis. And yes, I'm going to keep being an Ash-hole," I whisper, holding back the emotions that threaten to take over as I mention the nickname she always used for me.

My eyes scan across the room, and everyone smiles widely, clapping, until I get to Billie. I can't read her expression as the room fades to nothing.

I lift the trophy toward her with a nod and a smirk. "I won."

She rolls her eyes.

Typical.

After a few more seconds, I'm escorted off the stage, where I'm greeted with expensive champagne. Media wait in the hallway to get interviews for several business magazines. I stop for a few, being asked the same questions as usual. It's almost as if these interviewers are pulling from the same script.

Instead of heading to the after-party, I text my brother.

ASHER

I'm leaving.

NICK

No prob! Congrats. I saw you won! You did it.

ASHER

We did it. Eden would be so happy!

NICK

She would. I'm proud of you, little brother. I know she is too.

ASHER

Thanks. Means a lot.

I step outside and wait for the SUV to pull around. I get in, and as I buckle, the passenger door opens. My brows knit together when I look into Billie fucking Calloway's cold blue eyes.

"I don't want to deal with you privately," I tell her, knowing she's had too much to drink. I have too. "Get out."

"Absolutely not," she states. "Driver, please continue."

The SUV takes off. Her confidence made him listen.

"What do you want?" I'm rude toward her, giving her the same energy she always gives me.

"After all of that, why would you even consider helping Josh?"

I blink at her. "To fuck you over."

She scoffs. "I'd commit to making your life a living hell until the day I die. You'd become my personal project, Banks."

"Oh, you'd try and *fail*. Just like your business."

Her nostrils flare. She's pissed, as she should be.

"That speech was performative bullshit. Wow! Out of all things, I didn't think you'd be a hypocrite."

"Ouch." I hold my hand over my heart, pretending to be hurt. "For your opinions to fucking matter, I'd have to respect you. And I thought I'd made it clear over the years that I didn't. I have zero respect for you, Billie. Zero."

The vehicle eventually comes to a stop in front of my place.

I unbuckle and turn to her. "I only met with you this week

because I owed someone a favor. You declined. And, holy fuck, thank you *so* much for that. I won't feel any guilt when I burn your company to *ash*. It's the Asher Effect. Glad you get to experience it firsthand." I meet her eyes, trailing down to her lips.

Her mouth slightly parts. "I will *never ever, ever* beg for you, Banks. *Ever.* Not even if my life depended on it. I'd rather rot. Josh has a better chance of me taking him back, and when I say that will never happen either, I mean it."

"I really hope you're prepared to say goodbye to Bellamore." I sarcastically smile at her. "I look forward to burying you so you can rot."

I exit the SUV and slam the door harder than I intended. I move up the steps of my townhouse and unlock the door.

"Banks," Billie yells, climbing out of the vehicle.

I walk inside, closing the door behind me. I lock it and set my beautiful trophy on the mantel.

"Banks! Let me in right now!" she hollers on the other side, pounding against the wood like I just broke up with her.

I roll my eyes as I loosen my tie.

The neighbors on both sides of my townhouse are curmudgeons and will handwrite and leave strongly worded letters in cursive about the things I do that they disapprove of. They're worse than my parents.

I recently threw a party, and I received five handwritten complaints. If I'm watching TV late at night, I get a letter. I once had a half-dead plant on my stoop, and I got a letter. Now, if I hear a random bump in the night, I'm convinced I'll have an envelope tucked under my door in the morning.

"Banks! Seriously!"

I groan, pulling her inside with me, and close the door. She yelps as her body crashes against mine. Billie steps away from me, and her back presses against the cool wood.

We're close, but I cross my arms over my chest.

"What is wrong with you? Seriously? What? What do you want?" I ask, glaring down at her.

Her lips move into a firm line. "I seriously cannot stand you."

"Feeling is more than mutual right now. Now stop acting like an obsessed ex and leave. You're so annoying."

"I'm annoying? You bought the building across the street from mine to troll me. You try to drive me wild and frustrate me. You've had it out for me since college because your little ego was threatened by a woman being smarter than you. Now you've hung a gigantic sign that has everyone in the surrounding buildings talking. Not to mention, you're teaming up with someone who *hurt me*. You have *no idea* what he did to me. And after all that, you dare to call me annoying? Hilarious, Banks!" She takes a step forward, and her finger pokes into my chest. "You're a fucking *asshole*! Nothing has changed. Grow up. We're not eighteen anymore."

"Unbelievable. You come into my home and *try to* insult me," I say, grabbing her wrist.

My thumb is on her pulse, and I can feel her heart rapidly pounding. My gaze pins her in place, and her breath hitches. The meaner I am, the more she responds. Probably because no one has ever treated her with the same disrespect she offers the mere peasants who bow down to her.

"What do you plan to do about it?" she says angrily.

I take a step closer, pinning her against the door, moving her arm above her head. As I lean forward, my mouth hovers an inch over hers. I feel the warmth of her ragged breath on my lips as I lick them. One tiny movement is all it would take to taste the champagne on Billie Calloway's plump lips. Her eyes flutter closed, and I feel her heart still thrumming. But I don't move. I just glare at her.

"Mmm." My voice is a low growl. "You wanted it."

"Gross," she simply says, straightening her stance, and I see that flicker in her eye, the one that exposes her truths.

I lean in and whisper in her ear, "Why is your heart racing?"

"Because you're pissing me off."

"Liar." I breathe out, moving toward the kitchen.

Her back is still pressed against the door. She hasn't moved an inch since I walked away.

"So, that's it?" she asks.

I pull a glass from the cabinet and pour a shot of bourbon. I grab the remote and sit on the couch, kicking off my shoes.

Billie moves in front of the TV as soon as it flicks on.

"We were having a conversation," she says.

"No, *we* weren't. That wasn't a conversation." I glare at her. "Now kindly fuck off. Pretty please, fuck off? I don't know how to nicely ask you to fuck off, but do that immediately. Okay? F-U-C-K O-F-F. What does that spell? Fuuuuuck oooooff!"

"This is how you speak to a lady?"

"You are no lady," I state. "Now leave, little Calloway." I lower my voice. "You're drunk, and you need to go away."

Billie makes a face like she's offended. "You're so disrespectful."

"You wanted a villain, so I'm giving you one. And to think, *this* is just the beginning," I say, purposely being rude as I slam back my drink.

"The beginning of what, exactly?"

"The end."

A few seconds later, a knock rings on the door, and I hear a familiar voice call my name.

"Are you expecting someone?" Billie asks with her jaw locked.

I see something behind her eyes as I stand.

"Jealous?" I ask, moving toward the door.

Sarcastic laughter escapes her. "Absolutely not. I should send the poor girl a pity package. Must be desperate."

"Oh, you mean how Josh was with you?"

Her smile fades.

"Doesn't feel good, does it? You take every dig too, Ice Queen. Don't act innocent. I know you're fucking vicious. Just not vicious enough. I'm immune to your bullshit."

Her eyes don't leave me as I move out of sight. I unlock the door and step to the side as my across-the-street neighbor, Catherine, enters. Once a month, I play golf with her and her husband at one of my father's private clubs.

We're *just* friends. Nothing else. She is very happily married.

"Oh, *hello*," Catherine says when she sees Billie in the living room, where I left her. Catherine turns back to me and waggles her brows as she hands me a bag of food. "Apologies for interrupting. Dinner is served."

"You aren't interrupting anything. This nuisance was on her way out," I say, clenching my jaw. "Weren't you?"

"This conversation isn't over," Billie tells me, and then she moves toward Catherine. "I'm Billie Calloway. He has no manners and doesn't know how to introduce people."

"I'm Catherine. Oh, so you're *the* Billie Calloway?" she asks, grinning, taking her hand. "The diamond princess."

"The infamous," I say, understanding it's a dig. "But these days, Bills here goes by Ice Queen or Wednesday Addams of Fashion."

Billie turns to me. "Go to hell, Banks."

"I'm there anytime you're close to me," I state.

The comebacks just easily roll off my tongue. She makes it too easy.

"It was very nice meeting you, Catherine," she says politely, then walks past me with a groan.

The sweet smell of her perfume lingers in the air as the door snaps shut.

"*Finally!*" I yell, knowing she can hear me.

Catherine turns to me. "*Wow.* You two should date."

"Um, no. We very much hate each other," I explain. "There is no love lost, *trust me*."

She stares at me for a few extra seconds. "That's too bad. I sensed something."

"Yeah, too bad for *her*. Everyone knows I'm a catch," I say with a laugh, realizing she's not the first person this week who has paired me with Billie Calloway. It's maddening.

"That's why you should let me set you up with my sister. I'll have you married in a month."

"I'm good. But thank you for the perfect timing and the food. I didn't think she would ever leave, and I skipped lunch." I untie the plastic bag and pull out the lo mein noodles container and chopsticks.

"It's no problem. You do it for us when we don't want to leave. Oh, I charged it to your account. Murray got a drink to go. He says thanks," she says, moving toward the door. "Have a good night, Asher. You're sure you hate one another?"

"Yes," I tell her.

Paparazzi take pictures of her as she leaves. I send her a quick apology text. I didn't notice if they were out there when Billie left. If they were, I bet she was livid. I wish I could text her to ensure she made it home okay. Considering Billie lives two blocks away, I assume she did, especially with cameras in her face.

As I eat, my phone vibrates. I glance down at the screen and see a photo from Nick. More specifically, a screenshot from one of those anonymous gossip sites.

Blind Item #139

The diamond princess and the cocky billionaire marketer were flirting before the ceremony. After the nepo-baby award ceremony, they were spotted leaving together. He had also been seen leaving her office earlier this week. It's rumored they hate one another, but there's new speculation that they're secretly dating.

LAUGHTER ESCAPES ME AS I REPLY.

> **ASHER**
> Fucking hilarious how well these people will spin a narrative.

> **NICK**
> I wondered.

> **ASHER**
> It was the usual back-and-forth. However, this blind will make her panic. LOL.

> **NICK**
> The LOL makes you a dick.

> **ASHER**
> I know. A relationship rumor wasn't part of the plan, but I might be able to make this work to my advantage.

> **NICK**
> My previous statement stands. Total dick!

> **ASHER**
> No denial from me.

> **NICK**
> Apparently, everyone is talking about the two of you. What did you whisper in her ear? And what did she say back?

I think about how her breath hitched and the sweet, flowery smell of her skin.

> **ASHER**
> I told her maybe next time, and she told me to fuck off.

> **NICK**
> Always a competition with you two.

> **ASHER**
> Isn't that the best kind?

NICK

Billie isn't a game.

ASHER

Ah, but she is, and I'll test her limits every chance I get.

NICK

Hmm. Did you hear His Majesty reached out to her? Did she mention that? My stepsis told me.

Prince Louis has had a crush on Billie for at least a decade. The entire world knows it—even she does. However, she resists him like she resists everyone else.

ASHER

We didn't talk about her relationship status. Oh, wait, because I don't give a fuck! I don't care who reaches out to her!

NICK

You sure about that?

I read his text message a few times, my jaw locked tight.

ASHER

Yeah, positive. Anyway, good night.

NICK

Night.

Once I've finished eating, I go upstairs for a shower. I undress and step under the hot stream, closing my eyes and allowing my muscles to relax. As the water falls over me, I think about Billie, with her light-blue eyes and dark hair curled in those waves that perfectly twist around my finger.

Thoughts of her overtake me, and I grow hard.

"Shit," I hiss, grabbing myself, imagining shoving my cock into her smart-ass mouth and down her throat.

I'd fuck her humble.

Billie, my goddamn enemy, my thorn, my poison. When she walks into a room, my cock twitches from her sheer, infuriating presence. Her body is a weapon she wields without mercy—tight, toned, and dripping with the kind of curves that make me lose my fucking mind. Her perfect, fucking perky tits, little pebbled nipples, and that round ass are everything I dream of. I breathe out, caught up in the fantasy.

Those cold, calculating, crystal-blue eyes always mock me and look down on me like I'm nothing. Her lips are full and pouty, and she constantly smirks like she knows exactly what she does to me. She's a goddamn queen of chaos, and I hate her for what she stirs inside of me.

Which is why I'm here, in the shower, my cock in my hand, hard as fucking steel. My fist is wrapped around it like a vise, stroking slow and deliberate, wishing it were her mouth instead. I can almost feel her lips wrapping around my shaft, her tongue swirling around the tip, like she's savoring the taste of me.

Fucking hell, she'd hate it, but she'd also love it so fucking much as she took me in the back of her throat.

I grunt as I continue to stroke and picture her on her knees, her hands bound behind her back, her tits bouncing free.

She glares at me with those icy eyes, but I just laugh.

"You want this, don't you?" I say, thrusting my cock deeper into her mouth.

She wouldn't answer—she couldn't—but I'd know she'd say, *Yes*. Because, in my fantasy, she fucking loves it.

My hand moves faster now, the slick sound of my palm sliding over my shaft filling the bathroom. I'm throbbing, aching for release, but I won't come yet. Not until I've tortured myself with every filthy detail of Billie Calloway.

Fuck.

She's a drug, and I'm high on the thought of her, knowing it's awful for me, but it's the sweetest fucking torture. As it's always been. Just because I want to fuck her stupid doesn't mean I don't hate her. I do. I hate everything about how she makes me feel, knowing it would never fucking work between us.

Billie Calloway is the kind of woman who runs the world. Too strong-willed, hot-tempered, too much like me.

Fuck, I want to make her choke on me until tears stream down her cheeks.

Her nails dig into my thighs as she sucks me deeper, her throat tightening around me as I push past her gag reflex.

Once I have my fill, I flip her over, pressing her against the wall. I demand she put that perfect ass up in the air. I grab a handful of her hair, yanking her head back as I drive myself into her tight little cunt from behind. She screams my name, and I fuck her raw, pounding into her with everything I've got, just like she wants.

She can try to hide it, but her eyes *beg* for me anytime I'm near.

Right now, I wish Billie could feel every inch of me until she pleaded for mercy. But I'd give her none because Billie would never accept help.

The princess always saves herself.

"Who's in control now, huh?" I growl in her ear, my breath hot against her skin as I hold her against me.

She doesn't answer, just whimpers as I slam into her again and again, her body shaking with every thrust.

The fantasy consumes me, and my balls tighten. My cock throbs in my hand, but I stop before I come. Breathlessly, I need more of the fantasy before it vanishes.

I imagine her arching her back, her tits bouncing with every brutal thrust, her pussy tightening around me as she finally gives in to the pleasure.

"Come for me, you filthy slut," I snarl.

And she does. She can't help herself.

With a groan, I finally let the thoughts of her consume me.

Cum shoots out in thick white ropes as I picture it spilling across that scowl of hers.

*She's a mess—*my *mess—and for once, she doesn't have a single smart-ass thing to say.*

I brace myself against the shower wall, my chest heaving as I come down from the high. I gasp for air as the intensity rushes through me. Thoughts of her nearly smother me.

Fuck you, Billie Calloway. Get out of my goddamn head.

She's poison in my veins, and I hate her for it.

7

BILLIE

Paparazzi meet me on Banks's stoop like someone called and told them I was inside.

"Fuck," I whisper, temporarily blinded by the flashes as I take the steps to the sidewalk.

I hold up my hand, blocking my face as I walk past them. Pictures of me leaving his house are the last thing I need circulating, especially if he's working with Josh. I shake my head, pissed.

"Is it true you're dating Asher Banks?"

"Absolutely not," I state.

"But you went home with him?"

"You're aware of what assuming does?" I glare at the guy, and I think he shivers.

I roll my eyes, then walk away, realizing I should've never spoken. Tomorrow, a video of me saying that will be splashed across social media.

I pick up my pace, thankful I only live two blocks away. I didn't realize he was staying there again. Last I heard, he lived in his Upper West Side penthouse, but that was a few years ago. I don't keep up with him because I genuinely don't care. The farther he is from me, the better.

I'm sure he won't stay in this part of the city much longer. He usually avoids me as much as I avoid him. Although that doesn't seem to be the case anymore.

On my walk home, I text Harper, angrier and drunker than I imagined I'd be.

BILLIE
That was a mistake. He kicked me out of his townhouse. Paps were outside, waiting. What if that gets posted? Rumors are the last thing I need.

HARPER
Wait. Back up. You went home with Asher?

BILLIE
Not because he invited me. I forced myself into his car.

HARPER
OMG. Did you burst into his house too?

BILLIE
I pounded on his door, and he opened it.

HARPER
Like an obsessive ex?

BILLIE
Funny, because that's what he said.

I groan, feeling my cheeks heat.

BILLIE
I wanted to talk to him privately, but a woman arrived with food before I could, so I left.

HARPER
Is he seeing someone? Only a girlfriend or a fuck buddy delivers dinner. What did she look like?

> **BILLIE**
>
> Blonde.

She was very pretty and seemed kind. *Blonde. Petite.*

> **HARPER**
>
> Figures. To confirm, you didn't beg?

> **BILLIE**
>
> I won't. We should be able to have adult conversations without that.

> **HARPER**
>
> You and Asher Banks have an adult conversation? NEVER!

> **BILLIE**
>
> That's why working with him will be impossible, Harp. I'm sorry.

> **HARPER**
>
> I vote you bang it out. Don't underestimate the power of the pussy. It can make magic happen, trust me.

> **BILLIE**
>
> Now you're whoring me out to my worst enemy? 😒 Thanks, bestie, but I'm not that desperate yet.

> **HARPER**
>
> I've heard he's huge, like porn-star big. I've heard some call him Asherconda.

I tuck my lips into my mouth when she sends me a snake emoji.

> **BILLIE**
>
> Harper. Shut. The. Fuck. Up!

The last thing I need right now is to imagine Banks's gigantic cock.

HARPER

I've also heard he's very generous in the bedroom.

BILLIE

I'm about to come over to your house and kick your ass. There are billions of people in the world. Banks is the last man on earth I want to think about.

She sends a photo.

It's a screenshot of his Instagram profile.

He's shirtless, tanned skin glowing under the sunlight, standing in neon-green swim trunks and wearing Ray-Bans. He has abs for days with a dark happy trail that leads down to the sack in his shorts and muscular arms that are full of tattoos. The man looks like he was carved from stone.

HARPER

You're broken if you don't think that's hot.

My mouth suddenly goes dry.

BILLIE

I never said he wasn't attractive. His personality ruins it for me.

HARPER

They make mouth gags for a reason.

I laugh out loud.

BILLIE

Or duct tape.

HARPER

There's something between you. A spark. I saw it in your office.

BILLIE

There isn't.

HARPER

You're delusional.

BILLIE

I don't want a love prophecy.

HARPER

I wasn't giving one.

Harper's known for predicting our friends' relationships right before they get married. However, I've told her she can never tell me if I ever set off her Spidey-Sense. I want to fall in love unexpectedly.

Harper sends another photo. This time, Banks is surfing, his board cutting through a wave. Confidence oozes off of him.

HARPER

It wouldn't be the worst rumor to spread around.
What if you leaned into it? He'd never expect you
to do that. No one would.

I read her text message three different times, not sure how to respond.

BILLIE

If we're not out of this by midnight on my birthday,
I'll start my fill-in husband search.

HARPER

That won't be easy. That's next month.

BILLIE

Exactly. I'll start my search.

HARPER

Or you could give Louis a chance.

BILLIE

Prince Louis is an asshole.

HARPER

Just your type. 😊

Most men are intimidated or offended by me. I'm too assertive. Too pretty. Too rude. Too cocky. Too snobby. Too quiet. But still, it hasn't stopped the stalkers I've collected over the years.

Thanks to my dad, I don't care what anyone says about me. It's *their* problem, not mine. I was taught how not to be intimidated by *anyone*.

I'm a man's worst nightmare. I was trained to be ruthless. Josh and Asher are both aware of my upbringing. It will take two of them to destroy me.

Pathetic.

But Harper may be onto something.

BILLIE

Don't stress. We've got this.

HARPER

I know your Mensa mind will devise an infallible plan. You always do.

BILLIE

They'll both regret ever starting shit with me. I will play to the death. Anyway, I just walked into my place. See you on Monday.

HARPER

See you then.

I lock the door behind me and move straight to my bedroom, where I plug in my phone. I slide out of my ball gown and slip between the sheets, pulling the blankets over my head.

Asher's speech plays on repeat in my mind.

"She desperately wanted to help those who wanted to make a positive difference in the world. Eden was the embodiment of people over profits and wanted the good guys to prevail. That's now my mission. And I will

honor her with everything I do, even if many of you don't understand it at first. Eventually, you will."

"That's not fair," I whisper, staring out the tall window of my penthouse bedroom.

Thoughts of him take over, and the sweet torture of it makes me a masochist.

How can Banks sleep at night, knowing he's not keeping his word to his sister? She would never have supported Josh Lustre.

Hypocrite.

I've selflessly given the best years of my life to the fashion industry. I *am* the good "guy," and Banks knows that. He stays up-to-date with the top companies worldwide. If any one person can bridge the gap between a brand being national or global, it's Banks. He's the supervillain.

His sister, Eden, liked me. She would have offered to help me. That's just how she was—pure sunshine. Eden also loved my designs and believed in my vision before we were in the major leagues. Banks hasn't stayed true to what she'd have wanted, and I'll never forgive him.

While I'm having a pity party for one, my phone vibrates.

I stay where I am until the texts become a phone call.

"Leave me alone," I mutter to myself.

When it doesn't stop, I slide out of bed and grab it from the side table. Weston's picture flashes across the screen, and I answer.

"What?" I ask with a groan.

"Wow. What a way to greet your incredibly loving and caring brother."

The background noise is loud. Music plays, and he's surrounded by chatter.

"Rumor has it you're with Banks right now," Weston says.

I roll my eyes. "I'm home, and I'm very much alone."

"Blind item," he mutters.

"What?"

"Photos of you leaving here together were posted." Weston

clears his throat and lowers his voice. "Josh is livid. He thinks you and Asher have something going on. Easton explained that wouldn't happen until hell froze over, unless it has and ..."

"Be serious," I mutter.

"I'm asking," he states. "Tell me the truth."

"You asking is even more ridiculous."

"Is it?" Weston doesn't say anything for a few seconds. "I witnessed the two of you tonight with my eyes, sis."

"So what?" I tell him.

"You ... you had *the look*."

I growl, "That's absolutely preposterous."

"I'd never forgive him if he hurt you," Weston tells me.

"Aw, that's kinda sweet. But trust me, you have nothing to worry about. Wow! You're delusional, and I feel like I'm being gaslit by everyone when it comes to that asshole."

"Yeah, I feel the same because I know what I saw. You're my little sister. I only want the best for you."

"The best isn't Asher Banks, okay?" My thoughts wander.

"You have a type," he says.

I ignore him. "Do you think it's possible the paps were told to be at Banks's? There is no way they'd follow us there."

"You think it was planned?" He stays quiet. "A setup to control the narrative?"

"You've done it for years. Maybe this is part of his plan somehow? Why would he plant seeds of doubt about our relationship status?"

"I don't know. It's a genius plan," Weston says. "I'll find out."

"How?" I ask.

"I'll confront him," Weston tells me.

"Do not do that. Seriously. 'Never interrupt your opponent while he is in the middle of making a mistake.' This could benefit me."

"I'll watch this play out your way then," he says. "You're up to something. Don't make it personal, sis."

"It's too late for that," I mutter.

"Asher might not even work with Josh. He's still contemplating it."

I hear someone call his name, and he covers the phone and mutters something, but it's muffled.

"I gotta go, sis. Read the Blind Item. Okay? I'll be your ears and eyes the rest of the night."

"And no confrontations," I say.

"Agreed," he tells me. "Night."

The call ends. I flick open my web browser and type in the web address of the anonymous website where gossip is posted about the rich and famous. I scan over the last item submitted, and my heart races.

Blind Item #139

The diamond princess and the cocky billionaire marketer were flirting before the ceremony. After the nepo-baby award ceremony, they were spotted leaving together. He had also been seen leaving her office earlier this week. It's rumored they hate one another, but there's new speculation that they're secretly dating.

I take a screenshot and text it to Harper.

BILLIE

Weston said Josh is pissed about this.

HARPER

Yes! This is the best-case scenario. This may buy us some more time.

BILLIE

Harp, people will think we're secretly dating, and then I'll get zero dates. Eyes will be on us. Add the pics the paps got tonight. OMG. This could spiral.

HARPER

Or the world could take notice of how many powerful men truly want you? Asher Banks. Prince Louis. Josh Lustre.

> **BILLIE**
> Do you think Banks planted this story for some reason?

> **HARPER**
> I don't see how it'd benefit him. He really doesn't like you. He just likes to play dirty.

> **BILLIE**
> It's a strategic move. I'm sad I didn't think of it.

Who is smarter? Right now, Banks has me thinking about all of my options. I wonder if I'm playing into his hand.

> **HARPER**
> You need to do something he'd never expect. If your normal answer would be no, maybe you say yes, and vice versa. He's in your head already.

I hate that she's right.

> **BILLIE**
> So annoyed. I should've never gone to his place. I made everything worse. But he doesn't know me that well. Banks only knows my public persona.

> **HARPER**
> Okay, but you have to admit, there has always been a vibe. Like you'd choke each other while you banged.

I swallow hard, and a small smile plays on my lips. It's not something I'd ever admit. The two of us would be too destructive together. We're two tornadoes traveling down the same path. I'm not sure people like us can ever truly find happiness.

> **HARPER**
> I just hope you didn't eye-fuck him, like you usually do.

The Boss Situation

> **BILLIE**
> I do not eye-fuck him, except for when he wears Dior.

HARPER
Mmhmm. That's the only time?

> **BILLIE**
> Why does he have to dress so well? Another reason why I STRONGLY dislike him.

HARPER
Am I speaking to DB? Drunk Billie? Deb?

> **BILLIE**
> I love that you called my drunk personality Deb. I'm going to bed for real. Chat tomorrow. Night.

I lie on my back, staring at the ceiling, feeling my head swim. The champagne has taken over. As I drift off, I stupidly envision honey-colored brown eyes.

MONDAY MORNING

My alarm sounds, and I slide on a black pantsuit with my red fuck-you heels. I paint my lips the same color, brushing down my perfectly cut bob. It's just past seven, and I stop by Roosters and order my double shot of espresso. As soon as I round the corner, paps are waiting for me. They snap photos.

"Hey, Billie! Thanks for what you do," one of them says.

I ignore them, pretending they're not there. I step inside the coffee shop, exhaling. As I take a step forward, I look over broad shoulders and dark, clean-cut hair. Then I smell the faint hint of his cologne. He hasn't noticed me yet, and I know I could sneak out the door, but I refuse to change my routine for him. My headquarters was on this street first.

He orders, and just as he's about to pay, he notices me from his peripheral vision. "Satan, wow. You got another pass to leave hell? Two in a row?"

The barista snickers, batting her eyes toward Asher. I get it. He's attractive. I don't give him the reaction he wants.

"Whatever she wants is on my bill," he tells the cashier.

"No. Not necessary," I tell her, then turn to him. "You're not paying for my coffee."

"I am," he argues, then looks back at the girl behind the counter. "I am."

"Absolutely not," I argue, ready to tap to pay.

"Lady, let him buy you the whole damn store. You're holding up everyone," a guy rudely says behind me.

Banks smirks. "Everyone agrees. Now, please order your double shot of espresso that you drink every single day."

I glare at him, then huff. "I'll have a double shot," I say.

As he pays, I move to the end of the counter to wait for my coffee. He's the last man on earth I wanted to see this morning. Seconds later, Banks stands beside me.

"Why are you so close?" I ask, meeting his eyes.

"Because it makes you squirm."

"You're right. That's what happens when a pest moves into your personal space."

His eyes slide from mine down to my mouth. I hate how sexy he looks as he eye-fucks me from top to bottom.

"Take a picture; it will last longer," I say.

"You're absolutely right. *Great idea*," he says, pulling out his phone.

He leans in and snaps a photo of me and him together. He's smiling wide, and I'm looking at him, confused.

I reach for his phone. "Delete that right away."

"No way, Ice Queen. Putting this on my Instagram now that everyone is matching us."

"You think I did that?" I growl out. "I didn't."

A guy scoots past us and bumps us closer together. His hands are on me, steadying me. I look up into his eyes.

"You should really stop fucking looking at me like that," he mutters.

"Like what?" I hiss. "You're imagining things."

His brows crease. "You're in denial."

"Of what?" I whisper.

"I don't trust you," he snaps. "I never will."

"Black coffee and double espresso for Mr. and Mrs. Banks."

He huffs and grabs his cup, and I reach for mine.

I lean over the counter and meet the barista's eyes. "We are *not* married. That's not funny."

Banks walks away, thankfully, and I wait a minute before I step outside. To my surprise, he's patiently waiting for me. So are the paparazzi.

"You called your friends to join us," he says, pointing toward them. "Funny, they weren't here when I arrived. They're following *you*. I wonder why."

"This narrative about being with you is the last thing I'd ever want. It's what my nightmares are made of." My heels click across the sidewalk as I remove the lid from the cup.

A few seconds later, he's walking beside me. I stop walking, and so does he. We stand in front of one another, and our eyes meet.

"What do you want?" I whisper-hiss, studying him.

His jaw clenches. "You knew exactly what you did last night, getting into my vehicle."

"Explain it to me," I state, trying to walk away from him before he fully encapsulates me and pulls me into his orbit.

He grabs my hand and doesn't let me go. "You knew there would be rumors. You set up the pieces of this game."

I stare at him. "You really believe I did this?"

Something flashes in his eyes.

"What is it? What did you just figure out?" I ask him. "Whose game are we playing?"

"We can't discuss this here," he says, reaching for my hand and interlocking his fingers with mine.

"What do you think you're doing?" I ask under my breath. "Let me go."

He smiles, letting go of my hand and wrapping his arm around my shoulders. He leans in close to my ear. "The great thing about your fucking scowl is that you look the same whether you're having the time of your life or not. No one knows the difference," he says, nearly dragging me into my building.

We walk past security and move inside the elevator, where he lets me go. Banks takes a step away from me.

"Now who's acting like an obsessive ex? Seriously, what has gotten into you?" I glare at him, my back pressed against the wall opposite him.

"If you didn't do this and I didn't, then who did?" He shakes his head. "Relationship rumors are fucking low. Scum-of-the-earth lies. Exactly what a Calloway would do. It worked for your brothers, right? A relationship scandal. I should've known," he mutters.

I try to hold back a smile, but can't as I glance away from him.

"Wow, I think that's the first time I've ever witnessed you smile." He checks his pulse. "Have I fucking died?"

"I've finally found your Achilles' heel," I say, overcome with pure joy.

"Really? Which is?"

I tilt my head at him. "*Me.*"

The elevator doors slide open, and I step out, happy I'm wearing these heels. Right now, I'm dressed to rule the world, but I'm a cutie about it.

Maybe Harper is right, and I can get whatever I want from Banks. Would that make me a bad person if I exploited his personal weakness? Maybe Banks could help me kill two birds with one stone—destroy Lustre and marry me.

I laugh and shake my head. The thought is hysterically ridiculous.

Banks follows behind me, and we go into my office. He shuts the door, moving in front of my desk.

I sit, and he stares at me.

"Do you want me to ruin you?"

"I'll survive anything you throw my way," I tell him confidently. "I always bet on myself."

"I don't think you understand," he says, like a warning.

"I don't think *you* understand. I don't want anything from you. Ever." I meet his eyes. "You're doing this just so you can continue to humiliate me. Haven't you done that enough over the years?"

He acts cocky as fuck. "You hold the power, Ice Queen. Give me what I want. Decisions have to be made."

My lips part. "I'm going to say it for you very slowly, so then maybe you'll be able to comprehend my words. *Not no, but hell no.* I'm not afraid of or intimidated by you. And thank you for confirming I hold all the power. I know I have the ability to get whatever it is I want from you, or Josh, or anyone. You know that too," I explain.

"I will take pleasure in destroying your company and your huge-as-fuck ego. No corporation on the planet is too good for my help, but you're the boss. Good luck, princess. You'll need it."

I stand firm in my decision.

The door swings open, and I glance up.

"Good morning!" Harper says, moving closer and then stopping, glancing between us.

The tension is strangling me as I barely suck in air.

"Uh, did I interrupt something? Are the rumors actually true?"

"No," I tell her, my heart rapidly beating. "Banks was just leaving."

He stands, meeting my eyes. "Humble yourself, little Calloway.

And stop playing dirty before you get in over your head. I invented the game you're playing."

He adjusts his tie, moving toward the door. It clicks closed.

Harper stares at me. "What was that about?"

"He thinks I started the relationship rumors." I shake my head.

Harper's laughter fills the room. "If he didn't and you didn't, who did?"

"I don't know, but when I find out who keeps posting these blind items about my friends and family, I swear I'm going to make their life hell." I twist in my chair, staring at his office, watching his screen saver bounce across his monitor. "I think I've underestimated him."

"And what will you do about it?"

"I haven't decided yet."

8
ASHER

FIVE DAYS LATER

My door swings open, but I don't look up from my screen. My eyes are almost magnetized to it.

"Can I help you?" I continue typing my thoughts before I forget them.

When I glance up, I meet ice-cold eyes. Billie steps forward in those red fuck-me heels and stands beside my desk. I meet her gaze as she gently falls to her knees before me.

"Please. Asher. Please help me save my company. I'm begging you," she whispers, pushing my thighs apart.

Her hands rub my body, and I smile before she fades away.

My phone vibrates, and I lift my head from my desk. A puddle of spit has pooled on the wooden surface. I brush my hand over my face, realizing how exhausted I've been lately. That was a nightmare.

Fuck Billie Calloway!

I can't escape her. She storms through the hallways of my mind, wreaking havoc wherever she goes.

I spin in my seat, realizing it's dark outside. The ice queen is at her desk. Considering her light is the only one on, I assume she's there alone, per usual.

My door opens, and Nick abruptly walks in.

"Oh, good, you're here. Are you still meeting Josh tonight for drinks?"

"Yeah. Need to confirm he's not as bad as I remember."

"And Billie?"

"I'm *not* helping her. I've given her plenty of time, and she hasn't reached out," I say matter-of-factly, stretching. "I gave her two different opportunities, and now I'm bored. I thought maybe I'd shake some things up in the fashion world. Make her fight for it."

"You two should just fuck it out already. How long will you let this go on? Another thirteen years?" he asks, glaring at me.

"Not ever happening," I tell him.

He picks up the baseball on the edge of my desk, tossing it in the air. It's the same ball we used to play with as kids. It's my lucky charm.

"Don't underestimate the Calloways, little brother. Weston *will* help her, and so will Easton. They're called double trouble for a reason. They'll team up with Billie. The three of them together are dangerous. They're not who I'd want to be facing against with Josh Lustre as my partner. *Pfft*. He's an idiot. I'd rather punch myself in the face than have one drink with him." He throws the ball higher. "You're good, Ash, but you won't beat the Calloways. You know that, right?"

"I've planned for them to help her. But it's really not about winning or losing. Just trust me. Okay?"

"I know you don't want to work with Josh. I don't understand, and you won't explain it to me," he says.

"I can't. And don't ask me again." I give him a pointed look.

His face softens. "Do you think Eden would want you working with him?"

"I'm aware of the optics, and I'm okay with it. And the answer is yes. She would have approved of my decisions because she trusted me. People are already talking, and it's great for business. We've been flooded with contracts since the award ceremony a week ago. This is the feud of the decade," I confirm.

"Between who? You and Billie? Or her and Josh?"

"All of the above. Think about it: Billie Calloway's number one enemy teams up with her shitty ex to take her down," I tell him with a laugh.

"She's a warrior princess. Her cult will rise up and stand behind her. If you think the Swifties are sometimes unhinged, you haven't met a Billoway. They're her most faithful followers. Billie can do no wrong in their eyes. They will rise against you," he warns me.

Laughter bubbles up. "I almost forgot her little fan club was called that."

"It's not *little*." Nick isn't smiling. "I understand she's your perfect opponent, but these are billion-dollar corporations you're playing with. You could be adding gasoline to a social media fire that'd be much bigger than what our firm could handle. We don't want anything to do with this PR nightmare."

"Josh has a crisis PR team to manage that. The higher the stakes, the harder the fall. I'm actually really excited about the next quarter. I can't wait." I check my watch, realizing I should be at the bar right now, meeting Josh Lustre. "*Shit*. I gotta go."

"Do not do this," he says, following me to the elevator. "Your name doesn't need to get dragged."

"Look, I've made no decisions. I'm only giving Josh a fair chance. I gave Billie two. Thanks to the Blind Item that someone stupid posted about us, the games have already begun. I can't stop this," I explain.

"Either way, you lose," Nick tells me. "There isn't one scenario where you win this game."

"You're wrong and I can't wait to prove it to you," I tell him as I step into the elevator.

"You're so stubborn. I'm not cleaning up this mess!" he says as the doors slide closed.

After a ten-minute cab ride, I arrive at the tequila bar called Agave. As soon as I enter, I see Josh sitting on a stool at the end of the bar, flirting with the cute bartender.

Her eyes meet mine, and she offers me a smile as I walk closer. "I guess this is the guy of the hour you were just chatting about?"

"That's him. The best in the business," Josh says, grinning and giving me a firm handshake. "Almost thought you were gonna ditch."

"Nah, got caught up at work. You know how it is," I tell him, knowing had I not fallen asleep and had awful fucking nightmares, I'd have been on time. "Apologies."

"No problem at all," he says as I sit next to him.

"What are you having, sweetheart?" the bartender asks, wiping her hands on a spare towel.

"Mmm. Surprise me."

She leans in close. "I have a secret. It's tequila."

I chuckle, looking around the place that serves no other spirits. "I assumed. With salt, please."

A minute later, a double shot of liquid gold is placed in front of me with salt and a lime on the rim. Josh is given one too.

"To success," he says, lifting his glass.

"Absolutely." I down the tequila, and it's as smooth as water. "That's dangerous."

"Yes, it is," the bartender says, winking. "It's my family's brand."

She holds the bottle for me, and I commit the silver logo to memory. "With the right marketing, this stuff could take over. It's fantastic."

She laughs. "I know. It's great. My great-great-grandpa created the recipe."

I tilt my head at her. "So, you've got a story, and it's relatable. You have a family-values angle. What's your name?"

"Caitlyn."

I quickly text my brother.

ASHER

> Caitlyn, the bartender at Agave. Her family owns a tequila brand. Great-great-grandpa created the recipe.

He immediately sends me a thumbs-up emoji. Nick is used to my random texts like this. We have meetings about them at the end of each month.

Josh clears his throat.

I give her a smile. "It was nice chatting, Caitlyn. I'm Asher Banks."

"Asher Banks," she repeats with a smile.

Josh turns to her. "Just keep them coming, sweetheart."

I roll my eyes, giving him the attention he desperately needs right now. Instead of tequila, I should be drinking coffee. The booze makes me ... blunt. It doesn't help that I don't have patience for him—and haven't since he dated Billie so publicly. But I can't hold that against him any longer.

"Have you thought about my proposal?" Josh asks.

"I'm still deciding," I admit. "I read your article in *Businessweek*. Why did you feel the need to mention Bellamore like that?" My patience is at zero already.

"It was the truth. I do want to buy Bellamore. And I know it's not for sale right now. Eventually, it will be, and I want to make the first offer after I bankrupt her." He pauses for a brief moment, looking me over. "I don't know how to ask you this, so I will be direct. Are you fucking Billie?"

"No," I admit. "Considering she's your ex, you know how we feel about one another. Nothing has changed. Actually, I think I might hate her more than I did before."

"Ah, so she still despises you with a passion?" His shoulders relax.

"Still happily at the top of her shit list." I smile. "But let me be clear. If I were fucking her, it'd be none of your goddamn business. You wouldn't control what I did outside of our contract. Period. And you wouldn't begin to test that boundary. I might not be able to work with your competitors, but that doesn't mean I couldn't fuck them on my personal time. *Understood?" Fucking prick.*

"Yeah." His eyes narrow, and the tension grows between us.

This is pathetic.

I clear my throat. "Now, *if* I proceed with a contract, I'd be committed to your corporation. However, I've read your proposal, and I don't give a fuck about the numbers. What is it that you want for Lustre? Not the canned response that everyone expects to hear. And if you don't tell me the truth for the rest of this conversation, I won't work with you. Excuse me for being direct, but I don't have time for pleasantries. The sooner we can cut through the bullshit, the faster we can start working together. I'm not your friend, and I won't pretend to be, even if the tequila is good."

The bartender shoots me a wink and places two more shots down.

"I want to be the industry leader. I also know that as long as Bellamore is around, that won't happen. I need to erase her company's existence or purchase and merge it. Those are the two options."

I stare at him and realize this isn't about Bellamore. It's *personal* with Billie. And, fuck, I'd be lying if I said I didn't get it. It's the only reason I'm here. Billie is infuriating. She needs to be knocked down a few pegs, even if I know she'll rise after it. I will humble her, but I will also make her so much stronger. Now is not the time for her to relax and be complacent.

"And you cannot coexist with her?" I ask. It's a genuine question.

Josh takes a long while to think about it, and I appreciate that he does. It means he's digging deep to give me honest answers.

I won't work with someone who can't be truthful about what it is they want.

"No. I can't." He takes another shot. "I just ... *hate* how she's *still* under my skin. I can't stand how she's *always* on my mind. She haunts me in my dreams, and I wake up enraged because I can't stop thinking about her. I've tried to move on. I've tried to be with other people. And I can't. She broke me, and I wish I'd never met Billie Calloway."

It's then that I realize I'm no different from him. She's done the same to me. We down the tequila, and our glasses tap the bar top at the same time.

He grins widely. "At least we have one thing in common."

"What's that?" I ask, wondering if he can read it on my face.

"Common enemy. For now, at least."

Another round of shots is placed in front of us, and we swallow them down.

"Still dangerous," I say with a smile, referring to the liquid gold.

This brand could be huge in the party scene, especially with summer upon us. It's crisp and refreshing; plus, it has a nice story.

"You know, Billie was the best fuck of my life," Josh says, pulling my attention back to him. He stares off into the distance, as if sliding into their memories together.

Knowing she screwed this guy makes me sick to my fucking stomach. I thought Billie Calloway would have better taste than Josh Lustre. She deserves better than him.

"The way she sucks cock. Those soft moans. Fuck." He sighs.

My jaw clenches tight. Having to visualize it pisses me off.

"That's enough."

It's then I remember exactly why I can't fucking stand Josh. His locker-room talk has always been disgusting. My friends and I don't talk about this shit—*ever*.

The mood sours, and I can't stop thinking about the two of them being together. I think about his hands and mouth on her body. It's absolute fucking torture.

What did she see in this prick? Then a light bulb goes off.

Billie loves a douchebag.

I shake my head, knowing she's probably fucking creaming in her panties over me.

The bartender has been pouring doubles, and I need to cut myself off.

"What happened with you two?" I ask when I can't taste the limes anymore.

He tilts his head at me. "We had our differences and amicably broke up."

"Break it down to me like I'm a five-year-old. I need to know what I'm dealing with because this contract isn't about Bellamore. We both know that. Now, carry on. The truth," I remind him, waiting for him to explain.

Josh hesitates.

"I won't work with you if I don't know." I shrug.

"I cheated on her with the woman I dated before her," he says nonchalantly as chips and salsa are placed in front of us.

My brows furrow, and my jaw clenches tight. "With your ex? That's fucked up."

I can't believe Billie never leaked that to the public. *Why didn't she?*

"It was a huge mistake, and I wanted to work through it, but she couldn't forgive me. If I could go back and change things, I would. I'd marry Billie in a heartbeat," he says, and as sick as it is, I can tell he means it. "Whoever ends up with her, I'll be envious."

"Wait, are we talking about the same person? She's a *bitch*." I pick up my phone and text the bar's address to my driver. I doubt this will last another thirty minutes. Regardless, I'm ready to leave.

"The bitch thing is mostly an act," he tells me, his words slurring. "Her entire public persona is fake. She deserves an Oscar for the performances she consistently puts on. She's soft. Beautiful. Caring. Kind. Funny. Her laughter is like no other." He tilts his head. "I thought you knew her?"

"Oh, I do *know* her. The real her. The sneaky, conniving little smart aleck who doesn't know how to shut the fuck up." I sigh.

"She's also one of the smartest people I've ever met, and you stupidly cheated on her like a dumb fuck. She isn't soft, and a woman scorned is worse than me. People may call me the Boogeyman of Business, but if she hasn't forgiven you, she's not over it, and she will seek her revenge. She could ruin Lustre, Josh. Are you prepared for that? It's personal on both sides." I eat a few chips, needing them to soak up the alcohol.

Of course, Billie wasn't going to beg me to help her. She's up to something, and she doesn't think she needs me. But why? What has she figured out? What other dirt does she have on him?

She's a strategy game that I want to play.

The cheating allegation could be bad. Women don't play with cheaters, and that's his target audience.

"Tell me this. Why are you trying to take down her company if you would have married her?" I ask because I'm curious.

"Truthfully? I'm hoping this will help me win her back," he says, gulping down some water. "She loves an asshole who saves the day, and if I can rescue her company, the villain will become the hero. Bellamore will then be mine, and so will she. Then we'll live happily ever after together, where I'll have full control of everything, including her."

I glare at him, shocked that he'd think Billie would ever submit to him. Some of that woman's grudges are almost old enough to drink. This is the dumbest idea I've ever heard.

"You can't be serious."

He nods, and I have to stop myself from laughing.

"It's the *perfect* plan, and it *will* work, especially with your help. You get to be the bad guy." He pulls his black card from his wallet and clumsily slides it across the bar. "Let us cash out."

The bartender swipes the plastic off the edge.

"Josh, I have to warn you about how dangerous this is. Billie isn't playing a game of love with you. She will go for your jugular. Do you understand? You cheated. What if she tells everyone?"

"I'll deny it."

I laugh. "*No one* will believe you."

"I have the best PR team in the world. Who do you think named her the Wednesday Addams of Fashion?"

I stop myself from giving him a go to hell look. "You did that?"

"Yeah. Of course I did. When you dress like a professional Goth, it's hard to sell florals."

"She leaned into it though. It's a part of her brand now. Her *entire* persona. By pushing her, you made her *more* powerful than she had been. Please tell me you see that she's now an icon for wearing black every day of the year."

"Her profits have dropped by half since last summer. That's almost a year of loss. Doesn't seem that iconic to me," he says, cocky as fuck.

He doesn't understand he's hiking into enemy territory.

"I cannot guarantee your success," I confirm. "You do know that?"

"If I get Billie back, I don't care what happens," he tells me.

I shake my head. "I'm not running a matchmaking service."

"Then help me increase my profits while making her sweat."

I stare at him, realizing just how stupid he actually is. He has no idea who Billie is and what she's capable of. Underestimating her will be his downfall.

I follow him out the door.

"I'll let you know something by Monday morning. Do you have any questions for me?" I check the time, knowing my driver will be here at any minute.

"Great. Nah, man, no questions." He gives me a firm handshake. "Good to know you're not fucking my ex. I'd probably have to kill you."

"Don't you ever threaten me like that again," I say, ready to break his fingers.

"Hey, man, it was a joke," he says.

"I didn't laugh. I'll be in touch," I state just as my car arrives.

The Boss Situation

As I speed away, I lean my head against the seat, and then I text my brother.

ASHER
I'm going to help Josh. End of discussion.

NICK
I hope you don't regret this.

9

BILLIE

TWO DAYS LATER

After I grab my coffee, I make my way to my office. It's impossible for me not to notice the brand-new sign taped across Banks's window.

It's two banners, one stacked on top of the other.

Disrespectfully ...
You lost.

"What the fuck?" I whisper, staring at it with creased brows, wondering how long it took him to write that and then hang it.

My door swings open, and Harper balances her laptop on her arm as she moves toward me. She sets it on my desk and points at the headline. I don't like the expression on her face.

I read it.

Banks Advertising and Marketing Firm signs a multibillion-dollar contract with Lustre.
One billion dollars a month for the next quarter.

There's a picture of Banks and Josh together, smiling, both looking handsome as hell.

"This is a nightmare, right?" I sink into my chair with my hands clasped tightly into fists. "He's actually working with him," I whisper with an exhale.

"Which one are you shocked about? Josh knows how much you hate Asher, so I don't know which one is worse. Asher and you have always hated each other, but you'd think Josh would respect you enough not to work with him."

"He cheated on me, Harper. That man wouldn't know respect if it was tattooed on his forehead. Fuck! This is unbelievable."

Rage soars through me because I didn't think Banks would do this. Since he's friends with my brothers, I thought he'd show me a dash of compassion. Yes, we hate each other, but did we not have a mutual understanding? Assuming that is on me.

Bastard.

"We're screwed," Harper says, shaking her head. Then she sees the sign and screams as she reads it. "We are so fucked! I wish you had a thirteen-year-old vendetta against anyone other than him." Her voice is elevated as she moves around to the front of my desk. "I went to art school. Sometimes, I don't know if I'm cut out for this. I want to draw pretty clothes and play dress-up while making a ton of money. Is that too much to ask?"

"Proof that men ruin everything." I close my eyes, massaging my temples, searching for a solution. Our hole is deep, and I don't know how we'll dig ourselves out, but we will with time. "What are our immediate options?"

She shuts her laptop. "Other than finding you a husband, I'm out of ideas. Maybe we could pitch a new TV series to Hollywood. We'll call it *Dating a Calloway*. By the end of three months, we'll have you a husband and enough money for us to open a second location of Bellamore."

"Finding a husband will be harder than beating Banks and Josh at this. No one wants me, Harper. I scare men away because they're too intimidated."

I roll my head on my neck and dial Hannah's extension. She answers on the first ring. "Please cancel and reschedule my meetings today. Any other time this week is fine."

"Yes, Ms. Calloway," she says, and I end the call.

"You know who's not intimidated by you?" she asks, sitting in front of me.

I meet her eyes, and she glances behind me.

"Yeah, I know. He's so fearless. *So scary*. I'm fucking sick and tired of everyone telling me that. This is our industry, not his. *Ours*. We do it because we love it. Josh does it for the money and power. Even if we were broke as fuck, we'd still design. We'd still make clothes."

"You're right. I just don't want the bad guy to win," she says.

"Josh won't. Not this time," I tell her, growing more determined with every passing second.

"Why did you cancel your meetings?" Harper asks.

"I'm taking a mental health day. I have the urge to drink mimosas and get a deep tissue massage. Maybe a manicure." I look at my nails, which are cut short. It's usually a sign that I'm stressed. "Coffin-shaped ones so I can gouge Banks's eyes out the next time I see him."

Those honey-brown eyes…

She glares at me. "I can't with you. It's the wrong time to be making jokes. This is very serious."

"Oh, I'm not joking. I want to gouge his eyes out," I say with a sigh. "Do you trust me?"

"Yes, of course. And I know you have the best intentions and wouldn't do anything to ruin us. I also know Asher's taken down larger and more established companies than ours. We're at a major disadvantage, and we're barely making a profit. Our empire is on the brink of collapse."

"Then we prepare for war. Ruining them together would bring me so much satisfaction," I admit.

"War?" She lifts her brows.

"Our goal is to survive," I say, looking back at Banks's office.

He's standing, tossing a ball upward, laughing about something as he chats with his half-brother Nick.

"What have you heard from your stepbrother?" I ask Harper.

After her dad married Nick's mother, they became better friends. However, Nick has known Harper for a long time since he was besties with her older brother Zane. The two of them were never strangers.

"He said good luck."

I groan. "Did you know Banks is staying at his townhouse in Midtown? I know he held a party there, but I didn't realize he'd returned."

"He moved back there last summer. I thought you knew."

"I didn't. I must have done something awful in my past life to deserve this."

"Me too," Harper says and bursts into laughter. "I wouldn't want to bankrupt a company with anyone else."

"Me neither," I admit with a smile. "Anyway, I'll let you know what my brothers say."

She exhales. "Okay. Are you stopping by this weekend? Weston is having a get-together on Saturday."

"Really? I wasn't invited."

"He told me this morning in the lobby of Park Towers. Maybe he hasn't gotten around to it yet," she says.

Harper lives there, along with Easton and Lexi, and Weston and Carlee. I have a place there, but I prefer my penthouse loft. It feels more like home, and I'm surrounded by celebrities and musicians instead of the wealthy elite I like to avoid. I grew up around them and know they're not my crowd.

"We can't allow our family to rescue us financially, Billie. That was our agreement when we started Bellamore," she reminds me.

"I know. I just need them to give me some lessons at Petty University. We'll take their advice and execute without anyone's help. It will be the greatest comeback story in fashion history—the things those who come after us will talk about."

She nods. "Okay. I'm on board. If you have hope, I have hope. Don't forget, we have to finalize the fall line very soon. I'll continue forward with the design team. Business as usual?"

I lower my voice. "We have to ensure our upcoming designs don't get leaked before we announce them. If Josh doesn't know what we're doing, we can regain our share of the market he temporarily stole."

"It's not our concept artists. I can promise you that," Harper insists. "They're pissed. No one wants to be plagiarized like that. Lustre doesn't have a creative bone in its body. He continuously changes their release dates to match ours, as if no one notices. Everyone does. At first, it was cute; now, it's just pathetic, desperate behavior. I'm so happy you're not with him anymore."

"And everyone wonders why I have trust issues," I say with a huff. "Going forward, keep everything locked tight. Nothing regarding the line should be discussed over email or by messenger, only in the drawing rooms. I want fake concepts created, something we'd never manufacture. Final drawings and approved concept styles will only be seen by us. You and me only. No more storing things on the cloud. Communication gets locked down immediately."

"Great. You're mega paranoid," she says.

"No. I'm protecting us. It's not a virus, Harp. Our leaks are internal. I want an entire line of fake designs created, ones that are so awful that Josh's team won't touch them. Have marketing create promotional material with specific color palettes for our real designs, but give them nothing else."

She grins wide. "Do you think this will work?"

"It's worth a shot. Banks may be smart, but he's dealing with a literal man-child who doesn't know shit about fashion. My mother modeled when she was pregnant with me, and I was born to do this. This is our world, not theirs. He's been floating from our designs for nearly a year. I'm fucking done and fed up with it. We tighten it up, starting today. And if I ever find out who's responsible for this, I will fire them myself without regret."

"Okay, I can handle that," Harper says. "And you thought you needed lessons on how to be petty."

I move past her. "Weston is a thousand times worse than me. And Easton makes him look soft."

She smiles, and it's the first time I've seen her do that since this started nearly two weeks ago.

"You know, I really didn't think Banks would work with Josh. You know the old saying, *the enemy of my enemy is my friend*? You're now their common denominator."

I give her a small smile, and she follows me out of my office.

"I won't go down without a fight. We've worked too hard over the past decade to let two assholes take this from us. Pity Banks inserted himself, but he's just a distraction. Our real issue is with Lustre. We control what we can."

"I agree," she says as I step onto the elevator.

The doors close, and a few angry tears spill from my eyes. I quickly wipe my cheeks, overly frustrated and exhausted by this. Before I reach the bottom floor, my face returns to stone. While I seem unbothered to the public, I'm livid.

As I leave my building, photographers rush me, and I try to ignore them. My eyes scan across the golden letters for Banks's Advertising and Marketing before I slide into the waiting car.

I never could've predicted any of this would happen.

I just want these dark-haired billionaires to leave me the fuck alone and mind their business. Instead, they're forcing me into a competition I never wanted to join.

As soon as I enter the Calloway Diamonds Corporate office, I'm greeted like I'm royalty. My credentials allow me access to the top floor, where their offices are located.

Weston and Easton's secretary tries to stop me, but I enter Easton's office without pausing.

As soon as I walk in, I realize they're in a meeting.

"Billie?" Weston asks, his jaw clenched. "We're not finished. Ten minutes."

"Apologies," I say, moving back to the waiting room.

Their executive assistant shakes her head. "They're going to be pissed at me now. Thanks a lot."

"I'll make sure you don't get reprimanded. It's an emergency. Weston will understand," I explain.

Right on time, the men in suits exit the office, and I stroll in.

Easton stands with his arms crossed over his broad chest and glares at me. "What the fuck, Billie? You don't just barge into someone's office like that."

"What's going on?" Weston asks.

My brows knit together, and my nostrils flare. "It's an *emergency*."

"What's going on?" Weston asks.

I move to his computer and show him the article that Harper forced me to read before I left the office. Easton moves beside me and reads it.

"Worst-case scenario for you," Easton mutters, breathing out.

"It's not that bad," Weston offers.

"Really?" I ask.

"No, it's *really* fucking bad. I'm just trying to let you down easily." He laughs. "You should be flattered they chose you to fuck around with," Weston says, leaning back in his chair.

"Do I have a chance? Can I survive this?" I ask, glancing between my brothers.

"No," Easton says without hesitation.

I ignore him and focus on Weston.

"I think so."

"I came to claim my big favor," I say to Weston. "The one I earned for stealing Carlee's laptop. Now, let me be very clear. I don't want either of you to bail me out. I have to do this on my own, but you're both cutthroat. Teach me and guide me. Make me their villain."

Weston and Easton look at each other and smile wickedly.

"We'll make you a *monster*," Easton warns. "The way Dad always intended."

"Everyone already believes I'm one anyway. No more playing small," I state. "That's nearly bankrupted me."

"You're ready then," Weston confirms. "Just know that if you play with pigs, you'll get dirty."

"I'm prepared, and so is my publicist," I explain. "Alyssa and I spoke on my way here."

"Great," Easton says, taking a sip of his coffee. "Fill us in on Bellamore and tell us everything about Lustre that you know. Don't leave out a *single* detail."

Weston picks up the phone on the corner of the desk and dials an extension. "Cancel the rest of my and Easton's meetings for the day. Reschedule where you can."

The call ends, and my brothers stare at one another for a brief second, holding a silent conversation before turning to me.

"I'm sorry. You don't have to do that."

Easton shakes his head. "No one messes with our little sister."

"What he said," Weston says with a laugh. "No one."

10

ASHER

I adjust my tie, making sure I look sharp enough for the dinner party at Weston's tonight. It's the place to be this weekend, and only the elite were invited. When I got a last-minute invitation, I was shocked.

I'm on the Calloway family shit list for working with Josh Lustre. Nick thinks the invite might be an olive branch—a gesture to show we can still be friends, and that business is just business. I've been close to the twins for a long time, but I'm not buying that. Everything they do is calculated—it's in their blood, a true Calloway trait. They're so good at playing the game of life that they win without even trying, like chess masters who anticipate every move before it happens.

I know Weston.

I know Easton.

And I sure as hell know Billie.

The Calloways are testing me now. They've been waiting for me to make my move, and I finally did. The three of them are definitely up to something. Tonight could be a setup. They might pull off a media blitz to create the story they want everyone to see. It's totally possible.

My phone buzzes, signaling that my car has arrived. I slip it into my pocket and head out. As we drive away, I pull a flask from my inside pocket and take a sip of whiskey. Skipping tonight isn't an option.

Thirty minutes later, the car stops outside Park Towers, a towering high-rise on Billionaires' Row, filled with fancy penthouses on the higher floors. It has the best view of Central Park in the entire city. Photographers snap nonstop shots of me as I adjust my cuff links. Tomorrow, the media will definitely post pictures of me arriving alone.

When the news broke on Monday that I was helping Josh Lustre, more Blind Items surfaced about Billie and me being seen together. The story quickly turned into me sleeping with her to gather info for Josh. I've officially become a villain made from lies, the kind of character I root against in a movie.

Dealing with dating rumors wasn't part of my plan. The world knows we can't stand each other—a fact that's been splashed across gossip columns like a badge of dishonor. Still, I'll play every card I'm dealt to my advantage, even the wild ones—because in this game, you either play hard or go home.

Let's go, Calloways.

My heart rate is steady as I step onto the elevator, the shiny metal doors sliding shut behind me. Weston assured me multiple times that Billie wouldn't be here due to prior commitments. I just hope I can trust him because I really don't want to run into her. It's best if we keep our distance.

Security greets me in the foyer, which is standard for events like this. I check in, and my name is crossed off a list before I'm allowed into the penthouse.

As I enter, the music from the quartet and pianist fills the air. Chatter floats around the room, all bathed in a warm yellow glow that makes everyone look a little more glamorous than usual.

One thing about Weston: he knows how to throw a party. His penthouse was designed with one goal in mind—entertaining.

Before his first marriage, he hosted wild get-togethers, inviting A-list celebrities, supermodels, and world leaders. What happened at Weston's stayed within these walls. It's always been the code. I hope tonight follows that same tradition.

I'm happy to grab the room's attention as I make my way to the wet bar, weaving through clusters of laughter and clinking glasses. There's no line, and I could use a drink.

A cute bartender with fiery-red hair greets me with a smile as I approach.

"Hi there! Would you like to try our signature cocktail, created just for tonight?" she asks.

"I'd love one," I reply, returning her smile, feeling the buzz of the party.

Less than a minute later, she slides a vibrant blue drink my way, adding a splash of grenadine and a cherry on top.

I take a sip. "Wow, this is fantastic," I say, surprised by the burst of flavor.

"Glad you like it! It's called Revenge," she explains, her eyes sparkling with mischief. "Just because the water is clear doesn't mean sharks aren't lurking."

"Ah," I say, licking my lips, the sweet and sour flavors lingering. "Makes sense."

"I've always heard Revenge is best served cold." She winks just as Easton approaches.

He speaks to me first, clearly aware of the current boundaries. "How's it taste?"

"It's sweet, going down. Highly recommend," I respond with a smirk.

He meets my gaze, his expression turning serious. "Yeah, because you're an asshole with balls of steel, I now owe Weston a hundred thousand dollars. I didn't think you'd show your face. For once, I wish you'd been sensible. You know Weston loves chaos. Apparently, you do too."

"You bet against me?" I laugh. "You deserve to lose that money, Easton. Sorry, not sorry."

"Shit. You showed up," Brody hisses as he slips into line behind Easton, his voice filled with disbelief. "Fuck. Now I'm going to have to pay Weston."

"Not you too?" I glance between them. "Unbelievable."

"I *should* beat your ass for being here," Brody warns, his tone direct.

Even though he's not joking, I'm not scared. Honestly, for all the hell I'm giving Billie, I probably deserve it.

Brody is ex-military, built like a tank with muscles and tattoos that tell stories of battles fought and won. He's the perfect bodyguard for the Calloways—fearless with loyalty that runs deeper than blood. Plus, he's family, so keeping his cousins safe is personal. He's risked his life for them more than once, and somehow, against all odds, they're still safe and sound in a world that can be anything but forgiving.

"You might be seeing a lot of me," Brody admits as Easton grabs his drink and stands beside me.

"Why's that?" I ask.

"Billie's my new assignment, thanks to the shitstorm *you* started," he says casually, but I can see the frustration flickering in his eyes, like a storm brewing on the horizon.

"I didn't *start* anything," I reply, gulping down more Revenge, the bitter taste igniting a fire in my belly. "I was offered a contract and took it. You both would've done the same. Three billion dollars is a lot to walk away from."

Easton tilts his head at me. "I thought it was never about the money."

"Isn't that what we all say? Considering you're CEO of Calloway Diamonds, deep down, you know it *always* leads back to the bottom line. Doesn't it?"

His eyes narrow, and for a brief moment, I think he questions whether he knows who I am—like he's trying to remember the last time I didn't stir up trouble.

Before Brody can say anything, Harper steps up behind him. She sighs heavily when our eyes meet; her irritation with me is obvious.

"Asher, *great*! I can't believe I made a stupid bet with Weston. You're seriously the very last person I wanted to see tonight. Or ever. And I've dated some awful guys before," she says, hands on her hips, her voice dripping with sarcasm. She mumbles something under her breath that sounds like a curse.

"You three are the dumbest smart people I know. And let me be clear: the contract with Lustre isn't personal." I make eye contact with each of them.

"You saying it's not personal is total bullshit," Harper tells me, though there's no real anger in her voice. "The nerve you have to …" Her words trail off, and her expression changes.

Everyone facing me wears the same look. I turn, glancing over my shoulder, and that's when my eyes land on Billie. It's as if time slows down.

"You'd better be glad she showed up and saved our asses. Now we don't owe Weston a thing," Harper says, exchanging high fives with Easton and Brody.

I'm momentarily speechless.

As they celebrate, I realize Weston genuinely thought Billie wouldn't show up. That's why he made that bet with them. He'd have pocketed six hundred thousand dollars from three handshakes.

"Did you know she'd be here?" I ask.

Easton glances at me. "No. Weston was way too cocky when he said she wasn't coming. Sometimes, I get lucky and prove him wrong. Like right now."

I can't take my eyes off Billie as she turns toward the door. She bats her long lashes while speaking to someone who hasn't stepped into view yet. One side of her dark hair is pulled back, revealing the softness of her neck and shiny diamond earrings. Her plump lips are painted a deep red, and I can't look away.

She's captivating.

"Wow," Harper whispers. "She finally wore it."

"What is *it*?" Easton asks.

"It's a vintage Christian Stambolian dress that's *very* iconic. It was worn in the nineties by a royal and has been nicknamed the Revenge Dress. I find it interesting that she chose to wear it tonight."

The black dress is tight and fitted, hanging off one shoulder. It shows just the right amount of skin while somehow staying classy. The silk fabric highlights every perfect curve of her body.

Fuck. She knew exactly what she was doing when she slipped that on.

Billie's gaze meets mine, and she locks in on me. A ghost of a fucking smirk touches her lips as she reaches out her hand, pulling *him* toward her.

Prince Louis.

Give me a fucking break.

My jaw tightens as annoyance washes over me.

Harper gasps beside me. "Okay, I didn't see that coming."

Brody's and Easton's faces turn serious as the future king's bodyguards slide into the room, blending in like they belong. I glance at Weston; he looks just as shocked as everyone else, and I know it's real. No one expected this.

"Now, that's how you grab attention," I say, heading back to the bar for another drink, needing to drown out the noise.

Harper steps in front of me, urgency in her stride.

"I can't believe this," she whispers, her eyes darting around the room, still trying to grasp the scene unfolding.

"You didn't know?" I ask, pulling out my flask as we wait. The familiar metal is cool against my fingers.

She takes two big gulps, her frustration bubbling over. "This is your fault. You know that, right?"

"Stop blaming me for your friend's ridiculous choices," I reply, rolling my eyes but secretly enjoying this.

"We had two options: outsell Lustre or Billie needs to find a husband. Guess she's officially on plan B." Harper glares at me.

"That's a bit much." I take another swig from my flask.

"Come on, Ash. If Billie unlocks her inheritance, Lustre will be done, and so will you." She pauses, lowering her voice to a whisper. "Every girl dreams of becoming a queen."

My gaze drifts back to Billie, and I picture her and Louis ruling a kingdom together.

The thought nearly chokes me.

Billie approaches us with Louis glued to her side, his hand resting possessively on her back. That smirk is still in place, and I keep my eyes on her until she looks away. Something primal stirs within me.

Our drinks arrive, and when Billie gets close enough to hug Harper, she does.

Then she turns to me, giving me the dirtiest look she can muster. I fucking love it—that fire in her eyes that says she's ready for a fight.

Louis offers me a firm handshake, his shit-eating grin evident, as if he just won a game of chess. "Asher Banks. It's been a decade."

"Your Royal Highness," I reply, giving a mock bow, my voice dripping with sarcasm. "Good enough?"

Louis rolls his eyes, wrapping his arm around Billie's waist and pulling her close—a move that feels like he's claiming territory. But I'm not fully buying it.

"Why are you here?" Billie glares at me, her voice sharp like a knife.

"I'm questioning the same damn thing," I retort, my eyes wandering down her body, taking in how her dress clings to her curves.

Weston approaches, squeezing my shoulder tightly. "Chill out," he whispers, just loud enough for me to hear, his voice filled with concern.

He gives Louis a brotherly hug, and I finally unclench my fist and slip outside. Thank God I'm alone.

It gives me a moment to gather my thoughts as I chug my fresh drink. The cool liquid is refreshing against the heat of the moment. I set the empty glass on a table by the shimmering pool.

The water glows blue, and I try to calm down, knowing I can't bash in the future king's face at Weston's penthouse. The optics would be terrible, even if Louis deserves it. That's the last thing I need spreading around the internet. But, damn, it would feel good.

Moments later, I hear the patio door click closed, and I turn to see Billie walking toward me. Her expression is a mixture of determination and annoyance and something else.

"Go away." I face her, crossing my arms over my chest, bracing myself for whatever storm is coming.

"No. Why are you here? You never answered my question—something you're good at."

"I'm here because you weren't supposed to be. So, let me ask you the same damn question. Was that your plan? Say you weren't coming just to flaunt the future king at your brother's private party?" I give her a slow clap. "Round of applause for you. That's clever. I'll give you a point for that."

She grins, mischief lighting up her eyes. "Thanks. I thought you'd enjoy it. So, we're one to one. Got it."

"We both know you won't sleep with him," I say.

"How do you know I didn't before we arrived? Could be why I was late," she replies, playfully tracing her swollen lips with her finger. Her cheeks flush lightly as an evil grin spreads across her face. Billie steps closer, her hips swaying with a confidence that makes my heart race. "See, that's your problem, Banks; sometimes, you let your mask slip and—"

Before she can finish, her heel lands awkwardly on the pavement, and she yelps as she tumbles forward. Time seems to slow as I reach out to catch her, but she pushes me back. Billie screams just before we both plunge into the bottom of the deep end of the pool. It's sudden silence. My heart races, adrenaline flooding through my veins.

I quickly wrap my arm around her waist and swim upward, and her breath catches in surprise.

"Can you swim?" I ask, my voice steady as I hold her and tread water.

"Yes," she answers.

Our eyes are locked in a moment that feels electric, the world outside fading away.

"Finish your sentence. What were you going to say before you clumsily tripped and pushed me in?"

She chuckles as I hold on to her; our closeness ignites something that's hard to ignore.

"I don't remember," she says. "Let me go."

"Fine." I swim away from her, lift myself onto the edge, and stand, water dripping from my body.

Billie swims toward me, and I reach my hand out to her, my heart pounding.

She looks at it, then takes my help. Without hesitation, I pull her small frame out of the pool until her feet touch the ground. Standing in front of me, she laughs. We're completely soaked. Mascara streaks down her cheeks as she wrings out her hair, the scent of chlorine mixing with her floral perfume.

"I'm really sorry about the suit. It's a shame; the Gucci was really nice." Billie steps closer, unbuttoning my suit jacket to reveal the stunning crimson lining underneath. "This is one of my favorites."

I meet her gaze. "Your Revenge Dress might be ruined."

"It fulfilled its purpose," she replies, turning to walk away.

I can't help but watch her, captivated. As I glance past, I realize all eyes are on us, the crowd buzzing with curiosity.

"Fuck," I mutter under my breath, feeling the weight of their stares pressing in on me.

She leaves a trail of water around her feet, and just before she reaches the door, she glances back over her shoulder. "You're still an asshole."

"Your fucking favorite," I shoot back, and she gives me a small smile.

Billie walks inside, and Louis rushes over with a towel, wrapping his arms around her like he just pulled her from the depths of a stormy sea. He tucks her wet hair behind her ear and kisses her forehead, a gesture that almost seems real—except her eyes find mine instead of his, a silent challenge crackling between us.

I pull out my phone, realizing it was in my pocket. The last thing I want to do is turn it on, though I think it's waterproof. I hold it tightly as I grab my flask and unscrew the top. The familiar scent of aged whiskey greets me.

Seconds later, Weston joins me with a towel.

"I can't believe she pushed you," he says, shaking his head in disbelief.

"She tripped," I explain, trying to dry off as best I can, the fabric of my clothes sticking uncomfortably to my skin.

"That's not what she just said." His brows furrow in concern. "She mentioned you were jealous of her and Louis, so she pushed you into the pool. You pulled her in with you."

"Wow, she's really playing dirty," I tell him, taking off my coat jacket and tossing it aside, the fabric landing with a soft thud. "Looks like the games have begun."

"Why did you agree to work with Josh?" Weston asks, snatching my flask from my fingers and taking a swig. "I'm trying to figure that out."

"Nothing like a little friendly competition to bring out the best in this business. You and I both know that's when real progress happens. It pushes companies to step up and innovate. Only the strong will survive."

Weston shakes his head and smiles. "Billie's going to wipe the floor with you and Josh. You know that, right?" He laughs, giving me a light pat on the back.

"I have no doubts she'll give it her all," I admit, my mind racing with possibilities.

Weston nods, his expression turning serious. "Can we talk about what's going on between you two?"

My brows knit together. "Our feud?"

"We both know it's deeper than that." He leans in a bit, like he's about to let me in on a secret. "I'll only say this once: if you ever hurt my sister, I will ruin you without a second thought."

It's not just a threat; it's a promise. And I believe him.

"Let me assure you, what's going on between Billie and me is just business."

"For now." His smile disappears, replaced by a hard look. "There will come a time when you'll have to make a choice that could either break my sister or make her the happiest person alive. Choose wisely."

I loosen my tie. "Are you drunk?"

"I hope you know what you're doing," he says, suddenly making everything feel very real.

"Do you trust me?" I ask, searching his eyes for a sign.

"For some reason, I do. But please don't make me regret it. I'm the only one on your side." Weston glares at me before heading to the door.

"Did you know Josh wants her back?" The words spill out, tumbling from my lips in a rush. "This whole plan is to win your sister back." My voice shakes a little.

Weston spins around with his jaw locked. "That can never happen. He was awful for her. Plus, she's officially dating Prince Louis. This is much bigger than Lustre. The world is watching,

Asher. You wanted a stage. Now you've got one. What role will you play?" His voice is urgent.

Weston leaves me to myself.

I glance at Billie, still in Louis's arms.

Tonight was a trap, and I walked right into it, completely unaware of the disaster waiting to unfold. I finish drying off, knowing I cannot stay at this party soaked.

I don't care that everyone is sneaking glances between Billie and me while she lets the prince charm her.

If she wants to play games, let's fucking play.

11

BILLIE

The room is quiet, and all eyes are on me as Louis dries me off. Most guests whisper among themselves while sipping their Revenge cocktails.

"What happened?" Louis asks quietly, just as the quartet kicks off another song, this one more up-tempo, instantly changing the room's vibe.

"Karma," I reply loud enough for the eavesdroppers.

I can't pinpoint why I feel guilty. Maybe Weston is right; I just don't have the cutthroat edge needed for this. The pianist's notes drown out the murmurs spreading through the crowd.

I glance past Louis, locking eyes with Banks. He's still out on the patio, his face illuminated by the blue glow of the pool lights. His soaked coat is draped over a chair as he unbuttons his shirt and towels himself off, revealing more tattoos than I remember. When he looks up, his brown eyes seem to pierce right through me.

Louis snugly wraps the towel around me. "Are you good?"

"Of course," I reply, my gaze drifting back to the patio, where Banks stands shirtless.

Over the years, I've left countless parties because of him and his cocky attitude. I usually leave to dodge an argument, knowing he thrives on getting under my skin and getting me so flustered that I can barely speak.

Another reason I can't stand him? He makes me lose control.

"Stay focused on me," the prince murmurs in his charming British accent, pulling my attention back to him. "He's testing you."

"You're right. Thanks for the reminder." I smile, grateful that Louis knows how to help me shift my focus away from Banks.

My publicist believes that having a royal by my side will help redirect the rumors swirling online about me and Banks. Many think we had a fling—even Easton is convinced we did. But we definitely did not.

It was awkward as hell as I explained that I *would* help further humanity if Banks and I were the last two people on earth, but it would only be for the love of humankind. Weston jokingly dubbed us Adam and Eve.

I wring more water from my hair.

Weston finally strides toward me. When he's close enough, he leans in and whispers in my ear, "You have no idea who your opponent is."

Carlee pulls him onto the dance floor, and even though no one else is dancing, I know she's trying to divert attention from the drama brewing. I feel awful, especially since this is the first party they've thrown as a married couple.

"What did Weston say?" Louis asks.

I quietly repeat my brother's words as Asher redresses.

"Curious. I wonder what was said." His brow arches, and he glances past me.

Moments later, the patio door swings open and snaps shut. I turn and catch Banks's honey-brown eyes fixed on me. I've never seen that look on him before. His jaw is clenched, and he seems almost feral.

He steps closer to me, his body pressing against mine, and I can feel every fucking inch of him through the thin fabric of my damp dress. His strong fingers weave through my hair, as if he's rehearsed this moment a million times. He tilts my head toward him so gently that it feels choreographed. With his other hand, he grips my waist, his fingers digging into my flesh, like he owns me—like he's fucking claiming me in front of everyone. I should push him away, but instead, I arch into him, feeling the heat pooling between my legs.

His lips crash into mine, and, holy fuck, it's like an explosion. His tongue invades my mouth, hot and demanding, and I moan against him, my hands tangling in his hair. He tastes like revenge and sin, and I'm drowning in it, in him. His teeth graze my bottom lip, biting down just hard enough to make me whimper. Right now, it's just us, and everything else fades away.

He massages my scalp, a deep groan rumbling in his throat. I feel like I'm falling apart, crumbling to ash. He mentioned the Asher Effect before, and right now I'm spiraling, lost in him.

"Fuck." His voice is low and rough, sending shivers down my spine.

His lips find mine again, and this time, it's hotter, dirtier. His tongue twists with mine, and I'm trembling with desire.

When he finally pulls away, we're both gasping for air. Our gazes lock, and the room fades back into view. I snap back to reality and realize that everyone is staring at us.

My hair is still caught in his hand as he leans in closer, pulling my ear to his mouth.

"Tell me you hate me," he murmurs.

"Fuck you," I whisper, covering my lips with my hand, fully aware that they're swollen.

That line should've *never* been crossed.

Banks laughs and walks away, knowing he's rewritten the narrative I wanted for Louis and me.

Who will believe we're together now after that kiss?

As I turn, I meet Louis's gaze—his mouth slightly parted, eyes wide. It's the same stunned expression everyone else is wearing.

This is a living nightmare.

I quickly spot Harper.

She mouths, *What the fuck?*

I shake my head and rush out of the room. The elevator doors begin to close, and I slide inside with Banks.

I press the button to close the doors, then turn to him. If looks could kill, he'd be on the floor right now. He shrugs and tucks his hands into his pockets, acting like he couldn't care less.

"What is wrong with you?" I ask, frustration boiling over, aware that my panties are drenched.

Banks presses the button to stop the elevator. It jolts to a halt.

"What the fuck is wrong with you?" he retorts, his eyes sliding from my mouth down my body, which is currently on fire.

"You. You're what's wrong with me. Asshole!" I growl.

"Oh." He laughs sarcastically. "Because you're so damn innocent."

"Why did you do that?" My heart races, nearly bursting from my chest. "The last thing I need is a scandal with *you*."

"Too bad, Ice Queen. This is what you secretly wanted," he shoots back.

"No, it wasn't!"

"Aw, is the diamond princess mad because she always gets her fucking way, like a brat, but this time, she didn't? You've lost control. Just admit it."

"Why are you testing me?" I breathe out. "You're making this personal."

"It's been *personal* since the day we met."

He reaches past me, but I block his path to the button.

"You're infuriating as fuck," I whisper. "Do you realize what you've done? There are lines that shouldn't be crossed. That was one of them," I groan. "You just …"

He smirks. "You're having an existential crisis right now."

My brows crease. "Gross."

"Your words mean nothing since I heard you whimper."

I narrow my eyes at him. "I did *not*."

"Deny that shit all you want." He steps closer, and my back presses against the cool wall. He leans in, his hot breath ghosting over my lips. "And what if I kissed you right now?"

I try to respond, but my breath catches in my throat. My eyes flutter closed as his lips barely brush against mine. The metallic box suddenly feels too small, too hot, too fucking charged.

Heat radiates off Asher's body, his broad shoulders taking up more space than they should. His muscular frame exudes a raw, untamed dominance that makes my skin prickle. His cologne is unapologetically masculine, wrapping around me and nearly suffocating me.

I hate him. I *really* hate him. But my body betrays me as a flush of heat pools low in my belly.

His lips hover inches from mine, and I'm stunned by his level of control. I look up into his light-brown eyes, the intensity of his gaze nearly bringing me to my knees.

"Why are you doing this?" I whisper, my voice trembling, but the way my nipples harden against the fabric of my damp dress tells a different story.

"Tell me you don't want me," he mutters, his deep voice vibrating through my core.

Instead of protesting, I pull him closer. His lips crash against mine with a ferocity that steals my breath. His tongue slides into my mouth, claiming me again. And, damn, I hate how good it feels. How primal, desperate, and filthy it is to kiss him. Asher devours my lips, our tongues dancing together in a way that sends electric shocks straight to my core.

"I'm your karma," he murmurs as my fingers thread through his hair.

My hands should fly to his chest to push him away, but instead, I cling to the fabric of his shirt, pulling him even closer. I feel the hard ridges of his muscles beneath the wet material; his pecs flex as he deepens the kiss, gripping my hips with bruising force. His cock presses against me, thick, even through our layers of clothes.

I whimper against his mouth, hating myself for the needy sound escaping me.

"Mm-hmm. There it fucking was again."

Banks breaks the kiss just long enough for me to growl out a, "Shut up," before his lips crash back onto mine—this time even rougher and dirtier.

One hand slides down to grip my ass while the other tangles in my hair, angling my head for better access. My clit throbs with every rough touch. When Banks finally pulls away, my chest heaves, and my lips tingle.

He chuckles darkly, creating space as he presses the button for the elevator to continue down. We might not exchange any words, but the conversation is *so* fucking loud.

I place my fingers over my lips, still trying to process everything. The elevator stops, but neither of us moves.

His eyes burn into mine—wild and feral—and I know I'm in trouble. As much as I hate him, I can't deny the white-hot desire coursing through my veins. And judging by the look on his face, he feels it too.

The doors slide open, and Banks gives me that arrogant, infuriating smirk that makes me want to slap him and fuck him at the same time. He licks his lips and eye-fucks me for a few seconds before walking away. I don't realize I'm holding my breath until he's out of sight.

"Fuck," I whisper, balling my hand into a fist as I close my eyes tight. "*Fuck.*"

Kissing him was never supposed to feel like *that*.

When I return to the party, I'm frazzled. My heart pounds in my chest, and I desperately crave more of *that*—even though I absolutely shouldn't.

The imaginary spotlight on me feels blindingly bright.

Harper finds me, pulling me into the hallway, away from the crowd. She searches my face, eyebrows raised high. "What was that?"

"I don't know," I admit. "That wasn't ever supposed to happen."

"Why aren't you climbing into the car with that man and letting him rock your world until Monday morning?"

I place my hands on her shoulders. "Harper, we're talking about Banks."

She leans in and pinches me.

"Hey!" I wiggle away from her.

"Just making sure this isn't some weird dream," she says as Louis approaches us.

He immediately smiles, and Harper steps back, giving us some privacy.

"Everything okay?" he asks when we're alone.

He searches my face. My lips are swollen, and my mind is spinning.

"Yes," I reply, knowing I'm tipsy from Banks.

"Let's get out of here," he suggests. I know he wants to know more about the kiss, but he won't ask. At least I hope he doesn't.

"I'd love to. I *need* to."

Louis takes my hand, stealing the room's attention as he leads me toward the door. I glance back at Weston, who lifts his glass of Revenge with a smirk and nods proudly. Easton stands beside him, sharing the same expression.

We step into the elevator, and his bodyguards try to crowd in.

"Out," he demands, pointing his finger. "Meet me on the ground floor."

They reluctantly do as he says.

When we're alone, Louis smirks. "A love-triangle story?"

"That was *not* my doing, and not the media blitz I wanted. I *never* expected Banks to cross *that* line. I thought some things were off-limits."

"Asher has no boundaries. He's fearless in *everything* he does," Louis explains.

That soft look in Banks's eyes will haunt me forever. It's a memory that will be vignetted in my mind for all time. For a brief moment, he showed me a glimpse of the *real* him. I replay how we lost control in the elevator, right in the spot where I stand now.

He's poison in my veins, and I hate it.

"Did you feel something with him?" Louis asks.

"I need time to process what happened. I'm in shock." I feel like I committed a sin and should repent.

The elevator doors open.

Louis's bodyguards wait for us on the bottom floor. I glance at the prince, recalling the summer fling we had in our early twenties. We used to give his security hell when we snuck away together. They wear the same glares they did a decade ago.

"Proof that you're still a bad influence, Calloway," Louis says with a wink, flashing me his boyish grin.

With those light-green eyes and messy hair, he's an absolute dream.

He places his hand on my lower back, guiding me through the foyer of Park Towers and eventually outside, where a line of SUVs awaits. More men in suits stand on the sidewalk, and it's impressive. I smile at Louis with genuine admiration as the paps snap photos of us. He interlocks his fingers with mine, kissing my knuckles as flashes nearly blind me. It's all performative. It always is with us.

The vehicle door swings open, and we climb inside. I shiver, and he removes his suit jacket, handing it to me. It smells like the palace.

"Photos will be circulating within the next hour," he says. "Thank you."

"It's the least I can do. About tonight, I'm sorry it went off the rails so quickly."

He tilts his head at me. "No need to apologize. If I were Asher, I would have played the same card."

"Why?" I ask, confused. "I don't understand."

"To show you who's really in control. You completely melted

into him, babe. If you'd ever kissed me like that, I'd have *never* let you go. That's a promise."

I swallow hard. "Don't say that."

Summers ago, when it was time for me to return to grad school, we agreed to stay friends. The attraction is undeniable, but the real magic is missing. Lust doesn't last; we both knew it would only be temporary if we went any further. I could never make him happy the way he needs, and his commitment lies with his country.

So, now we're friends who make out and fake date whenever we want to distract the world. It's always worked until tonight. Maybe Banks knew Louis was my decoy.

Of course he did.

Louis laughs. "Say a prayer for him. Tonight, the Calloway Curse will take over."

I glare at him. "The *what?*"

"Please tell me I'm not the first one to mention this."

I burst into laughter, finding the information absurd. "No one has had the guts. Spill the details."

Louis shrugs. "Before we met, I was warned about you. The rumor is that any man who kisses you is doomed for life. Anyone you've ever been with wanders around like the Headless Horseman, but instead, he searches for his heart."

My laughter continues. "Please tell me you made that up."

"The curse is real, darling. I wouldn't say I'm personally doomed, but to this day, I still use our relationship as a benchmark to decide whether to pursue someone."

"Seriously?"

"You have no idea how unforgettable you are."

There have never been hard feelings between us.

"You are too," I admit, knowing I'll never forget that time with him.

We fell fast and hard, both in *and* out of love. Our relationship was an explosion, but it was over quickly after it began. I have no regrets.

"I've always sensed that Asher has been waiting for you on the sidelines. I think my presence unlocked something in him."

I laugh. "That's the most ridiculous thing I've ever heard."

"But is it?" he asks.

The SUV zooms down the street. I glance behind us and see at least eight other vehicles following closely. I'm used to security, but nothing like this.

"Will you tell me the name of the woman you're secretly seeing?"

"No," he replies, smirking.

I catch his reflection in the window. The prince is in love.

"Wow, you must really like her."

He glances at me. "I do. She's good for me. Stubborn. Fierce. Kind of like you."

"Why are you playing games?" I ask, confused.

"I could ask you the same about Asher," he says nonchalantly.

"That's not fair. I'm trying to save my business."

"Then why not focus on Josh?" he challenges. "He's the one responsible for Asher, isn't he? You should be playing the entire board, Billie, not just one piece."

"Weston said the same."

I've been avoiding Josh like the plague after he hurt me.

Louis smirks. "If you win over Asher, you take down Josh. If you win over Josh, you can stop Asher. You could destroy them both in the end."

"The last thing I need is the media painting me as some slut who saved her business by sleeping with powerful men."

He reaches for my hand. "All that matters is your happiness. Everything else is bullshit. Remember that, Ice Queen. Erase Josh socially by being with someone else. Maybe Asher could help with that," he suggests with a nod. "It *could* work."

"I don't think it can," I tell him. "He can't be around me because of the noncompete."

"He can't work with you, but there's nothing that says he can't *date* you," Louis counters. "Now, that's a scandal and a love story, wrapped into one. Find a way to monetize it, and you'll ruin Lustre. How badly do you want to save Bellamore?"

"I'll do whatever it takes to save my company without apology," I admit as the streetlights flash across his gorgeous face. "What are you suggesting?"

"If Asher falls in love with you, Bellamore is safe."

"Yeah, but if I fall in love with him, Bellamore is in danger," I tell him. "I don't play one-sided games with love. It always backfires."

"Do you think you're capable of loving Asher?"

I contemplate his question. "I don't want to find out."

The SUV pulls up in front of my building, and I take a deep breath as my door swings open. Cameras flash, and Louis escorts me to the main entrance. The doorman glances my way before quickly turning his back.

I lean in, brushing my lips softly against Louis's. The paparazzi snap countless photos, so we give them the show they crave. I do my best to make it look genuine.

"Thanks for tonight. I hope we achieved what you needed," I whisper, covering my mouth so no one can read my lips.

"Oh, we did—and so much more. Good night."

"Night," I reply, stepping inside, fully aware that those photos will be plastered across British tabloids before dawn breaks in New York.

12

ASHER

"Happy Monday," Lauren says unenthusiastically as she carries an elongated box into my office and sets it on my desk.

Papers whoosh around me, and a few flutter to the floor.

"What's this?"

The box exudes luxury—that much is certain.

"Not sure," she replies, picking up the mess. "It was just dropped off."

The sign I hung across my window last week is still in place.

Lauren glances at it, then meets my eyes. "This fight is a waste of time."

"That's your opinion," I reply.

I don't want to think about Billie today. That woman has been on my mind since I stupidly slid my lips across hers on Saturday night. Every waking hour has been pure torture, a living nightmare I can't escape.

I'd expected to feel nothing, but somehow, I felt it all. Suddenly, I was a twelve-year-old boy again, kissing my first crush. And I'm fucking *pissed* about it. Billie Calloway and I can never happen.

"Did someone burn both sides of your toast this morning?" She blinks at me, her eyes wide with curiosity.

"I didn't sleep well last night," I explain, recalling how I tossed and turned for hours.

"Okay. I hope you can get some rest tonight. You need it." She leaves me to myself.

I scoot the box closer to the edge, opening it, only to reveal tissue paper wrapped around something inside. On top is an ivory envelope with *Banks* written in elegant cursive.

Still thinking about that beautiful suit I ruined and how it was a crime against fashion. Please accept my apology—yes, I mean it—and this replacement.

-B

"ICE QUEEN," I WHISPER AS I PEEL BACK THE TISSUE PAPER TO REVEAL a charcoal-gray suit with a light-blue liner—exactly the shade of her eyes.

I pull the coat from the box, holding it up. It's Dolce & Gabbana, and considering her obsession with fashion, I know she went all out to find the best replacement.

I slide it on over my dress shirt, and it fits like it was tailored just for me. Considering who she is, I wouldn't be surprised if she texted my stylist for measurements.

I place the coat back into the box, along with the letter, carefully putting on the lid and tapping it closed. After a deep breath, I turn toward the window facing her office, where she's watching me. She lifts her hand to wave, and I walk over to the trash bin and drop the box inside.

The horror on her face almost makes me smile, but I maintain my burning glare. She shakes her head and returns to her desk.

I leave my office, not wanting her kindness.

This is a part of her game. We're all just pawns.

That's why Prince Louis was glued to her side on Saturday. He only shows up when he needs to shift the narrative about himself. I see through her PR stunts as if I directed them.

I waltz into Nick's office, and he holds up a finger, continuing his phone conversation.

"Yes, *Mom*. Ash won't do that. I get that the Alexanders are furious and worried about Harper's fashion company. Trust me, I know my brother better than *anyone*." Nick glares at me, clearly annoyed. "No, Mom. I don't think he cares about that."

Her high-pitched voice drones on.

"I know, I know. Anyway, I've gotta go. A client just walked in. Love you too," Nick says, ending the call. "My mom is livid. Harper's dad is pissed. Your vendetta against Billie and Harper was the topic of discussion at the country club on Sunday."

"Oh, I hope you told them I don't have any issues with Harper," I say, feeling pleased with my decision to be a bastard.

"They're business partners, and they have been best friends since they were five. They're a packaged deal. You hate one, you hate both."

I shrug. "That's unfortunate, I guess. Anyway, I need your help hanging another sign, please."

"Does this have anything to do with the articles about Louis and Billie dating?" Nick picks up *his* lucky baseball from the corner of his desk and tosses it in the air.

"Somewhat." I flash him a shit-eating grin. "Billie sent me a new suit and an apology for clumsily tripping and pushing me into Weston's pool on Saturday."

His brows quirk upward. "She apologized to *you*?"

"Right? I didn't know she was capable of that."

He leans forward, intrigued. "What's your goal with this, little brother?"

"Truthfully?" I ask.

He nods. "I just want to understand so I can help you better. I know you're up to something."

I sigh. "The ice queen has coasted through life for far too long. She's the smartest person I've ever met, yet she's become complacent. Since she would never work *with* me, I've decided to have her work *against* me. It's actually a lot more fun than I thought it would be."

He lowers his voice. "What if this doesn't work?"

"Then she'll lose her business," I confirm. "But I know her, and she won't give up because I'm involved. She'll fight harder. Billie wasn't concerned with Lustre until Josh hired us. What does that tell you?"

He shakes his head. "It tells me she knows you can polish a turd."

"Exactly. Now, Lustre is a real threat to her because of me. So, she'll wake the hell up and fight for her company or go bankrupt. I'm convinced Josh dated her just to infiltrate Bellamore. Now I'm her karma."

"Good karma or bad karma?" Nick asks.

"That's in the eye of the beholder. I see myself as good karma. She'd probably call me bad."

My brother's face softens. "I hope you know what you're doing."

"If fighting me makes her stronger, that's Josh's problem. My contract with Lustre will be fulfilled, and I'll have done everything I promised. But I also know Josh burns every bridge he crosses and messes up every great opportunity that comes his way. In ninety days, when my contract expires, Josh will see a spike in profits, but Bellamore will leave him behind."

Nick raises an eyebrow. "How can you be so sure?"

I smile. "It's personal for her. Oh, that reminds me. I need to swing by Lustre at some point to just randomly drop in."

My brother laughs. "This is unbelievable."

"I don't think it is. Eden would've helped her. We both know that. Now it's time to troll."

He follows me to my office. I grab the giant roll of paper stacked in the corner, and we spread it across the long table. I hand him a thick black marker as I decide what message I want to send to the world. It needs to pack a punch.

I'm surprised no one has mentioned the kiss Billie and I shared at Weston's. I've checked the Blind Items website like it's my religion. The posts only focus on her and Louis. While I suspect it's a facade, I also know they have a very real history. Is this a stunt or a second chance?

"If you keep this up, you'll end up falling for her," Nick says.

"No. It would never work," I admit, trying to push aside that flicker in the dark.

"But if it could?" he questions. "What if this mutual hating game is the greatest and longest foreplay of your life?"

"Somehow, I don't think so." I decide what I'll write on the sign.

"What happened at that party?" Nick finally asks since he wasn't there. He was hanging out with a friend from out of town instead.

Our eyes meet.

"I kissed her in front of everyone."

His eyes widen. "What?"

Nervous laughter escapes me. "And then in the elevator."

"What!" His voice jumps an entire octave. "Were you trashed?"

"I was pissed."

I think back to what Josh said about how he couldn't get Billie off his mind. Deep down, I knew the curse was alive and festering inside of me. Now I'm officially fucking doomed.

"This is so unprofessional," Nick says as he colors the lettering.

"This is old-fashioned trolling," I confirm, knowing Billie thrives on the constant push and pull.

I read over the gigantic sign, proud of what it says.

Does your boyfriend know about me?

Nick shakes his head. "Last week, you said this wasn't personal."

"It wasn't. But I changed my mind. I'm determined to go harder than she ever expected," I explain.

He stares at me for at least a minute. "Do you have a thing for her?"

I suck in a deep breath. "Define *thing*."

"*Wow*. You do."

I scoff. "I didn't say that."

"You don't have to. I know how to settle this." Nick cups his hands over his mouth. "Lauren! Lauren, come here!"

"Don't," I warn, raising my voice.

He moves toward the door, still yelling. A few illustrators stand from their cubicles and stare at us.

"Nick, you're making a scene." I don't want any unnecessary attention. Enough has been said about the firm over the last week because of the deal with Lustre. I'm not looking forward to dealing with new rumors.

Lauren enters, glaring at us. "Nicolas Matthew Banks. Don't you ever yell at me like that again. I was on the phone."

"I'm sorry. Just come in and close the door." Once she does, he continues, "Do you think Asher has a crush on Billie?"

"Calloway? Yes," Lauren answers.

My jaw clenches tight. "This conversation is a *joke*."

Lauren crosses her arms over her chest. "No one is laughing."

Nick doesn't take his eyes off me. "Holy shit. You're actually in lo—"

"Okay, that's enough," I cut him off before he can finish his sentence, but I know what he was going to say.

"Lauren, get out. Nick, help me hang this sign; then you can fuck off too."

He chuckles, completely unfazed. Lauren leaves, and I rip down my disrespectful sign, tossing it aside.

Nick grabs the new one off the conference room table, and we climb some step stools to put it up. Once we finish taping it, we both climb down.

Billie and Harper stare at us from across the way.

"Oh shit," Nick mutters as Billie storms out of her office.

Harper flips me off and rushes toward her.

"Guess it was the right message," I say. "Anyway, I need to step out and clear my mind. I'll be back this afternoon."

I grab my cell phone and head for the door.

"What if you could be together?" Nick asks again.

I glance back at him. "Stop with this. We'd destroy each other, and I wouldn't wish that on my worst enemy."

"But she is your worst enemy, and there is chemistry," Nick replies. "Can't believe you'd pass up love because you're too fucking stubborn to see it. Keep this up, and you'll end up just like me and Dyson. Alone."

I'm too pissed to have this conversation. I take the elevator down to the street, craving fresh air.

Paps quickly follow, their camera clicks giving them away. I roll my eyes, almost forgetting I'm on a watch list, thanks to the ice queen invading my space.

It wouldn't surprise me if she had them tracking my every move. I know her family's relationship with the media and how the Calloways love to spin their curated tales. Just like the Louis one.

A guy points a short-lensed camera in my face.

"Did you know Billie was with a royal?" he asks. "What happened with you two?"

I avoid eye contact and shove my hands in my pockets. In moments like this, when my thoughts are jumbled, it's better to stay silent. I'll play my cards close to my chest—at least for now.

While I grew up in the limelight, it was nothing compared to what the Calloways faced. The three of them were the picture of what wealthy American kids were expected to be. Billie had full spreads in teen magazines, detailing her academics and interests, along with her fashion sense.

Those who don't want to be a Calloway want to fuck one. There's no in between.

Roosters is just ahead on the corner, and I slip inside, relieved for the escape. As I rush in, I'm not paying attention and accidentally bump into the woman in front of me. I reach out to steady her and realize my hands are on the ice queen.

She groans. "Let me go. Jeez."

"Why are you *everywhere?*" I ask.

"I was here first. You probably saw me and decided to follow me," she says, glancing past me. "Oh, and you brought the paps. *Great.* Good job, Banks."

"*You* did. Had I known you were here, I wouldn't have come. Just like that fucking party," I reply, meeting her gaze. It's a mistake. It makes me miserable.

"Next time, I'll text you to let you know I'm leaving the office so we don't accidentally bump into each other. You're rude as hell. And your sign was stupid. No one was even talking about us," she whisper-hisses, clearly frustrated. "You're obsessed with the narrative."

"Obsessed?" I burst into laughter. "You fucking wish."

The barista stares at us, and I gently place my hand on the small of Billie's back, urging her to move forward. A jolt of electricity races through me at the slightest touch.

"Now order. I have things to do, and you're wasting my fucking time, per usual," I say, aware that pictures and videos are being taken of us.

This encounter, combined with my sign, is bound to get everyone talking. I can't help but smile at the thought.

Billie orders a hot tea—Earl Grey with a splash of milk. I guess she doesn't always grab a double shot of espresso.

"I'll pay for whatever he wants," she says, glancing back at me. Her eyes flicker from my lips to my eyes.

"Stop looking at me like that," I say, narrowing my focus on her.

"Like a human?" she retorts.

I take a step closer, leaning in to whisper in her ear, "Like you'd fuck me in the bathroom."

She draws a ragged breath. "You're projecting."

I know photographers are at the windows, capturing every moment.

"So, is that all?" the barista asks, annoyed but also invested in our exchange.

"You're *so* damn frustrating," Billie sneers. "He'll have a mocha, large, with two percent milk and one raw sugar. Extra hot because he loves to make my life a living hell," Billie instructs the barista.

The barista rings it up, and Billie swipes her card.

"How did you know what I order?" I ask, genuinely shocked.

"I know a lot about you," she mutters, not bothering to look my way as she moves across the room, away from me.

The barista glances at me, head tilted in curiosity, and I let out a sigh.

This is exhausting. My goal is to break *her* down, not the other way around.

13

BILLIE

"Earl Grey. Calloway," the barista calls.

I step up, grab my tea, and sit at the table by the large windows. I've got ten minutes to kill while my brothers finish their meetings.

My phone buzzes in my pocket just as Banks picks up his coffee from the bar. I meet his warm gaze and instantly wish I'd kept pretending he didn't exist. Not that it would've worked. The distinct scent of him envelops me as he moves closer and takes the chair across from me.

"Go away." I focus on my phone, reading a text notification.

It's Prince Louis's reply to the picture of the new sign I texted him before I left the office.

Prince Louis and his PR team are working overtime to sell our love story. I don't want them blindsided by the cheating love-triangle rumor that Banks is determined to sell to the public.

While it doesn't serve the prince, *I* can definitely work this angle.

Being seen with Banks and then having him announce his partnership with Lustre was last week's news. After the photos of the prince and me kissing on Saturday went viral, I've been drowning in positive press. It's boosting my image, even if it's just a temporary fix. When I woke up this morning, I considered it a win—one Banks is refusing to let me have.

This Monday is already shaping up to be a fresh hell, and it's not even lunchtime.

> **LOUIS**
> Please tell that bloody prick it would be in his best interest to piss off.

I snap a photo of Banks sitting in front of me and text back.

> **BILLIE**
> I'll let him know right away. Anything else you want me to pass along?

"Excuse me?" Asher leans forward and snatches my phone from my hand.

I stand up, swiping at him, nearly spilling my tea. "Give that back. Now."

"No." Banks laughs, extending his arm away from me.

"Seriously! I will fuck you up," I warn as he scrolls through our recent texts.

"Lots of flirting. And a fit check? Wow. How fucking special," he says, raising an eyebrow at a picture of me in a dress. His expression shifts, and he finally hands my phone back. "Love knowing the prince is jealous. This is perfect. Thanks for confirming."

"Wait, you actually think Louis's jealous of *you*? *Pfft*." I laugh so hard that I snort. "He's royalty. You're ..." My words trail off as my gaze drifts from his eyes to his mouth.

Sexy.

Banks leans in, elbows on the table, his dress shirt sleeves rolled to expose his muscular forearms, bringing him inches closer.

"If that mattered, you'd be across the pond, eye-fucking him instead of me. I know how you act when you're in love. Completely insufferable."

"I am absolutely not eye-fucking you." I pull back, creating as much distance as possible, refusing to let him turn the tables while the paparazzi are all over us. If anyone knows how to handle the media, it's him. "Just leave this alone. *Please*. I'm asking nicely."

His gaze is way too intense. Ever since he kissed me, I haven't been the same. Right now, I can't decide if I want to slide my tongue against his or slap him across the face. It's torture.

"Hmm. Naaah. I don't think I will," he says playfully, but I know he's serious.

"You're an *actual* menace." Frustration bubbles inside me.

He chuckles, and I hate that I enjoy the low rumble in his throat. To feel both hatred and desire so intensely might just be insanity.

"And to think all of this could've been avoided if you had just set your ego aside."

"You would have loved me submitting to you too much." I'm acutely aware of the eyes watching us from the windows.

"One thing we can agree on."

He returns my gaze, and it feels too intimate. I quickly look away.

"What happened to you?" he asks, pulling my attention back. "You've grown soft."

"I don't care about your opinion, and I certainly don't like you. Never have. Never will." My eyes flicker to his plump lips, and I momentarily get lost in the memory of our elevator encounter.

He raises a brow, as if he knows exactly what I'm thinking.

"Let's talk facts, shall we? Your business is failing. Your love life? Nonexistent. You have *one* friend, no pets, and zero hobbies. And that billion-dollar fortune of yours? Locked away until you find some unfortunate soul to endure hell with you for eternity. Look me in the eyes, and honestly tell me you think you're living your best life."

He pauses, and I can't deny I've been asleep at the wheel for far too long.

"What frustrates me is that you can change this, but you're too fucking busy coasting and blaming everyone else for your failures instead of looking in the mirror. This has been your MO since you and Josh split. *Mirror, mirror, on the wall, who's the biggest disappointment of them all? Hmm. Ice Queen.*"

My brow furrows. "How dare y—"

"I'm *not* your enemy, princess. Your self-sabotage has done a fantastic job of fucking you over." Banks removes the lid from his coffee to let it cool. "The girl I met at Stanford would be furious with you right now. To think, Billie fucking Calloway rolled over for a man who pretended to understand the fashion industry. He *used* you, and you let him. This is the consequence of your actions. Nothing else."

I glare at him. "My personal life is off-limits. Leave it alone. Stop prying. You have no idea what happened between Josh and me."

"I know you broke it off with him," he says.

"You don't know why."

The only people I've confided in are Harper and my brothers, and they're like vaults.

"That's where you're wrong, babe. I do know." He lowers his voice.

"Yeah?" I narrow my eyes. "I'm sure he gave you the same lie he tells everyone."

"He admitted to cheating on you with his ex."

His brown eyes meet my blues, as if trying to see me crumble, but he gets no reaction. My skin is thicker than steel.

"Josh told you the truth. Wow." My brows crease. I'd be lying if I said I wasn't shocked. "And even then, you still decided to work with him?" My adrenaline surges, and my face feels like it's on fire. I haven't been this angry in a long time. "You've officially lost the little respect I had left for you. Leave me alone, Banks. Seriously."

Josh has always claimed we mutually split due to business differences. It's an easier lie to navigate publicly, but when anyone tries to delve deeper, I avoid their questions. I'm ashamed and upset that I gave my heart to a mediocre man. Banks is right. Josh pretends to understand fashion and doesn't. That was the first red flag I overlooked.

"You do realize I'm immune to your reactions. I'm completely unbothered by your bitchiness; I actually find it kind of endearing." He waves his hand dismissively. "And if you must know, Josh seemed remorseful about his actions. He said he's still in love with you."

"He's manipulating you," I snap. "You can't love someone and also willingly sneak around and cheat and lie. That's not how it works. He's in love with the idea of me, with what I could do for him. He is not in love with me. And why are you telling me this? So you can use it against me? Planning to spin this narrative that I'm a horrible person who deserved to be cheated on? Then you'll play the white knight for Josh Lustre, right?"

"I might be a bastard, but I'd never do that. Not even to you, Ice Queen. Low-hanging fruit isn't my style. I stab people in the front with truths and real weaknesses. I look my enemy in the eye when I do it too. I may be sneaky, but if you pay attention, you'll always see me coming." Banks smirks and leans in. "Knowledge is power. Use what you know to your advantage."

We stare at one another for a moment too long. Banks is always calculated, and everything he does has a purpose. I just don't understand it yet. I can't believe I feel a flutter in my stomach while also being outraged.

"It's a shame that after all these years, you're still a weak little man who's intimidated by me."

"Oh, please. That's not what this is. We both know that. And I hope that wasn't your best attempt to hurt my feelings. Try harder, Ice Queen," he replies, unfazed.

I growl, "Don't push me. I have enough dirt on Josh to take

down Lustre Fashion, and your firm would be in crisis mode indefinitely." I smile sweetly. "You really don't know who you're messing with."

"You're an actual monster," he says, clearly impressed. "And a cutie about it too. This is going to be fun."

"Shut. Up."

"Breaking you down has become my new hobby. It might become my kink." He pops the lid back on his coffee.

"I'll never give in to you," I mutter. "Ever."

"Oh, I know. But just so you're aware, if you ever do, I'll never let you forget it," he admits.

I glance outside, realizing I've already overstayed my welcome with him.

Banks gives me a smug grin. "You're fucked."

"Are you offering?" I ask blankly, recalling how he kissed me with everything he had. "Did you tell your girlfriend you had your tongue down my throat on Saturday?"

He licks his lips. "About that, it was a mistake and—"

"Those are your words. Not mine." I scoff, hating that I feel anything at all in this moment. When he's near, my tight control slips away. It's another reason I can only handle him in short bursts. "I have to go," I mutter, grabbing my tea.

Time freezes. I've said too much, and I need to escape. So, I do.

"Billie," he calls as I push open the door.

I slide my sunglasses over my eyes, trying to block out the emotions swirling inside me.

Paps follow me, and Banks says my name again.

I ignore him. He catches up and matches my pace.

"That was messed up. I'm sorry," he mutters.

"Apology not accepted. Don't talk to me." I keep my head high and stride forward with purpose.

"This conversation isn't over," he warns.

"Stop putting on a show," I say, hearing the constant clicks of the cameras.

The photographers are capturing every moment. When I glance at Banks, I can't help but notice how his hair shines golden-brown in the sunlight. So do his eyes.

"Can we talk?" he asks.

"No," I reply, but I can tell it's the wrong answer.

He grabs my wrist, his thumb brushing against my fluttering pulse as he pulls me off the sidewalk and leads me inside a vacant building under renovation.

We're alone.

"Go back to pretending I don't exist." My words echo off the empty walls.

Something flickers in his eyes. "Since we met, there's never been a time when you didn't exist."

My heart skips, and my breathing grows ragged. I'm grateful my eyes are hidden behind my sunglasses.

"Do you really think kissing me was a mistake?" I ask, studying him, remembering the spark I felt when our lips collided. Even now, my body continues to betray me.

This is the first time I've found myself on the receiving end of a no-feelings kiss, and it sucks. Maybe Banks is right; maybe he is my karma, but what did I do to deserve this?

No answer is still an answer.

"Okay," I whisper.

Being rejected by a man I can't stand yet somehow want is a new low for me.

"You didn't think it was a mistake?" he asks.

"Fuck off, Banks." I pull my wrist from his grip, doing it with a little more force than necessary.

I push open the door, and the paparazzi anxiously wait outside. I ignore them and cross the street as the sunshine warms my cheeks.

This time, he doesn't follow, and honestly, that's for the best. Now I can break free from this ridiculous fantasy. That stupid kiss haunts me like ghosts in a graveyard, mingling with my other hidden skeletons.

I can't get tangled up with Asher Banks. But despite him threatening to destroy my business and ruin me, I still want to.

Is it simply because I shouldn't?

Maybe I'm the red flag.

I'm flustered as I take the next crosswalk. I have several blocks to go before I reach Calloway Diamonds headquarters, my escape route.

"You okay? Did he disrespect you?" my cousin Brody asks. "Want me to go back there and beat the fuck out of him?"

"No," I reply, rolling my eyes, though he can't see it behind my glasses.

"Were those sparks I saw?"

"Brody," I say through gritted teeth, "I will fuck you up."

"You'll try, little cousin. You've got a crush on Asher Banks. Wow."

"I will fire you," I warn.

"You can't. I don't work for you." Brody laughs and gives me space as he trails behind.

I enter the building without a hitch—my thumbprint grants me access to Easton and Weston's floor. I ride up in silence, trying to calm my racing thoughts.

As soon as I step off the elevator, I'm greeted by the familiar diamond shape surrounded by a triangle—a symbol my grandfather sketched on a napkin when he founded this company.

Their secretary meets me with a warm smile. "Easton's still on a conference call. He said five more minutes, but Weston is free."

"Thanks," I reply with a smile before heading into Weston's office.

I cross the room, aware that this could have been my prison if I'd accepted my father's offer. Large stacks of financial records are piled on the edge of his desk. He glances away from his screen, meets my eyes for a moment, then returns to his message.

Once he finishes, he looks up with a grin. "It's my favorite sister and future queen," he teases. "Should I bow down?"

I lift my sunglasses and shoot him a glare. "You know it's fake."

"I'm just practicing my acting skills." Weston winks, leaning back in his chair and crossing his arms. "They're all pining for you."

"Who?" I ask, confused.

"Louis, Asher, and Josh," he confirms.

I press my fingers against the bridge of my nose. "Is this a joke?"

"Nope." He chuckles sarcastically. "You're the centerpiece of their game. Don't you see? You're not Asher's opponent; you're the prize." Weston kicks his feet up on the desk. "After digging deeper, I'd bet money on it."

Just then, Easton enters, holding a tablet. He hands it to me and leans against the desk, watching intently. "Explain this."

I swipe through photos of Asher and me at the coffee shop thirty minutes ago. Our conversation is captured in a series of still frames. We look like a couple, sneaking a coffee date. If I swipe fast enough, it almost plays like a movie.

"What is it?" Weston asks, intrigued, leaning forward to get a better look.

I pass him the tablet, and his eyes widen in surprise.

"What is wrong with everyone?" I ask. "Why do you all give me the same reaction?"

Weston zooms in on a photo. It's from when our faces were just inches apart. I'll never forget what he said about me eye-fucking him instead of Louis. He saw right through me.

"Are you and Asher secretly working together?" Easton asks.

"Nothing's going on between us. I was there first; he showed up and wouldn't leave me alone. That's it. We're not conspiring."

Weston chuckles, swiping through more photos.

I glare at him. "What?"

"I can only imagine what he said to get you to give him that look. Shit. Deadly. You look just like Mom in that one."

Easton sighs, clearly uncomfortable with any family drama. He hates the extra attention, and I get it—I feel the same way. It's why I've stayed elusive over the years. The less the world knows about me, the better. It's been that way since I was a kid.

"Hmm," Easton says, a thoughtful look crossing his face.

"What?" I ask, instantly recognizing that cocky expression.

"I think Asher's helping you in some weird, fucked-up way," he says, nodding. "He's leading you to water."

"That's ridiculous." I shake my head.

He knew Josh had cheated and still agreed to work with him. Only someone who truly hated me would do something so low.

"Anyway, I believe Bellamore will be fine. I've been working on different ideas, and I'm on the brink of something big," I explain.

"He'd better not hurt you." Easton adopts his CEO, big-brother voice. "I will fuck him up."

He and Weston do that twin thing where they communicate without speaking. It used to annoy me as a kid.

"I've already told Ash—" Weston starts but stops mid-sentence when the door behind me swings open.

A stunning woman with reddish-brown hair strides in, wearing a vintage Chanel pantsuit and high heels. If I had to guess, it's from the 1996 collection. It fits her perfectly, and her fierce red lipstick completes the look. She enters, exuding a confidence that I wish I had.

Easton stands to greet her with a firm handshake. She offers him a gentle hello before turning her full attention to me.

"This is Stormy," Weston says with a mischievous grin.

She approaches me without a care in the world, extending her perfectly manicured hand. She clearly has money, evident from the eight-hundred-thousand-dollar diamond bracelet dangling on her wrist. Fewer than fifty of those were ever made.

"Nice to meet you, Billie. I'm your secret weapon and corporate fairy godmother."

"Hi." I'm not sure what to say, but she seems to have everything figured out. "Why have I never heard of you before?"

"I work in the shadows, staying hidden behind the scenes. My services are like Fight Club—only those at the very top know me when they need an expert to help them clean up a mess. Just to be clear, I'm only here because your brothers called in a huge favor. Technically, you don't qualify. But the Calloways have kept my family in business for decades."

I stare at her, realizing I thought I knew everything about running a successful company. If there are entire organizations I've never heard of that assist those at the top, what else is out there that I don't know?

"What does this entail?"

"How good are you at following directions?"

"Depends on who's giving them," I reply.

"You said you were willing to do whatever it takes to save Bellamore," Weston reminds me.

He's right; I did say that, and I meant it wholeheartedly. I'd do anything for my company. Well, anything except beg on my knees for Asher. I do have some boundaries after all.

Stormy sizes me up. She looks only a few years older than I am. In a different context, we might even be friends. As she brushes her hair behind her ear, I catch sight of a massive diamond on her finger—at least twenty carats, worth a few million dollars. So, her fiancé is definitely rich.

"You're a modern-day sex symbol, dressed like you're giving a speech at a funeral of a great-aunt you never met," she comments. "I don't get it."

"Damn, is being brutally honest part of your job as a publicist?" I ask.

"I specialize in crisis management," she explains. "I don't have time to sugarcoat things. We're on a tight schedule."

"We're already in crisis mode?" I ask, feeling genuinely annoyed with my brothers. "It's only been a week."

"We agreed that if one of us wasn't confident you could save Bellamore and outsmart Asher, we'd call Stormy," Weston clarifies.

"I'm sorry, but you need an expert. It's too risky to wing it," Easton adds. "I believe in you, but a road map is essential."

"Why the black wardrobe? Explain it to me," Stormy asks, completely ignoring my brothers.

"The media started calling me the Wednesday Addams of Fashion, so I embraced it."

"Embraced it or just lay down and took it?" she asks. "Do you know who came up with that nickname?"

"No," I reply, shaking my head.

"Josh Lustre," she says. "That's who I traced it back to. So, tell me this: will you keep playing his cards, or are you ready to play a different game? Your game."

My breath catches in my throat. "Tell me your plan."

14
ASHER

The sun finally sets, and my eyes burn from staring at the computer screen for two hours. It's been a long day of playing defense, and while it was expected, being "on" nonstop is exhausting. I have to be quick on my feet, ready to respond to any question at a moment's notice.

When I got back from running into Billie, I was thrust into an emergency meeting, followed by several conference calls. My publicists are losing their minds, and investors are low-key panicking, even though we're booked with clients for the rest of the year and have a long wait list. Gossip sites and media outlets have bombarded me, clamoring for a statement about the sign I hung for Billie, along with our coffee date. My timing couldn't have been better.

So many are desperate for me to confirm if we're secretly together. Others want to know if I think Josh Lustre can actually take over the fashion industry.

Absolutely not.

He was right about one thing: as long as Bellamore is active, he'll never be at the top.

I hop online and type in Billie's name. It seems like the prince and his team have worked overtime this evening to overshadow the headlines from earlier today. The fake relationship story has been twisted in several directions, but somehow, they're still losing to the secret relationship rumor that kicked off the night of the award ceremony. Just wait—I'm only getting started. Right now, I'm just pregaming.

I lean back in my chair, running my hand over my face. I can't shake thoughts of Billie and how she asked me if kissing her had been a mistake. She was looking for confirmation that I'd felt nothing, but I couldn't find the words. She snatched them away like a thief in the night. Now that I've seen her vulnerability—the part of her she keeps hidden from everyone else—I can't look away.

She felt something when we kissed. She showed her cards.

I can't pretend she doesn't exist, even if she begged me to. It's impossible. I've tried.

"Fuck," I mutter, realizing I need to halt this train of thought before I get too deep with her.

I need the ice queen out of my head, even though I know she'll never be out of my life. Our social circles are already too intertwined.

A knock on my office door pulls me from my thoughts. I'm surprised to see my brother.

Nick steps inside. "Wow. You're still here."

"Not for long," I tell him, realizing I'm getting nowhere. I lock my computer, signaling the end of my day. All I want is a bourbon, a hot shower, and a good night's sleep.

Nick sits in the chair across from my desk. "About earlier—"

"Don't apologize."

"I wasn't planning to. I'm genuinely concerned about you. You can't keep going at this pace," Nick says.

He's the only one who truly understands how hard I work.

"You've been saying that for the past year, and I'm still pushing through. Besides, why does it matter? This is all I have."

He crosses his arms. "You have no work-life balance. This

company is the cause of your current circumstances, not the effect, Ash. I know you work your ass off for Eden, and I respect the hustle, but somewhere along the way, you've lost yourself. All you do is work, eat, sleep, and repeat. It's a toxic cycle, and you're stuck in it. Our sister wouldn't have wanted this for you."

This is the last conversation I want to have right now.

"I have a lot on my plate. Once I finish the contract with Lustre, I'll take a vacation. I promise. Right now, I can't. Too much is at stake."

"Unfortunately, you don't have a choice. I'm really sorry, but," he says, sighing heavily, "the board thinks you've pushed things too far with Billie. You need to step away for a little while."

"Please tell me you're not enforcing this."

He raises an eyebrow. "Ash."

"It takes *your* vote, Nick," I say through clenched teeth.

"You're damn right it does. And you know who I thought about when I made my decision today? *Eden*. She'd have been furious, seeing you like this. You're exhausted, angry, and lonely. Wake up before you crash and burn."

"I'm wide awake," I snap back. "My eyes are open for the first time in years. Maybe even a decade. You have no idea what's on the line. Forcing me to take leave is a huge fucking mistake."

"We'll see in a week," he replies, unfazed by my outburst.

"That's too long." I glare at him.

"It can be extended to ninety days if this keeps up." He looks me over. "Humble yourself before I have to do it for you. Now, I know you're pissed at m—"

I nod, feeling my heart rate increase. "Oh, I'm *very* pissed."

"Yeah? You'll get over it. Anyway, I'm meeting some friends tonight at Diamond. Want to join me?"

"No," I reply.

"Come on. It'll be good for you. Trust me. For once," he says, and I catch a glimmer in his eyes.

"Why?" I see right through him.

"It would be in your best interest." He shrugs. "I'm leaving now. A car is waiting downstairs."

"I'm not staying long."

"I don't care," he tells me as I grab my phone, and we head to the elevator together.

I'm upset—don't get me wrong—but I know he wouldn't suggest this if he didn't think it was necessary. I'll find a way to move forward, whether it's from my office or my townhouse.

"Who's handling Lustre while I'm away?" I ask as we step into the metal box.

"Me." He smirks.

"This is bullshit," I hiss.

"Really? Did you know Stormy is working with the Calloways? Josh had a complete meltdown today over you and Billie possibly dating. Prince Louis is working overtime to prove he's with her. And you're just adding fuel to the fire. This could be viewed as a conflict of interest that might cost us a billion dollars."

I shake my head. Stormy is who high-level firms turn to when they're in too deep. She and her team are the absolute best in the industry. If Billie needed Stormy to help her dispose of a body, it would be gone within the hour, along with all the evidence. Is this more serious than I thought?

"You messed with the Calloways, Asher. What did you expect?"

"My actions are justified, even if they're not in the rule book."

"Your actions speak much louder than my words ever could. It looks like you're in it for personal gain."

"I don't care what it looks like. Time reveals everything," I throw back. My anger level rising.

"You'll eventually thank me," he says, his gaze locking on to mine. "You have to do things your way, and I have to do them mine."

"What do you know that I don't?" I whisper, wishing for fewer obstacles but knowing there will be more.

"I'm purposely ignoring your question," he replies, checking his watch.

"Once my mind is made up, I don't back down," I remind him.

"I'm aware. Just know I'm always on your side, just as you're on mine," he says.

As soon as we step out of the building, camera flashes blind us. I groan, shielding my face and rushing to the car, understanding this is my life—at least for now.

"Bet you're glad you're coming with me. Did you really plan on walking home?" my brother asks as we speed away from the firm, leaving the paparazzi behind.

"I don't know. I just decided to leave," I reply.

We zip across the city to an exclusive club in one of my favorite neighborhoods.

I adjust my tie as the car comes to a stop in front of the building, which sparkles like a gem. More camera flashes greet us, but my brother seems unfazed.

We slip through the double doors into a foyer waiting area. Diamond awaits with its soft, shimmering lights.

Security checks our IDs and scans them on a machine.

"Welcome to Diamond, Mr. Banks," he says to both of us.

We're granted instant access. Inside feels like stepping into a different world.

Only those on the exclusive list are allowed in. It includes A-list celebrities, royalty, athletes, and the who's who of the business world. Being part of that list is a privilege I was born into. Being a Banks opens doors that most people only dream of.

Inside Diamond, privacy is paramount. Those who breach it are banned for life, and no one with a social standing wants to risk that. It would tarnish their reputation—a clear sign they can't be trusted. The world is full of enough people who can't keep a secret.

Once we're upstairs, Nick quickly spots his friends—guys he went to college with. I've met them before, but it's been years since they were in the city. I follow my brother into the VIP section, and we join them at a large circular booth. Several bottles of bourbon and whiskey sit in the center of the table.

"Do you remember my little brother, Asher?" Nick asks, reaching for an empty glass.

They all chime in with an enthusiastic, "Yeah," as he pours himself a drink.

"I know it's been a while, so I think another introduction is in order. That's Jameson and Patterson; they're brothers. Callan, Hunter, and Smiley."

I wave and take a seat, thankful to be told their names.

The lights are low, and music plays overhead. The surrounding tables are packed with couples, and the bar has no open seats.

"Drink up," Hunter says with a nod. "Heard you've had a helluva day."

"What have you heard?" I pour a double shot of bourbon and down it in one go.

"Fucking around with a Calloway? You're gonna find out," Patterson says, shaking his head. "That's a death wish."

I chuckle. "I'll survive, trust me."

A moment later, a cocktail waitress with long legs approaches us, her eyes fixed on me. She's cute.

"Does anyone need anything from the bar?" she asks, smiling directly at me.

I swirl the amber liquid in my glass, smirking back. "I'm good. Thanks."

"I bet you are," she replies with a wink. "Let me know if I can help with anything."

She turns on her heel and walks away.

The guys look at me, eyebrows raised.

"What?" I ask.

"She wanted you," Smiley says.

"Too bad he only has eyes for one woman," my brother chimes in.

"That's how rumors get started." I shake my head. "And don't talk to me. I'm still pissed at you."

"Aw. Here's all the fucks I give," Nick says, opening his empty palm.

I can't help but smile. My brother is my best friend, always looking out for me. He's been protective of me since we were kids.

I take another shot, craving the liquor to hit me faster. Tonight, I want to forget my name. I need to temporarily forget Billie Calloway exists and that I'm being forced away from work.

"What did I miss?" Patterson asks.

"My brother thought it would be a great idea to get between the diamond princess and Josh Lustre. Now he's stuck in a shit show." Nick explains how he temporarily took over the company, grinning.

I roll my eyes. "You forgot to mention I'm not doing it for evil reasons."

"Then why?" Jameson asks.

It's tough to put into words what I'm after.

"I'm an asshole, and I'm bored," I say, slamming back another drink.

"Shit. You have a crush on the diamond princess." Hunter laughs, standing up to pour bourbon into all our glasses.

"No, I don't," I say, lifting my drink and tossing it back.

Jameson changes the subject, and we talk about nothing and everything at once. It feels good to shoot the shit. Maybe taking some time off will do me some good.

An hour passes quickly, and I realize I'm drunk, which can be both a blessing and a curse. Patterson keeps cracking jokes, and I can't stop laughing.

My eyes scan the room, and I nearly stop breathing when I spot Billie at the bar. She's leaning into the guy next to her, smiling, whispering something in his ear. My jaw tightens as I try to get a better look at who she's with.

"Did you hear me?" Nick asks, following my gaze.

I turn to him, and he tilts his head, as if he knew she'd be here. He must have heard it from Harper. Cocky bastard.

"Who's she with?" I ask, my voice dropping.

I take in the generic guy in a tailored suit. Broad shoulders. Dark hair. With that description, it could be anyone.

Nick shrugs. "Is that Prince Louis?"

"Not sure," I tell him.

I can't tear my eyes away from her. She's absolutely mesmerizing with her dark hair and light eyes. It doesn't help that she's right in my line of sight.

"I'll be right back," I tell my brother after slamming back another shot.

"Choose your moves wisely," he warns as I stand.

"Shut the hell up. I'm officially off script, thanks to you," I reply.

I stride across the room like I own the place. As I turn my head to steal another glance at Billie, she catches my gaze. Her plump lips part, and she doesn't look away. I shoot her a smirk and raise an eyebrow, the booze from the last hour swirling in my head.

I see you, Ice Queen.

She sees me too.

By the look on her face, I can tell I'm the last person she expected to see here. I can't blame her—my presence here is definitely unusual.

The guy turns to glance at her, and I confirm it's Prince Louis.

I immediately stop walking and glare at her. She leans in, whispers something in his ear, and I head toward the hallway that leads to the restrooms.

"What the fuck?" I whisper. *What the actual fuck?*

I move down the hallway and step into the bathroom to take a piss. My bladder is ready to burst after I drank for the past hour. Once I wash my hands, I stroll down the dimly lit corridor, where flickering lanterns cast a warm glow.

When I glance up, our eyes lock. She struts toward me like this is her runway. With one tall black high heel in front of the other,

her gaze fixed on me. The black mesh minidress leaves nothing to the imagination.

Damn, she's absolutely enchanting.

With flared nostrils, she glares at me. "Are you stalking me?"

I roll my eyes. "Oh, please don't flatter yourself, princess. You're the very *last* person on this planet I want to see right now."

It's not a lie. Being this close to her and smelling her sweet perfume is pure fucking torture. It always is.

"Your mouth says one thing, but your eyes say another," she replies smugly.

"Really? Tell me what my eyes are saying," I mutter, briefly falling into the abyss with her.

I swallow hard and step back, knowing it's for the best. But she quickly grabs my hand, pulling me back to her.

"We were talking."

Electricity crackles between us as she looks up at me.

"You told me to pretend you didn't exist. Let me do that," I say.

A small smile plays on her lips. "You're drunk."

"Thanks, Captain Obvious. Why are you here with Louis?"

She tilts her head, studying me. "Oh, I know you saw the headlines. We're officially dating now."

I take a step closer, and her back hits the wall. Leaning in, I whisper in her ear, "Why are you determined to keep lying about that?"

She swallows hard, grabbing my shirt and pulling me closer.

My stubble grazes her neck, making her breath hitch. A smile creeps onto my face as I trace her jaw with my lips, bringing myself close to her mouth. We're less than an inch apart as her eyes flutter closed. I brush my lips across hers, not pressing them together, even as she inches forward.

"Does your boyfriend know about me?" I whisper.

"Does your girlfriend know about me?" she shoots back.

"I'm not with anyone. Now it's your turn to confess," I mutter.

Seconds feel like minutes as I gently rub my nose against hers.

Our hot breaths mingle, and our lips are just a hummingbird wing's flutter away. I want to thread my fingers through her hair and capture her ruby-red lips, but I force myself to pull away, intoxicated by our closeness.

"You make me so mad and ..." she says in a low growl, unable to finish her thought.

"Die mad, Ice Queen," I reply, knowing I have Billie Calloway wrapped around my little finger.

The urge to taste her lips again nearly overwhelms me, and we can't lose control. I'm so damn tempted, but am I under her spell, or is it the bottomless bourbon shots I've taken?

"You still haven't answered my question," she says.

Her wall briefly falls, and for a moment, I'm completely star-crossed, almost picturing an entirely different life with her. We'd argue until we were ninety.

A small smile tugs at my lips as she gazes up at me, flustered, as if she's imagining the same thing. Her breathing is uneven.

"You should get back to your prince," I lean in and say close to her ear, running my fingers through her hair and giving it a slight tug.

Her fingers grip my shirt tightly. I slide my phone from my pocket, lift it, and snap a photo with the flash.

"You bastard," she growls, and I pull her closer.

"Say *ice queen*," I tell her, leaning into her with a grin. Then I turn to her with a chuckle. "Don't fuck with me, Billie. I'm playing to win."

"Win what?" she asks. "You have zero skin in this game."

"You're wrong about that. Micro versus macro." I turn back to her, opening my camera to snap another shot.

She looks gorgeous, even happy, as she leans confidently against the wall, staring at me with her fuck-me eyes.

"Delete those," she warns. "If not, I'll make you regret it."

"You're not in control," I say, flicking through the photos.

I relish the devious little smirk that plays on her lips, almost like she's daring me to post. There's another where her hair covers her face.

Billie moves toward me, standing right in front of me. "I suppose you're the epitome of control then?"

Her lips are so fucking close. They brush against mine, and I hold my composure, though inside, I'm fucking falling apart.

She pulls away, surprised. "Wow. You're immune."

"Try harder, babe," I mutter. "It'll take much more than that. Enjoy your date." I give a mock bow. "Your Royal Highness. Should I get used to addressing you that way?"

"You're an asshole."

"I know," I reply with a grin. "And you know it too."

I force myself to step back, knowing there's no antidote for Billie Calloway. I glance over my shoulder before disappearing from view, and I catch her watching me. She swallows hard, then heads to the restroom.

Our moments together are always brief.

My cock is rock hard, and I adjust myself as I cross the lavish room. In the center hangs one of the world's most extravagant chandeliers.

Louis locks on to me, and I pretend not to notice him. I don't owe him my attention, and frankly, I don't give a fuck who he is. He's another nepo baby, like the rest of us, except he gets to wear a crown.

I return to the oversized booth and take a seat. Nick looks at me, then glances toward the hallway. Billie comes into view.

Nick tilts his head, clearly tipsy. "Wait, are the rumors true?"

"I should probably bail." I pull my wallet from my pocket, grab some cash, and set it on the table.

Nick studies me closely. "Be careful, little brother. You're playing a dangerous game."

"Dangerous is my favorite," I say, downing another shot. I offer my goodbyes to Nick's friends. "See you guys around. Don't be strangers if you're back in the city, okay?"

They chime in at once, and I laugh. As I head toward the stairs, I text my driver the address, knowing I can't walk home in my current state, especially with the paps lurking outside. Diamond is a prime spot for photographers, always ready to snap shots of people coming and going. That must be why Billie chose to bring her prince here. It's another publicity stunt, another one that I ruined.

While I wait for my driver, I unlock my phone and search for recent articles about me. At the top, there are photos of Billie and Louis arriving at Diamond. Thirty minutes later, there are shots of Nick and me entering.

I knew he was up to something. My eyes scan down the list of articles.

I click on the top link LuxLeaks posted. LadyLux is an anonymous, divorced, middle-aged socialite who seems to know *everyone*. At least, that's the rumor. I'm skeptical about most things, especially when they come from hidden sources online.

The title—"What I Think about Asher Banks: Part 1"—catches my eye. I skim her words, some of which are a bit too raw for my taste.

I DID A LOT OF RESEARCH, AND MY QUESTION TO ASHER IS, WHY HAVE YOU and Billie hated one another since your Stanford days? I contacted several of your old college friends, who said this rivalry has lasted for years. Why? As I traced your steps over the years, it's clear that your paths always cross. I think you have a crush on her and realize you're running out of time. This is you trying everything to show her what you have to offer.

Do I think Billie should choose you? I'm not sure yet.

I REACH THE END OF THE ARTICLE.

. . .

Asher, if you're reading this, I believe what you're doing publicly is performative. I'm not convinced you two have ever had a private moment together. I guess this is me saying prove it *because I'm overly skeptical, but I know you won't.*

Remember, this post is my opinion about public figures based on information that's publicly available.

"Okay," I mutter to myself.

If she's skeptical, plenty of others are too.

I open Instagram and upload the photo of Billie and me; her face cleverly blocked. I had just whispered in her ear. The public probably won't have a hard time guessing who it is, even if it could be anyone. It's enough to make my point.

I type a quick caption. My finger hovers over the blue Share button as I debate whether to go this far.

I weigh the different outcomes, and then I disrespectfully hit the button.

"Thanks, LadyLux," I say proudly as the likes and comments flood in.

I will find out who you are if it's the last thing I do.

I scroll through the comments and notice people tagging Billie. I quickly go to my Settings and unblock her so she'll see every single one.

Your move, Ice Queen.

15

BILLIE

I lock myself in a stall, leaning against the cool door, hoping it grounds me.

It doesn't.

My heart races so fast that it feels like it might burst out of my chest. I squeeze my eyes shut, trying to understand why. It's never been like this with him before.

Banks kissing me at Weston's was one of the worst things that could've ever happened. For years, I'd searched for that first-love feeling again, and I'll never forgive him for forcing it upon me so abruptly. He should've never done that.

I take a deep breath to center myself and then leave the safety of the restroom with my head held high. Soft music plays in the background as flickering lanterns cast my shadow against the hallway wall. Even though privacy is expected here, it doesn't stop people from whispering in their tight-knit circles.

Banks shouldn't be here, especially with the ridiculous rumors swirling about us. He's ruining everything. I roll my eyes at the thought. He's in my head, and I can't stand it.

As I make my way to the bar, I spot Banks in the VIP area. His jaw is clenched, and his gaze sharpens as he chats with Nick. The guys with them look familiar, but I can't recall any of their names.

Expensive liquor bottles are clustered in the middle of the table. How long have they been here?

I approach Louis, and as I get close, he wraps his arm around my waist. We give everyone a show to reinforce our dating story—at least for a few more weeks, if Banks will allow it.

"I think I need to go," I whisper, feeling overwhelmed. The two martinis I had aren't helping.

"Whatever you want," Louis replies, pulling me closer with a firm grip on my waist for those watching our every move. "We made our appearance and accomplished our mission," he whispers in my ear.

I pull away and give him a small smile, relieved that he's the one I'm fake-dating. He leads me through the room toward the exit. I catch a glimpse of the empty seat where Banks was sitting. This is what happens when we're in the same building—one of us always leaves. For years, I've avoided him, and now I find myself at a crossroads with no clear path ahead.

"How long will you fight this?" Louis asks as we descend the stairs to the ground floor.

"What?"

"The crush."

I roll my eyes as he reaches for my hand, gently pulling me closer.

"You'll need to try harder to hide it from those who know you. Your eyes give you away," he says loud enough for me to hear.

Louis knows me inside and out. I choose to ignore him.

His entourage falls in line behind us, as they always do.

As we approach the exit, I'm mesmerized by Banks casually leaning against the wall, laser-focused on his phone, a smirk playing on his lips. The glow of the screen highlights his chiseled features. I can't help but notice his long lashes and the curve of his lips.

"Mm-hmm," Louis says, glancing toward Banks.

"Whatever," I whisper as the double doors swing open, and we step outside to the relentless clicks of cameras.

In public, we look like a power couple. The media have already written our story; we just have to stoke the flames a little longer.

An SUV pulls up, and I catch Banks in my peripheral vision.

"Smile, Ice Queen," he says as he walks by, reaching for my free hand. His fingers brush against mine, sending butterflies fluttering in my stomach.

Louis pulls me away, guiding me to the car. I glance back at Banks, who flashes a smile before disappearing into the vehicle.

My heart pitter-patters. He's performing for the public and trying to ruin my fake relationship. The problem is, he's so fucking good at it. That's what frustrates me the most.

Grr.

I let out a long sigh of relief once we're inside the car.

"I almost forgot Asher's a brave bastard," Louis says, pulling his phone from his pocket.

"It's unfortunate, if I'm being honest."

"You're his perfect opponent." Louis opens a text and replies to someone saved in his Contacts with a fork emoji.

> LOUIS
> I'm free now. Are you?

He tucks his phone back into his pocket.

I want to ask him who she is.

When our eyes meet, he smiles as if he can read my mind. "I don't kiss and tell. Ever."

"I'm just curious. But I get wanting to keep secrets."

"I've learned that before I take any relationship public, it's important to really get to know someone," Louis says, chuckling softly.

"You're testing her," I say, raising my brows.

"Always. I'm looking for a wife and a suitable queen," he replies with a playful flick of his brow. "It could be you."

I grin widely. "If I'm not married by forty ... I'm still all yours."

"You won't make it to forty," he counters. "Our plan is working. People are more interested in your love life than your business. You're gaining global attention right now, Billie. I hope you realize how big this is."

I run my fingers through my hair, tucking it behind my ears. "It's the perfect distraction while I figure out my next steps," I tell him. "I'll do almost anything for Bellamore."

"Not to your detriment, I hope."

"It's my kingdom. If my castle is on fire, I'll stay with it until it's nothing but ash. I'll mourn the loss and then rebuild it bigger than it ever was."

He nods. "If you ever wonder why Asher chose to play games with you, *that's* why. You don't quit."

I sigh. "He has to know this love-triangle rumor only benefits Bellamore, right?"

Louis meets my gaze. "I think he's focused on the bigger picture, not just Bellamore. I've tried to make sense of it, and that's the only explanation that fits."

"Hmm. And what's the big picture?" I ask, still not quite following.

Asher said something similar, and so did my brothers.

"You," he says simply.

"I want everyone to stop with that," I respond firmly, knowing there's no way. "He felt nothing when we kissed. There's nothing there. He's trying to hurt me."

"Oh. I'm sorry," Louis says, his expression softening. "He's a bellend."

"Yes, he is," I confirm.

The car slows at the curb, and Louis walks me to the door. Paparazzi are camped out, snapping pictures of us.

He gently kisses me for the cameras and then tilts my chin up. "Don't stress. You'll make it through this. You always do."

"My choices are to fight or give up. I can't let Josh win," I whisper.

"Trust me, darling, right now, he's losing big. Heard he had a meltdown earlier today." Louis holds the door open for me.

"Really? Good." I smile. "Thanks for everything." I brush past him and into the lobby.

"Night, Billie."

"Night, Your Royal Highness."

I blow him a kiss, and he grins as he heads back to his car.

If *only* things were different.

Once inside my penthouse loft, I kick off my heels and unzip my dress, letting it fall to the floor. I unsnap my bra and drop it, too, before heading to my bedroom and stepping into my closet.

I throw on some comfy shorts and a cutoff graphic T-shirt that shows off half my stomach. I retrieve my phone from the pocket of my dress and pour myself some rosé in the biggest glass I own. The sweetness hits my tongue, a delightful blend of sweet and tangy.

I light a candle on the counter and briefly watch the flame dance. It smells like strawberry shortcake.

Settling onto the couch, I get comfortable and catch up on what people have been saying about me today.

Most outlets are reporting on my night at Diamond, detailing my supposed romance with Louis and portraying Banks as my jealous secret lover. My nostrils flare as I see photos of our hands brushing together.

The articles speculate that Louis is just a cover while Banks and I plot to take down Josh.

I gasp, realizing that might be why Josh had a meltdown today. Does he really believe this? Could Banks be double-crossing him and somehow helping me in his own twisted way? It's possible. Easton thinks so. I'm not convinced.

Right now, no one knows the real story. One thing that's not being discussed is Bellamore versus Lustre Fashion, and I want to keep it that way, so I'll continue with this angle.

I quickly text my bestie.

> **BILLIE**
> I think I'm entering my villain era.

> **HARPER**
> You entered that era when you turned twenty-one, and nothing has changed.

I burst into laughter.

> **BILLIE**
> Okay. I'm moving into my supervillain era.

> **HARPER**
> Are you drunk?

> **BILLIE**
> Tipsy.

I snap a picture of my half-full glass of rosé and send it to her.

> **HARPER**
> What's your plan?

> **BILLIE**
> I'm going to reach out to Josh.

> **HARPER**
> DO NOT DO THAT. BAD IDEA.

> **BILLIE**
> Hmm.

> **HARPER**
> Sleep on it. Don't make any decisions about your shitty, lying, cheating ex while you're rosé drunk. Please. Promise me. If you still think it's a good idea tomorrow evening, I'll back you up.

BILLIE

> Okay, okay, I promise. Now, back to my mindless scrolling!

HARPER

Thanks! Have fun!

I open a new browser window and type in *Asher Banks*.

The first article that catches my eye is from LuxLeaks. I can't help but smirk as I click the link.

FROM THE DESK OF LADYLUX

LuxBabies,

Today, we're talking about a billionaire baddie I haven't mentioned before. Meet Mr. Asher Banks, brother of ex-hockey superstar Nicolas Banks, who has officially made it onto my radar. We've touched on Nicolas's problematic behavior before, but now it's time to dive into his little brother. Since Asher seems to be desperately seeking attention, I figured I'd give him some. If you're new here, just know that this post is based on speculation about public figures, using information that's readily available online. My opinions are my own and purely for entertainment purposes.

Don't mess with me, Asher.

I CONTINUE READING ABOUT THE CRUSH SHE THINKS HE HAS ON ME. It becomes too much, and I can't take it anymore. I lock my phone, set it down on the coffee table, and then chug the rest of my wine. It's not enough, so I head to the kitchen and grab the bottle from the counter. With my bottle of rosé in hand, I open the door to the terrace, inhaling the fresh air, which cools my lungs and brushes against my skin.

"Bastard," I hiss under my breath, squeezing my eyes shut.

He's all I can think about.

Playing hard to get is clearly part of his game, but why is it working?

I gulp down more wine, leaning on the rail. My thoughts spiral, and I wish they wouldn't.

"Ice Queen?" I hear a familiar deep voice from below.

I turn, blinking twice, as if I might be imagining him.

I groan loudly. "Wow, still stalking me!"

"Still flattering yourself. I picked up a pizza," he says, holding up a box I didn't notice.

I take another swig of wine. "What kind?"

"Pepperoni and mushrooms with extra cheese," he replies.

"That's my favorite. Now you're trying to win me over with food? Who told you? Harper?" I ask.

"No. It's how I order it. I would've pegged you for more of a pineapple-on-pizza type of girl though."

I scoff. "I could say the same about you."

He chuckles. "You're good at that."

"Why did you walk by my place, knowing the next block is faster?" I ask.

"*Pfft*. The next block only seems faster. It's not. The distance is the same; the scenery is all that changes." He shrugs, opens the box, and grabs a slice. He takes a bite but immediately spits it out. "Yep, too fucking hot. I know it's a lame complaint, but I'm starving."

"Patience is a virtue." I laugh.

He tilts his head, watching me. "You should do more of that."

"Deliver proverbs from my balcony?" I ask, though I know he means letting loose—laughing, smiling, enjoying life.

We share a moment.

My gaze drifts over him, and I notice he's still in the suit he wore earlier. It's a textured cashmere silk that fits him perfectly. I can still smell his lingering scent on my skin. If we could just talk, maybe we'd find common ground instead of trying to tear each other apart.

I clear my throat. "Do you—"

"Fuck off, Calloway." He smirks, cutting me off before I can finish.

"Only if you fuck off first," I retort, walking inside and gently shutting the door.

I attempt to drown my worries in rosé and take several big gulps.

Banks looked at me like he was hungry for more than just pizza. I know I wasn't imagining it.

I pick up my phone, return to LuxLeaks, and finish the rest of the article.

Asher, if you're reading this, I believe what you're doing publicly is performative. I'm not convinced you two have ever had a private moment together. I guess this is me saying prove it *because I'm overly skeptical, but I know you won't.*

Edited to add: Proven wrong. Asher's response.

SOUNDS OF ZOOMING CARS ECHO OFF MY BUILDING. I CHUG MORE wine and click the hyperlink, which opens my Instagram app and takes me straight to the photo on his account.

"What?" I whisper, realizing I'm no longer blocked.

My mouth drops open when I spot the picture of us in the hallway, but my hair and his profile cover my face. His fist is buried in my strands, showcasing his big hand and plump lips close to my ear. His gorgeous face steals the show, eyes closed. The photo radiates intensity, much like the moment itself.

"Oh no," I whisper, realizing he just sealed the deal.

If he can convince LadyLux ...

I swallow hard, staring at the photo, recalling how his warm breath felt against my ear and the way his voice rumbled in his throat. My thighs instinctively squeeze together. I sit up straight, my breathing becoming erratic as I read the caption, meant for me —*Pretending you don't exist.*

Butterflies swarm in my stomach.

I scroll down to the comments and notice some accounts even tagged me. Most of the comments mention me directly. My face flushes crimson, and my entire body feels like it's on fire. I stand and pace my living room, having a full-blown panic attack as I scroll. He posted it thirty-five minutes ago, and it already has thousands of comments.

The hair grab ... wow.
Tap out, girl. I'll trade you.
Is this how you let the world know you're secretly together?
This woman has a choice between a literal prince or Asher. I honestly don't know who I'd pick.
I'm convinced Billie Calloway is God's favorite.
This was tonight at Diamond! OMG, does Louis know?
I bet Josh Lustre didn't see that coming. Yikes.
Thank God! I was hoping she'd choose you. Prince Louis is a douche!
This is the only time I've ever seen a hair out of place on her head.

This will take over the internet tomorrow.

The comments continue on for what feels like a mile.

My jaw locks tight, and I feel my temper rising as a soft knock echoes on my door.

I set my phone down, happy for the escape as I move to answer it.

I glance through the peephole, hoping it's Harper because she randomly stops by. But it's not my best friend. It's my mortal enemy.

Banks.

16

ASHER

"Special delivery," I say, knowing she's peeking at me through the peephole. I take a step back and lift the lid. "Okay, you have to admit, it looks good. I'm *not* talking about the pizza."

She groans on the other side of the door. "Go away!"

I lean in closer to the crack. "You don't want me to."

Billie immediately swings the door open. She's rocking bright yellow shorts that cling to her like a second skin and a graphic T-shirt that she transformed into a stylish grunge look. It shows her stomach and the curve of her hips. Proof that she can make anything look sexy.

"What do you want, Banks?" she asks, raising an eyebrow.

"Wait." I pause, letting my eyes slide down her body and back up again. "You actually own clothes that aren't black? *Shocking*."

She rolls her eyes. "How did you get past the doorman?"

"I have my ways," I explain.

"You're so annoying," she counters.

"Would you like some?" I hold the box open, letting the mouthwatering aroma of cheese, pepperoni, and freshly baked dough waft into the hallway.

"Are you talking about the pizza this time?" Billie licks her lips

172

and pushes the door open wide enough for me to step inside. Her blue eyes glint with mischief.

"Are you drunk?" I ask, knowing that when she drinks, she can get wild.

I remember countless college frat parties where my eyes stayed glued on her all night. There was no way I'd let any of my friends near Billie. Every last one of them wanted to bang her, but they'd have used her. Un-fucking-acceptable.

"Don't make me change my mind," she warns.

I walk past her without hesitation.

"Wow," I whisper, stopping to admire the vibrant paintings on the walls and the vintage furniture.

This building was a bookbinding shop in the late 1800s, and it's been remodeled into several penthouses and loft-style apartments. Plenty of A-listers, artists, and fashionistas call this place home.

"Not what you expected?" she asks, shutting the door behind her.

"I just have one question." I glance over at her. "Where do you keep your portal to hell?"

A small smile dances on her lips as she walks past me, giving me an enticing view of her curves. I force my eyes to stay forward, but I'm tempted to memorize every last inch of her. The lights are dim as she leads me into the kitchen. She has an open floor plan with high ceilings, exposed brick, and wooden beams. It feels cozy, lived in.

"A candlelit dinner. How unexpected," I mutter, following her into the kitchen.

She almost laughs.

"Stop doing that," she says, opening a cabinet and pulling out two plates.

"Doing what?" I ask innocently.

"You're flirting," she replies.

"This isn't flirting. Raise your standards." I shrug.

She glares at me. "Every day, I wonder why my brothers choose to be friends with someone like you." She's annoyed, yet she hands me a plate.

"Yeah? How long have you been holding that rant in?"

She groans. "You anger me."

"Feeling's mutual," I admit. "But don't pretend to be all kind and thoughtful. Your reputation precedes you, Calloway. You're not soft. You're cold as ice."

"Then why are you here? It's almost like you enjoy me tearing into you," she counters, unbothered.

"And what if I do?" I challenge. "What if getting under your skin is the highlight of my day?"

She shakes her head. "Find someone else."

"Nope. It's me and you, Ice Queen. This has been going on for so long. No way I'm calling it quits now. I'm way too invested."

She grabs a few napkins for us.

When I glance over, I see her phone is unlocked, displaying the Instagram post of us. I pick it up and smirk.

"Nope," she says, rushing toward me and snatching it from my hand. "Why would you post that? What is wrong with you?"

Laughter bursts from me. "For this reaction. Totally worth it."

"This isn't funny, Banks! You're ruining my life. For the last time, leave me alone." She almost sounds desperate.

"No can do, princess." I move deeper into her kitchen and spot a few bottles of bourbon on the counter. One is my favorite. I remove the top and take a swig. "This is the best. You've got good taste," I say, settling into a seat at the nook. "In everything except men and the dumb-as-fuck sculptures you have at Bellamore."

She looks at me like she wants to rip my eyes out. "Rude as hell. Don't talk about my art that way."

"How much money did you waste on them?"

Her mouth drops open. "I *made* them. You fucking prick."

"Oh, you made them? So, you're fully responsible for the sleek, curved dildos in Bellamore. If that's not a sign of sexual frustration, then I don't know what is."

Billie sits on the stool at the end of the breakfast nook. She's so far away that I wouldn't be able to touch her if I reached out. Maybe that's for the best.

"They don't look like dicks," she mumbles, taking a bite of pizza. "You shouldn't be here. The paps are watching the building."

"Aren't they always?" I ask.

"Still performing for LadyLux?"

I grin. "Wasn't her article enthralling?"

She rolls her eyes. "It's inaccurate."

"Those are your words, not mine," I remind her, echoing what she said to me.

I know what LuxLeaks posted—there were truths sprinkled in, even if some things were exaggerated.

This catches Billie off guard; it shows on her face.

"Why did you unblock me on Instagram?" she asks, then shakes her head. "Actually, why did you block me in the first place? That's a better question."

I take a bite of the pizza I tried to eat earlier. "Ah. Now, that's a great question," I say, just as a few knocks sound on Billie's door. My brows furrow. "Are you expecting someone?"

"My boyfriend," she tells me, and I can't tell if she's joking.

She moves toward the door and glances back at me. The knocking continues. She looks in the peephole, and her demeanor shifts.

"You have to hide," she says, moving back to me as the knocking persists. Billie grabs my hand and pushes me down the hallway. "Hide in my bedroom." She points at the door at the end of the hall. "Five minutes."

"And if I say no?"

"Please don't do this to me right now. Please." She's serious.

"Who is it?" I ask.

"Go," she instructs.

I move toward her bedroom that's lined by dark brick walls. Her high heels are scattered on the floor, like she undressed the moment she got home. I pass the sexy dress she was wearing, along with a strapless bra. I enter her bedroom, amazed by how she designed it.

"Nice lair, Ice Queen."

A king-size four-poster bed rests against a light-gray wall, neatly made with fluffy white blankets and stacked pillows.

A deep voice pulls me away. I leave the door cracked open, straining to hear, but I can't make out the words.

"What do you want?" Billie asks, her tone laced with venom and an anger I've never heard before. It's surprising, considering I've witnessed some of her worst moments over the years.

The muffled voice returns.

"It doesn't matter if I'm alone or not. We aren't together. We are never getting back together," she states firmly. "No! I will never forgive you."

My heart races as I listen. If she raises her voice one more time, it's over.

"No, no," she says.

I hear footsteps approaching. I quickly slip into Billie's closet. It's dark, and the silhouettes of her black clothes surround me.

"I know he's here," the guy says, and I instantly recognize the voice—Josh Lustre.

"It doesn't matter. We're not together. Why the hell are you here?" she retorts. "I thought I'd made it clear that I never wanted to see you again."

"I miss you," he confesses. "You and Asher—"

"Are nothing," she snaps. "We will never be anything. Why are you so damn concerned about him? You know how I feel about him, and you still hired him! What the fuck, Josh?"

"Then why is he here? Apparently, it's not hate if you're eating pizza with him."

"Get out," Billie demands. I can picture the glare on her face, her cold eyes piercing into him.

"I've requested to no longer work with him."

"Are you stupid?" she shoots back. "Asher is the best thing that could have ever happened to you, considering what you've been doing."

He scoffs. "I don't know what you're talking about."

"Yes, you do. And I promise you, if you don't stop, I will take everything you own. Your company will go to hell in a Birkin bag, and I will ruin your reputation worse than you ever could."

"Empty threats," Josh replies dismissively.

"And that will be your downfall," Billie counters without missing a beat. "Leave."

"Bill—"

"Do not call me that. I fucking hate it. I've always hated it," she says firmly. "You shouldn't be here. I have nothing else to say to you."

"I'm sorry, baby. Please forgive me. I'll do anything if you give me another chance," Josh nearly begs.

My jaw clenches tight.

"You weren't sorry when your dick was buried in your ex while you were with me."

Almost a minute of silence passes.

Then the door swings open, and I'm face-to-face with Josh.

I exhale sharply, aware of how this must look, even though it shouldn't.

"You bastard!" His fists start swinging.

Billie tries to pull him away, but it's no use. Josh lunges toward my head, and I duck just in time. With a fierce growl, he charges at me, rage radiating off him.

"You don't want to do this," I warn. "I'm not dating Billie."

"You're clearly fucking her!"

I let out a laugh. "I've already told you once that it's none of your damn business what I do in my free time."

He swings again, but this time, I fight back. My knuckles connect with his face, and he stumbles back. He trips and falls to the floor, and I tackle him, ready to finish this once and for all.

Years of resentment bubble up inside me for how he treated Billie when they were together.

"Don't do it, Asher," she whispers, reaching for me. "He's *not* worth it. I promise."

I lock eyes with her, then glance back at Josh's pathetic face. "You're so lucky she's logical."

Josh growls as I release my grip on him.

I stand, pinning his shoulder down with my foot, increasing the pressure. "Next time you pull some shit like that, you'll really regret it."

"Don't threaten me," he says, trying to sound tough.

"It's not a threat," I assure him.

"I'm so sorry," I tell Billie as I leave her room, knowing this was a mistake.

She follows closely behind me.

"Please don't leave," she whispers.

"Are you begging me to stay?" I ask teasingly.

Her lips part slightly, and just as I'm waiting for her response, Josh appears behind her, face flushed with anger. He moves toward me, using all his strength to slam me against the wall. Billie screams for him to stop. His fists fly, and one connects hard with my jaw.

"Get out, Josh!" she yells as she rushes for her phone.

I throw a few punches into his cheek, but he trips me up. Moments later, we're rolling on the floor. The front door bursts open, and when I look up, I see Brody. He's livid, turmoil swirling in his deep blue eyes.

"What the hell? How did he get in here?" Brody yanks Josh off me, putting him in a headlock and guiding him out the door.

Billie locks it behind them as they start yelling at each other in the foyer.

"I should have you arrested for breaking your restraining order," Brody threatens.

I furrow my brows, staring at Billie.

She steps closer, gently grasping my chin to get a better look at my jaw. "Wow," she says, studying me. "Why are you helping me?"

"I need to go," I admit, realizing my spontaneous decision was a terrible idea.

I pictured a nice pizza dinner, filled with conversation. Tonight has shown me that pushing boundaries with Billie is a bad call. Maybe Nick was right; I really do need a vacation because I've completely lost the plot. I am crashing out.

Billie moves to the counter, grabs the pizza box, and hands it to me with a sweet smile. "Thanks for the slice."

I take it from her and open the lid. "Want another?"

"I'll take the one on your plate. That's enough."

"Okay," I say, forcing myself to walk away.

I head toward the front door, and she follows me.

I step outside, turning to respond. As I open my mouth to say something, she interrupts.

"Fuck off, Banks," she snaps.

I give her a single nod. "Fuck off, Ice Queen."

She slams the door in my face.

I try to hold back a smile but fail as I walk a short distance down the hallway and press my thumb against the reader of my loft. The one I secretly purchased after I took over my sister's agency.

The knob clicks open. I step inside and flick on the lights. I've always loved the architecture of this building. The brick and exposed wooden beams are my favorite features. I set the pizza box down on the counter, no longer hungry, even though I was starving.

This loft, with its three bedrooms and four baths, isn't a place I visit often. It feels empty inside, like most of the property I own—except for the townhome a few blocks away, which feels a bit more like home.

I suck in a deep breath and loosen my tie. I rummage through cabinets and drawers, even the fridge, which is stocked only with bottled and canned drinks.

As I shrug off my suit coat, a loud knock pounds at my door.

I look to see Billie with her arms crossed tightly over her chest. She's mad.

I crack the door open just enough to see her. "Can I help you?"

"You're my fucking neighbor? Do you realize that I've been trying to find out who owned this place for the past four years?"

"Mmm. What did you discover?" I ask. "That it's an umbrella company within an umbrella company within another?"

"Exactly," she replies through gritted teeth. "Do you get off on buying property right next to me? First, the building for your business, and now this? What's your actual deal?"

"I only bought it to enjoy the seventy-one-foot indoor pool in the winter," I explain. "I prefer my townhome to the loft though."

"You paid twenty million dollars just to swim in a pool?" She narrows her eyes at me.

"Yep," I say. "My trust fund more than covered it."

"You're incredibly annoying."

"Thanks. I *try*." I close the door in her face, then watch her through the peephole.

She scoffs and blinks at the door, slowly shaking her head. I think she's in shock.

Billie places her thumb over the hole.

"You're such a …" She stops talking. "You've been my neighbor, and I don't even know what to fucking say. I can't believe this."

I chuckle. "There are more revelations just waiting for you, princess."

She pounds her fist against the wood. "It's not funny. You're terrorizing me!"

I swing the door open. "You're literally the terror in this situation. Am I at your house, having a meltdown?"

Billie inhales deeply. "You know what? You're right. You're

absolutely right. I am having a breakdown at your door because you pushed me to my fucking limit. I hope you're happy."

A grin creeps onto my lips as I lean against the door. "I'm the happiest I've been in a long time."

"Now I'm convinced you're the actual devil," she says, attempting to walk away.

I grab her hand, pulling her back in front of me. "Is that why I'm so bad for you?"

"Maybe," she says, her brow lifting playfully. "There are plenty of other reasons why."

"List them," I challenge, intrigued. "Tell me why you hate me, little Calloway. I'm still not sure."

Her breath hitches as her chest rises and falls. Her nipples are hard, clearly visible through the thin fabric of her almost-vintage T-shirt. The elevator dings open, and Mrs. Chambers, our other neighbor, catches sight of us. Her silver hair glimmers in the foyer's overhead light. She immediately beams at us.

"I figured I'd run into you two," she says with a wink. "Wait until LadyLux hears about this."

"Mrs. Chambers, please, it's not what it looks like," Billie interjects.

She's a feisty old woman, a widow of an oil tycoon from Wyoming. Her brother owns one of America's most successful cattle ranches.

"Hand me your phone," she says, holding out her palm.

I pull it from my pocket, and she opens the camera, snaps a photo, and hands it back.

"What does that look like to you?"

Billie glances at the photo, and a grin spreads across my face.

I step forward and hug Mrs. Chambers. "Thank you so much for this."

"Honey, I want what you've been drinking."

"Delete that," Billie pleads, reaching for my phone, but I lock it.

"No way," I counter, blocking her every move. "This is gold."

Mrs. Chambers strolls away. "Just have sex already."

Moments later, we burst into laughter. Mrs. Chambers's words linger in the air like a dare, a tempting call to sin, and then she's gone, her door closing with a finality that feels like permission. Billie's eyes lock on to mine. I study those lust-drunk, hate-filled eyes that have always shot daggers toward me. Now they're molten, searing into my skull.

"No," she breathes. Her voice trembles, as if she's already losing the battle *she* started.

"Absolutely not," I growl back, my voice rough, my cock straining against my pants.

Then she leans in, taking every damn risk in the world.

Her body slams into mine, pinning me against the doorjamb with a force that leaves no doubt who's in control. Our lips crash together—hot and hungry—and our hate for one another evaporates like cold rain on scorching concrete. I open my mouth wider, giving her everything she craves. Logic vanishes as our tongues tangle in a filthy dance that nearly brings me to my knees.

I fucking hate the way she makes me feel. I want to ruin her, but in the best goddamn way possible.

"Asher," she whispers against my lips, her voice ragged.

That undoes me.

She has never called me by my first name, not even when we first met.

17

ASHER

I grip her hips as I pull her into the loft with me, pinning her against the closed door while we lose ourselves in the kiss. My hand slides down to her perfect ass in those tiny shorts that drive me insane. I yank her closer, pressing the hardness in my pants against her, and she moans into my mouth—a sound so fucking obscene that it sends a jolt straight to my dick.

My fingers slip under the hem of her shorts, finding the wet heat of her pussy waiting for me like a fucking feast. She's not wearing panties, and she's soaked through the material. Her slickness coats my fingers as I push one inside her. She moans with pleasure, giving me soft pants. Her walls clench around me like they're trying to steal my soul. I'd willingly give it to her for more of this—for *her*.

"*Fuck*," she gasps against my mouth, nails digging into my scalp as I add another finger, curling them just right to make her legs shake.

Her clit is swollen and begging for attention, and I flick it with my thumb, the rhythm brutal and relentless.

Her pussy is bare and perfect, and I want her on my face, riding my tongue.

I messily slide my mouth across her cheek to her ear. "You hate me, huh?" I snarl, my breath hot against her skin as I work her harder and faster.

She gives me several little moans, an approval as she grinds into me with her back arched.

"You fucking hate this so much that you want more? Mmm. Greedy fucking girl."

"Yes," she desperately answers.

Her whimpers betray her as her hips buck against my hand. Her pussy is a vise—slick and tight—and I can feel her trembling, that telltale tension building as she teeters on the brink of coming all over my fucking hand. She rides me almost to the edge. When every muscle tenses and her breathing morphs into moans, I stop.

I pull my fingers out of her with a wet sound that makes her cry out in frustration. Her body jerks like I just ripped her heart out. Her eyes fly open—wild and desperate—and I smirk, placing my fingers deep into my mouth just to see her squirm.

"You taste so fucking good," I say, my voice dripping with venom and satisfaction. This is proof that I have control, not her. "But it seems like the ice queen needs to cool off."

"You're denying me?" she grits out breathlessly, staring at me, nipples hard as hell.

If looks could kill, I'd be dead, laid out on the floor, staring up at her sexy body with stars in my eyes. Billie is a constellation of beauty, even if a storm surrounds her.

Her disdain for me is so obvious that I find it entertaining. This woman has never been denied a thing in her life. Just like the other Calloways, she has always gotten everything she wanted. Her father made sure of it.

Her plump lips are swollen from my rough kisses, her hair a glorious mess. I want her. I need her. But I also know we've been drinking, and I will respect her in the most disrespectful way because she responds to it. She's a spoiled brat, and taming her, showing her she isn't in control, will be a challenge.

The Boss Situation

I chew on my lip, smiling at how dripping wet she is. My princess is soaked.

"I hate you so fucking much." She smooths down her shorts.

"Good. It's best if you keep it that way."

"I will get you back. And it will be so much worse," she snaps.

"I honestly can't wait," I tell her.

"That was the first and last opportunity you'll ever get with me, Banks. I won't make that mistake again." She seethes, opening the door.

"Can't wait to make you eat a shit sandwich full of your words," I mutter, my voice gravelly as I watch her from the doorway.

I cross my arms over my chest. She flips me off as she walks away with trembling legs, wet shorts, and nipples so hard that they could cut glass. Anger radiates off her, and I can tell she's turned on.

Unfortunately, I'm not immune; my cock throbs painfully in my pants. I'm tempted to go to her, lift her into my arms, and carry her back to my bedroom. I'd fuck her until she couldn't walk, imprinting my cock so deep inside her that she'd know she belonged to me from that moment on. No one else. Even if we hate each other.

Billie enters her loft and slams the door.

I chuckle, loving how well I've learned her.

I escape inside, feeling like a stranger here.

My cock is a goddamn ticking time bomb, throbbing like it's got a heartbeat of its own. It's so hard that it's practically begging for mercy, but I'm not in the mood to give it any relief—not yet. I fumble with my pants, fingers trembling like a fucking teenager as I unbutton and unzip. The second my dick springs free, it's like it's got a mind of its own, standing at full attention, pre-cum already pooling at the tip, like it's ready to explode.

I'm a mess, and it's all because of her.

Billie. That bratty, spoiled little queen who's been driving me insane for years. Ever since we met, she's been the thorn in my side, the itch I can't scratch, the fire I can't put out.

And tonight? Tonight, she was here. In my apartment. Those icy-blue eyes that see right through me, those full lips that could ruin me if she ever decided to use them properly. We had drunk too much, and she let me touch her. Fuck, she wanted me. I almost kept going. I almost gave her what she desperately wanted. Afterward, I'd have fucked her senseless.

Now I'm here, alone, with nothing but memories, the scent of her on my fingers and the taste of her on my tongue.

I bring my hand up to my nose and inhale deeply. She smells like sin and salt, like something sweet and dangerous that I know I shouldn't want but can't resist. God, she tasted even better—like trouble that could destroy me if I let it. I want her to ruin me, to take me apart piece by piece, until there's nothing left but the sound of her name on my lips.

I storm into my bedroom, stripping off my clothes like they're on fire. The sheets are cool against my skin as I slide between them, but they do nothing to calm the heat burning through me. My hand finds my cock again, and I don't waste any time. I wrap my fingers around it, squeezing just hard enough to make my breath hitch, and start stroking. Slow at first, just to tease myself, because I know I won't let this end anytime soon. Not yet.

I close my eyes, and there she is. Billie.

Fucking Billie.

Her black hair falls around her gorgeous face as she looks up at me from between my legs, those blue eyes locked on mine, like she's daring me to stop her. Her tongue flicks out, catching the pre-cum on the tip of my cock, and I swear I can feel it—hot and wet and so fucking perfect.

"Fuck," I growl, my grip tightening as I imagine her swallowing me down, taking me so deep that I can feel the back of her throat.

My hips buck up into my hand as I stroke harder, faster, the sound of skin on skin filling the room. I can almost hear her moaning, those soft little noises she makes when she's losing control, and it's enough to make my balls tighten.

But I'm not gonna let myself come.

Not yet.

Not until I've imagined every detail of what I'd do to her if I had her here right now.

I start with her mouth. Those lips wrap around me, sucking until I'm dizzy. Then I flip her over, spread her legs, and bury my face between them until she screams my name. She tastes like heaven—I know it; I can feel it. She's so fucking wet for me, her pussy clenching around my tongue as I lick and suck and tease her until she begs me to fuck her.

And I would.

Oh, I fucking would.

I push inside her, inch by inch, until she's full of me, until she's gasping and clawing at my back like she can't get close enough. I fuck her until she's a whimpering mess, coming so hard that she forgets her name.

And then I do it again. And again. And again.

But she's not here. She's in her apartment, probably lying in bed, thinking about me, just like I'm thinking about her. I bet she's touching herself right now, fingers sliding in the slickness I caused between her legs as she thinks about what we did tonight. She's such a fucking brat, but she can't help herself—she wants me just as much as I want her. She has to. Otherwise, she wouldn't have let me touch her. She liked watching me taste her.

My hand moves faster now, my hips jerking up into my grip as I imagine her riding me, taking control like the spoiled little princess she is.

She's so fucking tight, her pussy gripping me like a vise as she rides my cock, her tits bouncing with every movement.

I can almost hear her moaning my name, begging me to fill her up, to make her mine. That's what she really wants. That's what her cold eyes say each time they meet mine.

But I can't. Not yet.

I force myself to stop, my hand stilling just as I feel the edge of an orgasm creeping up on me.

My body screams for release, but I deny it, squeezing the base of my cock to keep myself from coming. This isn't about relief; it's about control.

About proving to myself that I can resist her, even if it fucking kills me.

I collapse back against the pillows, chest heaving as I try to catch my breath.

She's buried deep under my skin—that much is clear.

And one day, when she's ready—when we're ready—I'll make her mine.

But until then? This is all I get. This is all she gets.

And it has to be enough.

I have to know when to hold them and when to fold them. Too much is at stake.

18

BILLIE

I slam the door shut, leaning against it as my heart races.

I'm so wet for him that it's nearly dripping down my leg. The worst part about the entire thing is that he knows I'm putty in his hands. Asher so quickly brought me to the very edge until I was ready to spill over for him like some desperate whore. I was. Oh my God, I was. And had he not stopped, I'd have completely lost myself.

"Fuck," I breathlessly say, wanting that man out of my mind. Somehow, I also want him buried deep inside me. I'm a fucking mess.

With my back pressed against the door, I slide down to the floor, my thighs trembling like a fucking earthquake.

My cunt's still throbbing, slick and swollen—a damn traitor, begging for more of Asher.

He's a beautiful, infuriating bastard who has me weak in the knees.

When his fingers were deep inside me, curling just right, it felt so fucking good. I wanted it. I needed it. And he knew it—that was why he stopped. That asshole left me hanging, my pussy clenching around nothing, my body screaming, *begging* for more of him.

I'm not in control.

I bite my lip hard as I shove my hand down my shorts, my fingers sliding through the sticky mess between my legs. I'm so wet, my juices soaked completely through the material. I picture him—his smirk, those honey-brown eyes that see right through me, that stupidly perfect jawline with scruff that makes me want to punch and kiss him at the same time.

My fingers desperately find my clit, swollen and aching, and I rub it in slow, deliberate circles, wishing it was his tongue instead.

"Shit," I whimper as I slide two fingers inside myself, my walls clenching tight.

I'm so fucking needy, so desperate, and I hate him for it. I *hate* how he makes me feel, how he can reduce me to this—a horny, writhing, panting mess on the floor of my loft. I curl my fingers, searching for that sweet spot, and when I find it, I moan loudly, my head falling back against the door.

I picture his large fingers—big, rough, slamming deep inside me. I think back to how his body was pinned against me, his thick cock pressing against me as he whispered in my ear.

My other hand sneaks up to my breast, pinching my nipple hard; the sharp pain only makes the pleasure more intense. My hips buck against my fingers; my pussy clenches as I fuck myself faster, harder, desperate for that release he denied me.

"Asher." I moan his name like a prayer, but he's more of a curse. My voice trembles.

That coil in my belly winds tighter and tighter until I'm shaking, nearly begging to come.

I'm close—so damn close—and I move from my nipple down to my clit.

It hits me so violently.

My entire body tenses and convulses as I come, my pussy spasming around my fingers. Waves of pleasure crash over me, nearly drowning me as I imagine being with him. I bite my lip to

The Boss Situation

stifle the scream that threatens to escape, my thighs clamping around my hand as I ride it out, gasping for air.

When it's over, I'm sweaty, sticky, and still so goddamn turned on.

I pull my fingers out slowly, watching as they glisten with my juices, and realize I squirted. That's never happened before. I can't help but wonder what would have happened had he made me come. I might have begged him to fuck me to oblivion.

I felt how hard he was for me, how desperately he wanted me. Asher *tasted* me.

My thighs clench together as a fresh wave of heat floods through me. I'm still so turned on and horny.

Damn. He's ruined me.

Absolutely fucking wrecked me.

And the worst part? I'd let him do it again in a heartbeat.

The chase has me in a choke hold, and it may kill me.

I pick myself up off the floor, my yellow shorts drenched, and move to the bathroom. I turn on the shower, slide out of my clothes, and step under the hot stream.

Right now, I need a hefty dose of reality and to wash the smell of him off my skin.

The steam floats and curls around me like a lover's breath, hot and heavy. My body still buzzes from his touch.

I'll never forgive him for this because now, I'm physically craving him.

My skin prickles with a delicious ache that only he can satisfy.

Asher. His name alone makes my cunt clench like a fist, for him, for his touch.

I let the hot water run over me, my nipples still in hard little peaks, begging for more attention. My fingers trail down my stomach, dragging through the slickness between my thighs, as I picture his hand instead of my own. But that isn't enough. Not nearly enough.

I reach for the showerhead, detaching it from the wall and adjusting the pressure until it's a light and steady stream.

Perfect.

I lean back against the tiled wall, spreading my legs wider as I bring the nozzle closer to my already-sensitive clit. The second that warm, relentless stream hits me, I moan out, my head falling back as pleasure shoots through me like a bullet.

I close my eyes and let myself drift into the fantasy of him again. *It's always him.*

His towering frame looms over me, his chest broad and sculpted, every inch of him hard and dangerous. Asher has always lurked in the shadows of my mind. Right now, he's at the forefront.

His golden eyes burn with intensity as he pins me against the shower wall, his cock thick and heavy between us, pressing against my stomach.

"You already came for me once. Come again, princess."

I can almost hear his low, gravelly voice, and it sends shivers down my spine.

In this fantasy, he's touching me; his fingers circle my clit with a precision that makes me cry out.

I feel his other hand gripping my hip, holding me in place as he drives me closer to the edge.

Stars explode behind my eyes as the water pulsates against me in a rhythm that matches the fantasy of Asher I've conjured.

My breath comes in ragged gasps as I fantasize about his hot mouth on my neck, his perfect teeth and plump lips grazing my skin while he whispers filthy promises in my ear.

"I want to feel you come on my cock," he murmurs in this vision of mine, his voice dripping with need. "I want to fuck you so hard that you actually hate me."

My thighs tremble as pleasure builds inside me—hot and unrelenting. The second orgasm hits me so fast and hard that I nearly lose my balance. Waves of pleasure crash over me again and again, and my cries echo throughout my bathroom. What I feel is raw and guttural. It's almost an out-of-body experience.

When I finally come down from my high and regain some amount of consciousness, my legs feel like gelatin. Each ragged breath heaves through my chest as I steady myself.

I place the showerhead in its holster, feeling somewhat satisfied, though I have an itch only one person can scratch. But even as my body relaxes, thoughts of him linger—the memory of his hands, his mouth, his thick cock in his suit pants, pressed against me—leaving me craving more. And deep down, I know this isn't over. Not even close.

Maybe Josh had a right to be jealous. Tonight, I confirmed Asher is attracted to me. That alone gives me an upper hand, but also changes things.

I dry myself, then go to my bedroom and slide between the sheets. I stare at the ceiling, wondering what he's doing right now. I hope he's stroking himself to me.

"Whoa," Harper says as she bursts into my office, her voice echoing in the space.

I snuck in five minutes earlier, not ready to face the day after my night. My throbbing hangover blends with my double shot of espresso that hasn't magically worked yet. Weeknight drinking isn't something I usually do, but I needed to ensure Louis and I stayed relevant. Asher fucked that up.

Actually, he's messed up a lot of things for me.

I didn't sleep well and tossed and turned in bed over thoughts of *him*. Today, I'm mentally and physically exhausted.

"I have a question for you," I say to my best friend.

"Sure."

"Do you think my sculptures look like dicks?" I ask.

She bursts into laughter. "Kinda. But I still like them."

I shake my head. "Bastard."

Harper's lips curl into a mischievous smile. "You're glowing like Edward in *Twilight*. Spill it."

I refuse to meet her gaze, my eyes locked on the meeting request blinking on my screen, asking me to accept.

"Not sure what you're referring to," I say, my tone as nonchalant as my attempt to ignore the growing chaos swirling inside me.

She approaches my neat desk and slides her phone toward me.

I glance down and see the photo of Asher and me standing in his doorway. His hand is on my hip, and I'm looking up at him like he's *everything*.

"OH MY FUCKING GOD!" I scream, instantly pissed as I quickly scan over the caption.

This is her definition of hate.

My head pounds harder as I glance over the comments.

Hate? Look how you two look at each other.

Holy shit! I was today years old when I realized Billie Calloway doesn't always wear black.

THIS is Billie Calloway? Ice Queen? No way. She's a smokeshow.

You bring out the best in her.

Ho, is that the diamond princess?

Where can I get those shorts? And that shirt combo?

OMG. Billie Calloway is a fashion icon without even trying.

Is she smirking? Whoa.

Never seen her happier.

I shake my head, pushing it away, feeling like I might throw up. There are thousands of comments, and it was posted forty minutes ago.

"This is bad. This is the worst-case scenario."

My thoughts start to spiral. With one post, Asher officially unraveled my and Louis's fake relationship.

Harper sits in the chair in front of my desk. "I think this is the best thing that could've ever happened to us. The shorts you were wearing are a part of our spring line. We sold out of every size in yellow."

"What?" I look at her, puzzled. "We couldn't *give* those shorts away."

"Seems like you're the magic. And Asher. We're not through our financial issues, but we should end this quarter much higher than we forecast, which is a start. Maybe we really can turn this around? You're a genius. This is actually working," she states. She waves her hand in front of my face as I zone out. "Are you still with me?"

"I'm sorry. I'm shocked, and I'm livid. I didn't do this. I can't take credit for this. Right now, I don't have control of the situation, Harp. That scares me," I admit. "This will hurt Louis and anger Josh. Why would Banks do this? He's trying to destroy everything," I growl, standing. "I *hate* him so much!"

She's looking at me, confused. "Hate? After this photo?"

"*Especially* after that photo." I remember what followed after—how he had my body begging for him. I would've given him every part of me.

I glance over my shoulder at his office. The lights are dark, and his computer is off. The sign he hung last week is still securely in place. And of course, he's conveniently late.

"I need to speak to him. Right now."

"Let it be," she says. "It will all work out. But I do have one question. Who took the picture? Brody?" she asks.

I huff. "Nosy Mrs. Chambers stepped off the elevator as I was telling Banks to go fuck himself after I learned he purchased the loft across from mine!"

Her mouth falls open, and her eyes are as wide as saucers. "Asher owns that loft? He's your neighbor?"

"When I watched him leave my place and unlock that door, I realized he owned it. I lost my shit, and Mrs. Chambers snapped a photo of the aftermath to prove a point, apparently," I explain, understanding the optics of how this looks. I almost hyperventilate.

"No one will believe that I'm with Louis after this! I wouldn't be surprised if Banks had set this entire photo up with her."

"He does seem to know you really well."

My nostrils flare. "Fuck Asher Banks!"

Harper gives me a cheesy grin. "I would."

"Shut up," I tell her, placing my head on my desk. "I don't know how to fix this. What are my options other than going into hiding until the Lustre contract expires?"

She chuckles. "All you have to do is make Asher uncomfortable."

"Impossible," I mutter. "He has no boundaries."

"He *acts* like he has no boundaries, but everyone has a limit, a weakness, even him. Just live in the moment, B. Take the punches and start saying yes to situations instead of no. The spotlight is on you."

"That's the part I don't like. Necessary evil."

Harper stands with a grin. "You've got this, boss."

"*We* do. I won't let you down, Harp."

"Oh, I know," she says, walking toward the door. "I want sushi soon."

"Me too," I tell her.

"You are going to the gala this weekend, right?"

I nod. "Shit, yes. I need to let Weston know."

"You were supposed to RSVP by last week," she reminds me.

"It's Weston. He'll make an exception."

The next few hours are hectic. The two pictures that Asher posted of us have gone so mega viral that Perez Hilton is now covering my alleged relationships. The palace wants answers, but Louis has denied everything, calling this a media setup by his firm to twist the narrative.

At some point, Louis won't be able to continue doing that because right now, no one believes him. We might have another week of this charade, at best.

My assistant has worked overtime to handle the inquiries regarding my relationship status. I'm spiraling, realizing how much of a toll this attention is taking. Every twenty minutes, I spin in my chair, checking if Banks has arrived. He hasn't.

A looming feeling hangs over me, and I'm trying to ignore it. If I had his number, I'd text him, but I can't ask anyone for it. Not even him. It would confirm too much, and he'd never allow me to live it down. It's not a conversation I'm dying to have with anyone either, not even myself.

I go to Harper's office and peek my head inside. "I think I'm going out for lunch."

She's on the phone, and she waves me inside. I sit in front of her desk.

"No comment," she says.

A moment later, the call ends.

"Your fake relationship with Louis is one headline away from exploding after Asher posted that photo," she confirms. "My phone has—"

It rings.

She unplugs it and returns her attention to me. "Silence." She sighs. "Finally. How are you holding up?"

I shake my head. "I'm at my limit."

Harper can read me so easily, but that happens when you've had the same best friend since you were five years old. "Why don't you take the rest of the day off? Go home, have a nice hot bubble bath, draw some on your iPad," she suggests.

"Maybe I will," I tell her.

"It's an order. Being here, surrounded by this, isn't productive. You're on the brink of something monumental, bestie. I can *feel* it," she says.

Harper is very intuitive. She has been known to make love prophecies and predict things before they happen.

"I really hope you're right."

"I am. I *always* am," she confirms. "Now, go relax. I'll see you tomorrow."

I stand. "Thank you for being the best business partner and friend I could ever have."

"Right back at you," she says, waving me away. She plugs her phone back in, and it immediately rings.

I leave her office, feeling like a tangled ball of yarn, knowing things are a mess. As soon as I leave the building, paps are on me. I hail a cab and climb in. Before we pull away, the door opens and closes.

When I glance over, I see Nick.

He gives me a boyish grin, looking at me with the same expression Asher wears sometimes. "What a surprise."

"You can say that again," I mutter.

"Where you goin'?" the driver asks.

I give my address.

"I can be dropped there too," Nick says, then glances at me.

I stay silent, not knowing what to say to him. He's always been very nice to me, but he's closer to my brothers' age than mine. Nick used to snowboard and play hockey before he was injured, and then he began working with Eden at the advertising company. He's flirty, attractive, and a walking red flag.

"Do you realize there will be pictures of you and me posted together now?" I look into his eyes.

"Oh, that's fine. I'm not concerned," he admits, and the car grows quiet again.

"Of course you're not concerned. My life is a fucking wreck because of your asshole brother."

"I'm aware. And I apologize."

I stare out the window, wishing there weren't so much traffic on the road, but it's midday in Manhattan. It's to be expected.

"Where is Asher?" I ask.

"He didn't tell you? You were clearly together last night." His brows crease.

"*Nothing* is going on between us."

"I'm not here to debate it. I don't give a fuck if you two are or aren't together. I'm concerned that he's going to make a stupid mistake and mess up our company. A lot of people's livelihoods depend on our success, and I can't let them down. Because of that, Asher has been put on leave for seven days. He won't be back at the office until next week."

My eyes widen. "You put him on probation?"

"I did, and it can be extended up to ninety days. *You* are a conflict of interest," he says nonchalantly. "The board doesn't appreciate anything Asher is doing, and they do not like the public attention being drawn to the company. Also, Lustre is very upset about the two of you. Now I'm going to have to deal with that dumb fuck until things settle down. The last thing I need is a major lawsuit on my hands."

"I didn't ask for this." I shake my head.

"It's not you. It's my stubborn brother. He listens to no one. Ever."

The car takes a sharp curve onto the highway where the traffic is heavier but there are fewer lights. I'm not upset about it. I want out of this car right now.

"You know he's still going to give Josh his all," I say.

"Yeah. But he'd also give his all to fucking with you, and that can't happen. He needs to take some time to clear his mind, and by the looks of it, you need to as well."

"Glad I asked for your opinion," I say. "Is that a Banks trait?"

"The response I expected." He chuckles. It's soft and kinda sexy.

I see the allure, even though sporty guys aren't my type. They're too douchey, even for me.

The car slows outside of my building, and Nick pays for the ride.

I reach for the handle, and Nick speaks in a lowered voice. "He's at the Hamptons house. It's where he goes when he needs to clear his head. Whatever is going on can't be public as long as Asher is working with Josh. Do you understand?" he says, his eyes pinning me in place.

"Send that message to your brother. I know how to keep my personal life private." I give him a small smile and step out.

I enter my building, rattled, and I want to speak to Asher right now.

As I take the elevator to my loft, I know exactly what I have to do.

Looks like I'm taking a drive to my family's Hamptons home. It's three doors down from his.

Of course it is.

19
ASHER

I sit on a blanket on the beach as the chilly wind surrounds me. The fire I built roars to life, the air causing the hot flames to blaze through the dry wood faster than I expected. Luckily, I gathered enough supplies to last me through the bottle of whiskey I've been nursing since the sun set an hour ago. I shake my head as "When a Man Loves a Woman" starts playing on my phone, the familiar tune pulling me deeper into my thoughts.

Drinking alone while the waves crash in the distance, while listening to music from a different time, refreshes my soul. I can't deny that memories of Billie occupy my mind like a stubborn shadow. This feud between us is fueled by a mix of annoyance and admiration, and it's hard to untangle one from the other.

Lifting the bottle to my lips, I take several gulps. It goes down smooth, like water on a hot day, and I can feel the warmth spreading through me.

The stars are out, even if the glow from the city still lingers behind me. Being here is an escape for me, a sanctuary where I hid for months after Eden tragically passed away. When I'm lost, I always find my true self here.

A chill travels over my skin, and I pull my hoodie tighter over my baseball hat to cover my ears. I'm barefoot, still in shorts, completely unguarded. Alone.

I let out a deep breath, and when I look up from the flames, I notice a figure walking toward me. My eyes stay locked until they move closer, and I'm convinced I'm imagining things. I've drunk so much that I'm starting to hallucinate, believing Billie's really here. I have it so fucking bad.

"Didn't expect to see the angel of death tonight," I say, trying to keep my voice light, but the weight of my words lingers in the air.

Billie stands across the fire, the flames casting a warm glow around her, like a halo. I stare up at her, the whiskey still tight in my grip, as my heart pounds in my chest.

I might be *finally* losing it.

Her dark hair dances in the breeze, and her eyes lock on to mine with an intensity that sends a thrill down my spine. I take another swig of whiskey and set the bottle beside me on the blanket, my focus solely on her.

"Are you wasted?" she asks, moving closer, her gaze daring and teasing, like she's challenging me.

"Come here." My voice is low and gravelly, filled with a yearning that surprises even me.

"No," she says, crossing her arms over her chest.

"Now," I say as I reach my hand out to her.

Though she wants to act like a brat, she does what I asked, gliding across the sand toward me. I pull her down onto the blanket with me, and she settles on my lap.

"Why the fuck are you here?" I ask, desperate to touch her, needing to know she's real, that this moment is real.

"Because I have a fucking bone to pick with you," she says, her voice barely above a whisper. "Nick told me you were here."

I chuckle, shaking my head. "He's a bastard."

Electricity swarms between us as I lean in, breathing her in. I want her so fucking bad that it hurts.

"You smell good."

"I'm really mad at you," she admits, her mouth set in a firm line.

"Aw, what else is new, Ice Queen?" I lift an eyebrow, smirking.

She turns her head to glare at me.

"Why did you post that picture? What's wrong with you?" she snaps.

I laugh. "You have been the highlight of my day."

"You've created a shitstorm," she says desperately, her voice a mix of frustration and something else. "You are ruining my life!"

"No, I'm just forcing you to live a little," I admit, tracing her bottom lip with my thumb, feeling the softness beneath my touch. "I have no fucking regrets."

The wood crackles as the waves crash in the background. I'm feeling too vulnerable, and I shouldn't be around her in this state. We shouldn't be this close, but honestly, I don't have the fucks to give to put any walls up as I wrap my arms around her. She places her hand on my cheek and turns her body until she's straddling me, the heat radiating between us.

"I'm supposed to hate you," she softly says as I tuck her dark hair behind her ears, getting a better look at her and the freckles that are lightly sprinkled across her nose, a constellation I could get lost in.

"If this is hate, I can't wait to see love," I say, turning my hat backward so I can better nibble on her bottom lip.

"I'm not supposed to want you like this. It angers me." She sighs, grabbing my hoodie tight in her fists, as if holding on for dear life. "Nick told me to stay away from you."

"I know. It's because you're really fucking bad for business," I say, trying to sound serious, but the allure of her is overwhelming. I lower my voice. "I'll tell you a secret though—I don't care."

"You should care. Because of you, no one will believe I'm with Louis. Josh is literally spiraling out of control. The media are having a field day, digging up timelines of all my relationships. My office has been swamped with inquiries. This is a mess. One you created."

"Anything worth a damn is messy, babe. In the end, it will all work out, trust me." I study her, admiring how pretty she is. "But Nick is right. You should stay away from me. You shouldn't be here right now."

The fire crackles like it's laughing at us, mocking the tension that's been simmering between me and Billie for years.

"Tell me to leave," she whispers. "Tell me to leave, and I will."

She gently grinds into my cock, which is rock hard, like she's testing how much I can take before I snap. Her lips are inches from mine, and her breath smells like sweet wine.

I should push her away. I should, but against my better judgment, I don't. I've lost my willpower, and damn if I'm not ready to embrace it.

"You're such a fucking coward, Banks," she whispers, her voice dripping with venom and something else—something raw and desperate. Her hand slides up my chest, nails dragging over the fabric of my hoodie, like she's marking me. "You can't answer my questions. You can barely look at me. Why?"

"You remind me of what I can't have," I admit, not having a single fuck to give. My heart thumps hard as I drown in her ice-blue eyes, feeling the weight of her gaze.

"Wow. I finally get it," she says, low and throaty, studying me with a fierce intensity. She finds truth in the silence that hangs between us. "You don't hate me. You hate that you can't have me."

"Projecting again, princess? Bet that pussy is already drenched for me. Isn't it?"

Our mouths slam together, and we're not soft or gentle. Right now, it's fucking war. We grow more greedy, more desperate, and she has no idea how right she really is. I grip her waist, pulling her closer, craving more.

"You don't have to admit anything. I can see it in your eyes, in how you look at me."

Her tongue invades my mouth like she's claiming territory, and I let her. I let her fucking take it because it's hers.

"I feel it in your touch. In how you give me all of you when you kiss me."

Billie thrusts her hands in my hair, pulling hard enough to make my scalp sting, and I groan into her mouth because it feels too damn good.

"I love that sound," she whispers in my ear, her breath hot and inviting. "That's you surrendering to me."

"Is that what it is?" I laugh against her mouth, knowing this is what dreams are made of as she pushes me onto my back with determination.

I slide my hand up her sweater, realizing she has no bra. I tweak her perky nipple, and she sighs, the sound sending a rush of heat through me.

Her lips are swollen and wet, and she looks at me like she wants to devour me whole. "Tell me you don't feel anything. Confirm it so we can go back to how things were."

Billie wants me to deny her, to push her away. It would be easy, but instead, I shake my head, the truth burning in my chest.

"I can't. There's no going back. You and I both know that."

"We still can." She breathes out, her thighs pressing against my sides like a vise.

She grinds down on me, and even through the layers of clothes, she finds pleasure. Her hips move in slow, deliberate circles against my cock, which is straining in my shorts. Her chest rises and falls, and she rocks against me as if her life depends on it.

I grip her ass, bucking my hips up into her, letting her take what she needs. She's so worked up, so horny, and by the look on her face, I can tell she's ready to finish right here on my lap.

"I want you buried deep inside me," she whispers. The sound of her voice sends a jolt straight to my cock.

She reaches down to my shorts, and I grab her hand, halting her.

"Not like this," I say, looking seriously into her eyes, not letting her hands go. I want her to understand.

"Don't you want me?" she asks, confusion flickering across her features.

"I do. So damn bad. But I can't treat you like a fuck toy."

Her forehead presses against mine, and I know she's trying to fucking break me as she rocks against me, trying to push my boundaries. I can sense her trembling and hear her breathlessness. Sliding my hand between her thighs, I rub slow circles on the outside of the joggers she's wearing. A gasp escapes her lips, sweet and needy.

She wraps her arms around my neck and kisses her way up to my ear.

"Lose control with me," I say, giving her what she craves.

"I always do."

It's the most honest thing she's ever said.

"So. Close." She tenses under my touch.

The sound of the sea drowns out her desperate cries as I slide my hand into her panties. It doesn't take long before she's losing it. Billie kisses me as she falls apart, her body shaking as she comes hard, her thighs clenching around me like she's trying to milk every last drop of pleasure from this moment.

When it's over, she collapses against me, her chest heaving like she just ran a marathon. I hold her against me. I smile, running my fingers through her hair, inhaling the sweetness of her skin. As she comes down from her high, Billie pulls away, her dark, fucked-out eyes meeting mine.

"You're different tonight." She rests her chin on my chest, looking both satisfied and contemplative.

I lift my brow, tucking my arm behind my head, capturing her in my memory. "I'm also fucking trashed on whiskey. Wonder if I'll remember this tomorrow."

"You know I'm unforgettable," she says.

She moves off of me, and we sit up.

Billie glances at the bulge in my shorts, smirking like she won a twisted game. "I like knowing I drive you wild. I think it's the confirmation I needed."

I lift a brow. "Really? What will you do with that information now that you have it?"

"I'm not sure." She runs her fingers through my hair. "Will you always deny me?"

She breathes out, and the mood grows serious.

My smile widens. "Probably."

"Asshole response. Typical," she says, rolling her eyes.

"That's because I *am* an asshole. You know that. But so are you. That's why this works," I say.

"Hate to fuck around and run, but I'm exhausted." Billie's face softens, her eyes heavy.

I pick up the bottle of whiskey and take a long pull.

Her face softens, and she dips down, tasting the whiskey on my lips.

"Can we talk tomorrow morning before I leave? No bullshit. No arguing. No masks. No whiskey," she says, her voice dropping to a whisper.

"Before I agree to anything, I'd like you to tell me how that shit sandwich tastes? Seems like the other night wasn't my last chance, was it?" I ask.

She leans over and paints her lips across mine again.

I'm desperate for her.

"Hmm. It tastes like satisfaction," she says, her hot breath on my cheeks.

Billie pulls away and stands. As she walks away, her hips sway like she knows I'm still watching, and I can't help but admire the view.

"If you want to talk, meet me right here at sunrise," I tell her, trying to sound casual, though my pulse quickens.

She glances back at me over her shoulder, a playful smile dancing on her lips. "Good night, Banks."

"Fuck off, Ice Queen," I say with a grin, and this time, it earns me one in return.

MY EYES FLUTTER OPEN, AND I ROLL OVER TO CHECK THE TIME. As I reach for my phone, the alarm buzzes to life. I'm impressed I remembered to set it, considering how much I drank last night. I'm not sure if it actually happened or if I dreamed it.

I immediately turn it off and slide out of bed, feeling more energized than I should, especially since I'm running on five hours of sleep. But what else is new? I'll sleep when I'm dead.

I sit up and look out the windows of my suite, which faces the beach. It strangely feels like a brand-new beginning, the kind that makes me believe anything is possible. After last night, I'm convinced it is.

I slide on a sweater and some joggers, grabbing a cozy blanket. I open the sliding doors and walk to the beach, letting the salty air fill my lungs. The sun breaks the horizon as the whooshing of waves surrounds me like a familiar song. I spread the blanket on the cool sand and make myself comfortable, glancing around the private beach. A few people are jogging along the shore, but there's no Billie in sight.

I lie on my back, staring up at the light-pink and purple sky, wondering if she changed her mind. If she did, I totally understand. Cutting through the tension hasn't been easy. Maybe she has regrets.

The sun is halfway up now, and I close my eyes, soaking in the sounds of waves crashing, trying not to dwell on being stood up.

I'll make her regret it. The thought makes me smile.

Moments later, I feel someone standing over me. My eyes flutter open, and I look up to see her smiling down at me.

"Good morning," she tells me, her voice warm and inviting.

I can't help but grin. "Ice Queen. You are *so* lucky you didn't stand me up."

"*Pfft.* Not letting you get out of this conversation that easily."

I sit up, and she settles beside me, so close that our skin brushes together, sending a little spark through me. I open my arm, and she leans her head against my shoulder as we watch the sun fully rise together. It feels surreal, like I'm dreaming.

Being this close to her is a whirlwind of emotions. It feels too vulnerable as we sit silently, listening to the waves crash rhythmically against the shore. The sky morphs from golden pink into a soft purplish-blue. I hold her like she might vanish at any moment, like this is nothing more than a fleeting moment. It could be. I don't want it to be.

My fingers gently trace circles on her skin as she breathes me in. Words aren't needed because our silent conversation is loud enough. Somehow, I find comfort in her presence and don't want this to end.

We hold one another for what feels like an eternity, maybe forty-five minutes, before we both release a long sigh of contentment at the same time. We glance at each other, then quickly look away, a little shy.

Weston was right; we're so much alike.

"I have to leave in two hours."

"Let's get our day started then," I say, standing and holding out my hand for her. I gently pull her to her feet. When she's in front of me, I smirk. "You said no bullshit today."

"No bullshit," she replies, her eyes sparkling. "We have to get each other out of our systems."

"You think that's possible?" I ask, grabbing the blanket and shaking out the sand.

"I don't know," Billie answers honestly, a hint of uncertainty in her voice. "I feel like I don't know who you are."

"You know *exactly* who I am." I tuck a stray strand of hair behind her ear, studying her, as if trying to memorize every detail. "Now, come on."

I fold the blanket, leaving it on the edge of the boardwalk, and then I take Billie's hand, leading her to the wet sand. Our chemistry is almost too much as the cool water slides over our feet, sending little shivers up our legs.

"Would you rather never feel fear again or regret?" she asks.

"Regret," I say without missing a beat. "It's something that only comes after making the wrong decision. I enjoy being right. All the time."

Her face cracks into a bright smile, the kind that lights up her whole being. "I like that answer."

"What about you?" I ask, genuinely interested.

"I'm not sure," she says. "Fear has stopped me so much that I don't even make the decision to regret."

"Really?" I furrow my brows, surprised. "I've always thought you were fearless. No fucks given."

She chuckles. "No one is completely fearless. Not even you."

"Except Easton and Weston."

"Okay, you're right about that," she says. "I love my brothers so much. It's been difficult, growing up in their shadow though. I don't get to be Billie. I get to be Easton and Weston's little sister. Little Calloway. Diamond princess. What is my identity?"

"You're the ice queen who runs her fashion empire from her Crystal Palace. I don't think you see yourself the way everyone else does." I wish she could see what I do.

She smiles, and we focus on the water. Sunshine sparkles across the surface like a thousand tiny diamonds.

Billie breathes in the salty air, closing her eyes for a moment before turning to me. "What are we doing, Asher?"

"Exploring our options," I reply, keeping it real. It's the truth after all.

Her brows lift in curiosity, and a grin sweeps across her pretty face. "Does this feel strange to you?"

I shake my head, swimming in her ice-blue eyes, feeling like I could get lost in them forever. "No. It feels inevitable."

Our laughter fades, replaced by a heavy silence that hangs in the air, charged with unspoken words. It's raw and honest, the kind of moment that leaves me breathless and terrified, as if I'm teetering on the edge of something monumental. I gently cup her face, our eyes locking in a silent promise that hangs between us like a fragile thread.

"When we return to the city, we'll have to put our armor back on," I whisper, my voice thick with certainty.

She exhales, her understanding evident in the way her gaze softens. "I know."

20

BILLIE

Asher pulls bacon and eggs from the fridge while I settle onto a stool at the breakfast nook. Seconds later, he slides a double shot of espresso across the countertop toward me. I've been in this house before, a very long time ago. The decor and colors are just as I remember them. I've always loved this home and how close it is to the water. I fondly recall the older couple who lived here when I was a kid.

"Had I known this house was for sale, I would have bought it," I admit, feeling a twinge of nostalgia.

"I'm sure you and hundreds of others would have. It has a vibe, doesn't it?" Banks has a knack for snatching up properties fast. It's one of the perks of being an heir to one of the most successful financial firms in the country.

"It's strange. I never expected you to be domestic." I blow on the espresso, admiring the contours of his arm muscles in that snug black T-shirt that he was wearing under his hoodie.

"I have many other skills," he says, glancing back at me with a smirk.

"Really? Like what?"

He tosses the bacon into the skillet, then looks over his shoulder at me. "I can juggle."

I snort. "No way."

Asher picks up three oranges from the counter and tosses them into the air effortlessly. "Grab another and give it to me."

I move to the bowl of fruit and do what he said. "I just ... throw it to you?"

"Yes, do it now," he says.

I toss the orange. He continues flawlessly and catches it, adding it to the mix, and it makes me giggle.

"It's official. You're a clown," I say, genuinely impressed.

Laughter bursts from him as he catches each orange and sets them on the counter. "I'd have to be a clown to think hanging out with you is a good idea."

"Hardy har har. You *enjoy* my company. You crave it. Even when I'm busting your balls."

"*Especially* when you're busting my balls," he corrects, flipping the bacon with a wink. "It's one of my favorite pastimes actually."

I return to the barstool and rest my chin on my palm as I quietly watch him navigate the space. I sip my rich espresso, enjoying the moment as the savory smell of bacon wafts through the large, open space. The salty breeze drifts through the open windows, and for the first time in years, I feel like I'm living.

It's surreal being here with Asher like this. It's comfortable and relaxed in a way I could've never imagined, like slipping into a favorite old sweater that still fits perfectly.

He catches me daydreaming, and a teasing smile plays at the corners of his perfect lips. "Enjoying the view?"

"Yep. The beach looks gorgeous from the windows." I lift my brows playfully, glancing past him at the shimmering waves.

"Once a smart-ass ..."

"Always one," I say.

A few minutes later, Asher slides a plate toward me, leaning across the counter casually while handing me a fork. "Go ahead. I want to make sure the princess is fully satisfied."

I bite the fluffy scrambled eggs and close my eyes in delight. "Not bad, Banks. Not bad at all. Compliments to the chef."

He sips his coffee, his golden-brown eyes piercing through me. "I know it's fucking good. Thanks for the confirmation though."

"Your confidence is dangerous," I mutter, picking up a crispy slice of bacon and crunching into it.

"Only because it's your kryptonite." Asher fills his plate and sits on the stool beside me, so close that our legs touch.

Being this close to him is overwhelming but exciting—a reminder of how quickly things are changing. We're first-class passengers on a runaway train that neither of us can stop. If I could, I'm not sure I would.

"I'm really happy you're here," he says between bites.

"I am too."

Time feels like it freezes as our gazes briefly lock. Heat rushes up my body, and my cheeks grow hot. It's like he sees me in my rawest form. Asher always has.

I swallow hard, trying my best to maintain my composure. It's a losing battle, especially when the walls we spent over a decade building sit crumbled at our feet.

"Careful. If you keep looking at me like that, you might tempt me to fuck around and find out," I tell him.

He tries to hold back a smile but fails. It's warm and gentle and so goddamn sexy that I can barely handle it.

"I think you're currently fucking around and finding out."

I grin as a comfortable silence takes over. We eat and exchange random glances, enjoying the simple pleasure of each other's company. I reach for my phone, checking the time, knowing I need to head back to the city within the next hour. He notices but doesn't say anything.

The seconds continue to pass, and neither of us can stop them. Time—it's one of our most precious commodities. No matter how many zeros are at the end of my bank account balance, I can never buy more of this.

Asher picks up our empty plates and carries them to the sink.

"Let me help," I offer, standing.

"You're my guest," he says, rinsing them clean before popping them in the dishwasher. He dries his hands with a towel, the muscles in his arms flexing as he moves.

"Thanks for breakfast. It was great," I offer, genuinely appreciative.

"Anytime. Fun fact: breakfast is my favorite meal of the day."

"I usually skip it," I admit.

"It's the most important meal of the day," he reiterates, giving me a playful nudge with his elbow as I stand beside him.

I lick my lips. "Caffeine is more important."

He shakes his head. "You're so damn stubborn."

"You are too."

Being this close feels oddly intimate. Being here is a secret I'll keep close to my heart. I almost wonder if we could be a part of one another's world.

"What's on your mind?" he asks, as if he can sense my shift in mood.

I swallow hard, trying to dismiss the thought. "Nothing."

"Come on, little Calloway. I know when your mind is wandering."

My heart flutters when he looks at me with patience, care, and a hint of adoration.

As I open my mouth to speak, my phone buzzes in my pocket, pulling me away. I glance down and see it's Harper. "I'm really sorry. I need to take this."

"No problem," he replies, his voice casual but laced with a hint of disappointment.

I quickly answer and walk away, knowing this conversation isn't over. I step into a large common room with high ceilings and an air of elegance. In the center stands a grand piano, the polished wood gleaming under the soft light. Turn-of-the-century paintings adorn the tall cream-colored walls, adding a touch of class to the space.

"Yes?" I say, trying to sound composed.

"Oh, thank God you picked up! Are you on the way to the office?" Harper asks, her voice brightening.

"Um, no. I'll be there after lunch," I remind her.

She huffs. "Fine. I really wanted some of those pink doughnuts they have at the shop around the corner from your loft. But I'll just send an intern."

"Anything else?" I ask.

"Actually, yes," she says.

My heart races as I think about Asher waiting for me in the kitchen.

"Spit it out, Harp. I don't have all damn day. I'm in the middle of something."

"Where are you?" she asks. "I know you're not home."

Lying to her isn't possible, but giving her as few details right now is. "I'm in the Hamptons," I explain.

"What? Oh my God. Are you with *Asher?*" Her voice rises an entire pitch, causing my stomach to twist. She must've spoken to Nick and known Asher was here.

"What. Do. You. Want?" I ask through gritted teeth, my patience wearing thin.

I've told no one where I am but her. I slipped away from the city without a word.

"It's times like this I wish I would've FaceTimed you. No way you could lie or avoid answering when I can see your face. I *know* he's there. Nick told me Asher was in the Hamptons."

I refuse to admit anything. "Harp, please."

"Okay, okay. I know you told me you'd be at the benefit gala this weekend, but you didn't RSVP with the museum, and I got a call from a very pissed-off Weston. He said you were avoiding him after you fired someone. Who did you fire?"

The Boss Situation

"Shit. Yes, please confirm with him officially. Louis is my plus-one," I explain, sidestepping her final question. "Anyway, I gotta go. Do you need anything else?"

"No, but—"

I end the call abruptly, and when I turn around, I find Asher leaning against the doorway with his arms crossed over his chest, a knowing look on his face.

"You'll be at the benefit this weekend?" he asks, a hint of curiosity in his voice.

"Of course. Weston wouldn't let me live it down if I missed. You know how obsessed he and Carlee are with the arts."

He fully enters the room, pulls out the piano bench, and sits. I focus on him.

"Do you play?" I ask, genuinely interested.

"Sorta," he replies, a hint of modesty in his voice.

I smile and take a seat beside him. He places his fingers on the keys and begins playing "Can't Help Falling in Love." It's flawless, and when he reaches the second chorus, I join him, playing a lower octave on the keys.

"You sorta know how to play?" I tease as we transition into the pre-chorus. "Lies. What other secrets are you hiding?"

"It's not a secret, princess. You just never cared enough to find out," he says, finishing the song and leading straight into "La Vie en Rose."

The notes twinkle under his touch, creating a light, dreamy atmosphere. It's a timeless song about falling in love. His brow quirks up as he watches me, and the world around us slowly fades away as he plays just for me.

"Who are you?" I whisper, suddenly realizing I might have misjudged Asher. A chill runs over me, and I think Weston might have been right about this man.

Asher removes his fingers from the keys and turns to face me. "Stay with me until Saturday morning, when I leave."

I focus on him, noticing how his hair falls messily across his forehead. I can't help but admire his long eyelashes framing those intense eyes. "I have a meeting after lunch today."

"And I give a fuck, why? You're the boss. Reschedule it," he tells me nonchalantly. "Reschedule the rest of your week while you're at it."

A sly smile slips across my lips. "Only if you beg. On your knees."

"Ah. Well, unlike you, I'm not too fucking proud to do what it takes to get what I want."

Asher stands, pulling me to my feet, and then drops to his knees before me.

"Wow," I whisper. I didn't realize how incredibly hot this would be.

He grabs my hand, and I look down at him, feeling a rush of exhilaration. The room, the piano, the paintings—everything disappears but us. Right now, it's intensely personal, and I swallow hard as he looks up at me.

"Pretty, pretty fucking please, stay with me until Saturday." His gaze narrows. "If you walk away from me now, you'll spend the rest of your life wondering what could've been."

My breath catches in my throat. Asher gently lifts my sweater, sprinkling soft kisses on my stomach. My fingers thread through his hair, and I know I can't deny this feeling.

"Okay," I whisper.

I can't walk away from him.

I don't want this to end. Not yet.

"Was that a yes?" he asks, his eyes sparkling with excitement.

"Yes," I confirm.

"Good fucking girl." He stands, grabs my cheeks, and smacks a kiss on my lips that leaves me breathless. "Now, since we have days to spend together, I have some things I want to discuss first."

He takes my hand, leading me away, and suddenly, the mood grows more serious than I expected.

My phone buzzes in my pocket again, breaking the spell. I pull it out, seeing it's Harper again.

"I'm so sorry," I say, annoyed.

Asher snatches the phone from me and answers it. "Harper, we're really busy right now," Asher barks.

He pulls the phone away from his ear, and I can hear her excited screams echoing through the receiver.

"Shh. Listen to me carefully. Billie is out of the office for the rest of the week. She went on a self-discovery retreat. Have everything rescheduled. And anything else can wait until Monday."

Harper says something back, and Asher ends the call, handing my phone to me with a sigh.

"Are you insane?" I ask, half amused, half shocked.

"Yes," he replies with a grin, squeezing my hand. He leads me through the house and out to the back porch.

The fresh breeze brushes across my cheeks, and we both inhale deeply at the same time, then burst into laughter.

Asher guides me over to the hammock setup. He lies down on it first, then opens his arms for me.

"I'm afraid," I admit, a flutter of nerves dancing in my stomach.

"I've got you," he says, his voice steady as I roll into him. He wraps his arms around me, and the hammock sways violently back and forth.

"What if it flips?" I ask, a hint of panic creeping into my voice.

"Then we'll fall together," he reassures me, carefully brushing hair from my face. It doesn't feel like he's referring to the hammock.

We're in a cocoon, hidden from the outside world, just the two of us.

"Are you comfortable?" I ask, knowing my weight is bearing down on him.

"Most comfortable I've been in years," he replies, threading his fingers through my hair.

I rest my head on his chest, listening to the rhythm of his rapidly beating heart.

"Your heart is racing," I whisper, feeling his pulse quicken beneath me.

He swallows hard, his fingers trailing down my skin, sending shivers through me. "You always do that to me."

I meet his eyes and breathe in deeply, inhaling his familiar scent, wanting to bottle it up and keep it with me forever.

"This feeling scares me," I whisper, vulnerability spilling from my lips.

He softens, a gentle smile spreading across his face. "It's fucking terrifying."

"What are we supposed to do?"

He smirks. "Survive. That's all we can do."

"I can't fall in love," I admit.

He barely leans forward, swiping his soft lips against mine. "You don't get to decide, Ice Queen. Neither of us does."

I huff, and he chuckles, holding me tighter.

"Little Miss Needs to Control Every Aspect of Her Life has no control."

I groan. "So, what is it that we need to discuss?"

I return my head to his chest, and he twirls my hair around his fingers.

"No matter what happens over the next few days, on Saturday, when we're around one another, you have to promise me that you'll keep up appearances."

"And keep hating you?" I ask, meeting his gaze with an arched brow.

"Yes," he says with a playful grin. "But try to make it believable. None of that eye-fucking shit you do."

"To be completely fair, I don't even realize I'm doing that half the time." I slightly reposition myself so I can better see him.

"Double down on your fake-as-fuck relationship with Louis and hate me. That's all I need you to do. Help me help you."

"Well, I was already doing that," I admit with pride in my voice.

"Terribly. Make it so good that the Crown believes an engagement is on the horizon. Make Josh believe it."

"The Crown won't believe it as long as you keep posting pictures of us together on Instagram."

He chuckles. "I know. That stops too. I'm going to archive the posts and make it very clear that I'm single so you can continue on with princy."

"And my being with Louis won't bother you?" I ask, a mix of concern and curiosity creeping in.

"It doesn't matter. Macro, not micro, babe. I'm thinking of the big picture." His smile fades, replaced by a serious look. "Just please promise me you can do that."

I nod, feeling the weight of his words. "What does this accomplish?"

"Ah. I can't tell you that. *Yet.* If you're asked to give a testimony, I want to make sure you can tell the truth. I will never put you in a position where you'll need to lie or put your career or reputation on the line for me. There are things I cannot and will not discuss with you until this is settled. To protect you."

"Asher," I say firmly, "I don't need your protection."

He chuckles, a warm sound that makes my heart flutter. "You do, trust me. One day, when the time is right, I promise to tell you everything. Oh, also, we cannot be seen together. When we leave here, no one can know we were ever together."

"I planned to keep this—whatever this is—a secret. Well, other than Harper knowing because you literally confirmed it for her, but she's a vault. She'd cut her tongue out before sharing anything personal. Anything else, sir?" I add with a teasing lilt.

"Mmm. I kinda like it when you call me that," he says. "But no. Also, I know you're working with Stormy."

I gasp, repositioning my body. My sudden movement sends the hammock twisting and flipping until we're both lying flat on our backs, staring up at the porch.

"Fuck, I'm too old for that," Asher groans, his laughter bubbling up.

I roll over to face him. "You know about Stormy?"

"Everyone who's anyone knows about Stormy. And the fact that she chose to work with you to fight against me? Honestly, I'm fucking honored. If Easton and Weston called her for a major favor, they were scared for you." He chuckles, pleased with himself.

"Okay, well, I fired her."

Asher props himself up on one elbow, his mouth falling open in disbelief. "What?"

"Yep." I shrug, trying to play it cool.

Asher shakes his head as he stands, then gently lifts me to my feet. Carefully, he guides me over to the steps, where we both settle. The sun is shining brightly, and its warmth beams against my skin, making me feel good. My eyes scan the beach, and I'm happy it's private access.

"Have you ever watched *Pulp Fiction*?" he asks, his gaze drifting to the rolling waves in the distance.

Seagulls swoop and dive above us, their cries mingling with the sound of the surf.

"With John Travolta and Samuel L. Jackson?" I respond, soaking up the warmth. Even though I'm known as the ice queen, I can't help but enjoy a good dose of sunshine.

His eyes slide over me, drinking me in. "Yeah. So, you know when Vincent and Jules blow that dude's head off in the back of the car and there's blood everywhere? You know who Jules calls to help clean up that disaster because it's an absolute nightmare situation? He calls Winston 'The Wolf' Wolf, and the guy made the entire mess disappear like it never fucking happened."

"Yes, and what's your point?" I ask, raising an eyebrow.

"Stormy is The Wolf in this scenario. She would've brought you to places you'd only dreamed of being. Her contacts are endless. It was an incredible opportunity, Billie. Why would you do that?" he questions, genuinely puzzled.

"You sound exactly like Weston and Easton. Seriously?" I sigh, a bit exasperated. "I did it because I don't need her. She's wrong." I study him for a brief second, searching his eyes. "Her plan included me never speaking to you again. She wanted me to sign an unbreakable contract that erased you from my life. And even though we argue and purposely drive each other insane, I knew I couldn't do that in good faith. I know I said I'd do anything for Bellamore, but I can't ..." I swallow hard, setting my jaw. "I don't want to erase you, even if she believes you're very bad for my business."

He doesn't take his gaze from me, his expression serious. "She said that?"

"Yes. And so, after her pitch, I told her to get fucked. Then I told Easton and Weston to fuck each other. The looks on their faces—so priceless. I walked out of Calloway headquarters, furious that they thought they could control me. This is my life. This is my business. And I will win in the end," I explain. The mood grows more serious. "There are other ways for me to come out on top without resorting to that, and I will find them."

He shakes his head. "Why would you choose me over your company? Why would you do that?"

"Because when you kissed me, I felt something I hadn't felt before," I confess. "Even if you piss me off and try to destroy or ruin me, I can't deny how the world faded away. It was the only sense of calm I'd experienced after living in a fucking storm for years, not knowing if I'd ever find that again. I will never be able to deny that, even if I wanted to." My voice cracks, and I'm overcome with emotion. "So, if this is all a game to you, Asher, now would be a really fucking great time to tell me so I could avoid heartbreak."

His lips crash into mine like a fucking wrecking ball, and I'm already gone, lost in the heat of him. His mouth is hungry, savage, like he's been starving for me and I'm his first fucking meal in years. His tongue slips past my lips, claiming me with a possessive urgency that makes my knees buckle. I grab on to his shoulders, digging my nails into the fabric of his shirt, wanting to tear it off, to feel every inch of him against me.

His hand grips my waist, fingers digging into my flesh like he's marking me, branding me as his. I can feel the heat of his palm through my clothes, searing into me, and I'm already soaked, my panties clinging to me, slick with want. His other hand slides up my back, pulling me closer—so close that I can feel the hard ridge of his cock pressing against my stomach, and, holy fuck, it's huge.

I whimper into his mouth—a stupid, desperate sound that I can't control—and he growls in response, low and feral, like an animal. His lips move to my neck, teeth scraping against my skin, and I can't think, can't breathe. All I can feel is him—his hands, his mouth, his body. Together, we're everything and nothing.

"You chose me," he whispers against my throat, his voice rough and raw.

"Yes," I gasp, arching into him, wanting him to take me right here, right now, on these fucking steps.

His hand slides down to my ass, squeezing hard, pulling me against him, and I can feel every inch of his cock pressing into me, demanding, relentless. My mind is spinning, my body on fire, and I want him so bad that it hurts.

"Asher, please," I moan, his name tasting like sin on my lips.

He kisses me again, deep and dirty, his tongue fucking my mouth like he's already inside me.

His hand slides under my shirt, rough fingers skimming over my stomach, and I'm shaking, trembling with need. He cups my breast, thumb brushing over my nipple through my bra.

"Fuck," he mutters against my lips, his voice ragged, and I can feel him hardening even more against me.

I'm ready to beg, ready to drop to my knees and take him in my mouth, ready to let him fuck me raw right here in the sunlight. But then—

"Asher!"

The deep, angry voice cuts through the haze like a fucking axe, sharp and sudden, and he pulls away from me, breathing hard, his eyes dark and wild.

"Dammit," he mutters in a completely different tone, and I can see the frustration in every line of his body.

"Is that Brody?" I ask, my head swimming. "Shit. I forgot to tell him I was leaving the city."

I want to scream. I want to grab Asher and pull him back to me to finish what we started. But he's already standing, turning toward the house, and I'm left on the steps, wet, desperate, and aching for him.

"He's worried. Take a rain check. You've survived not having me this long," he says, his voice full of promise, and I can only nod, my body still throbbing with need.

But damn, I want him now more than ever.

My skin feels alive with the memory of his touch, the heat between us still sizzling in the air, and I can't shake the feeling that we've only just started.

All I can think is, *Please don't break my heart. It's currently taped together.*

21

ASHER

The back door swings open, and Brody bursts out onto the porch, clearly in a panic.

"Fuck. There you are." He strides toward Billie, worry radiating off him.

Billie glares up at him and stands to her feet, crossing her arms over her chest. "What are you doing here?"

"You promised you'd tell me if you left. Well, this funny thing happened, where you fucking left and didn't tell me. I'd trusted you to be honest with me. Do you know what I had to do to track you down? Your brothers are freaking out, and so are your parents. You can't leave without telling anyone. How did you get here?"

He's livid, and I haven't seen him this upset ever.

"Please tell me you didn't drive that fucking motorcycle here."

Her jaw is locked tight, and her eyes are zeroed in on him. Like a tiger, she's contemplating her next move. Go for the jugular or give it to him easy.

Billie continues her cold glare. "You drove two hours to treat me like a fucking child? You will watch your tone when speaking to me. Family or not." Her voice is calm. Slow. It's frightening.

"I was extremely concerned about you. You're not safe,

The Boss Situation

wandering around without some sort of detail while you're *dating* Prince Louis," Brody sarcastically says between clenched teeth, glancing back at me. "If something happens to you on my watch, I'll never be able to live with myself. I trusted you, Billie. My ass was on the line, and you disrespected that. I'm sure Easton and Weston will be more than fucking pleased to know where you are. Your parents too."

"Brody, please. Please do not tell anyone that I'm with Asher. I will forgive you if you keep this part to yourself." Billie's not backing down. She's fierce and flustered.

My eyes slide down her body, and I memorize her.

"I'm nearly thirty-one years old, Brody. You're literally ruining one of the greatest moments of my life. Please be invisible," she whispers, and then he takes a step back.

With disdain, he walks away. As he passes me, his nostrils flare. "You hurt her, and I'll fucking kill you," he says to me, then walks back through my house and disappears.

A few minutes later, I hear an engine roar and growl as it takes off.

"That went surprisingly well," I say to her, breathing out.

I don't know if any of the Calloways would be happy to discover we've been fucking around. Another reason why it's best to keep it to ourselves. This situation gives me the courage to finally admit something I should have a long time ago.

Although we're alone again, the mood is spoiled.

Billie breathes out and closes her eyes. "Have you ever wanted to disappear from this life? To just live? I'm so envious of people who have a normal life."

"Yeah. All the time. We didn't get a choice, did we?"

"No," she whispers.

I give her a smile and nod, loving how she thinks.

"I come here a lot to escape," I admit, moving close to her, resting my hands on her shoulders as I face and meet her blue eyes. "It's my safe space. When Eden passed away, I left everything in the city and disappeared here for three months. It healed me in ways I hadn't known I needed. Anytime life becomes too much, I'm here with the sand between my toes and the saltwater breeze on my skin. Luckily for me, now you're here, too, and we get to escape life together, even if it is just for a few days. Sometimes, that's all you need."

I kiss her forehead, and it feels so natural. She wraps her arms around me. I hold her for a long time, and she holds me back. And it's just us with no other worries in the world as the sun beams down on us, kissing our cheeks.

Billie eventually pulls away from me. "Did you buy this home because my parents' house is in this neighborhood?"

I laugh. "Actually, no. This beautiful turn-of-the-century mansion belonged to my mother's parents—my loving grandparents. Your father actually purchased the Calloway estate because of them." I tilt my head at her. "Wait, do you not remember meeting me when we were, like, twelve? Best summer of my life. My grandparents threw huge parties, and all the adults got wasted. And at the end of the summer, we did too."

Her brows furrow. "What? I met you at Stanford."

"That's not completely true. We got drunk on spiked punch and put a blanket on the sand at the end of the boardwalk. We counted satellites in the sky and made wishes on stars. And I *totally* kissed you." I chuckle. "It was a standout memory for me. It was the summer I was made a man."

She stares at me. "No. His name was Max. Max Holly. His parents were in Africa that summer."

I nod. "My parents were in Africa, trying to rekindle their failing marriage, so I was dropped off at my grandparents' house. That summer, I forced everyone in my life to call me Max. And I stopped being a Banks. It's short for my middle name, Maxwell. It was cool. Hip. Three letters. Unforgettable," I say.

"Oh my God," she whispers.

"It was my tagline," I say with a laugh.

Billie shakes her head. "I don't believe you."

"Hold on. I have proof."

I pull my phone from my pocket and quickly find the photo my mom texted me a few months ago when she was going through photo albums, reminiscing like I'd had a perfect childhood. It was dysfunctional. I hand my phone to Billie. It's a picture of the two of us, and we're dressed in Hawaiian shirts. My arm is around her, and she is smiling widely. Later that night, twelve-year-old me made a move, and a part of me never got over her.

"Aw." Then she pokes me hard in the chest. "I've searched for you since that summer. *Jerk!* Why didn't you say something sooner? Not a hint? Nothing. You just kept this information for … for … nearly twenty years?" She takes a step back, really studying me. "You went from a chubby, braces-wearing, four-eyed kid with pimples to a Greek god in six short years when we met again?" She gasps. Realization washes across her face. "*You* were my first kiss." She covers her face with her hands. "I might have a mental breakdown."

"I thought you recognized me the day we ran into one another at Stanford. When our eyes met, I immediately knew it was you," I admit. "I didn't know how to be like, *Hey, remember me? I stuck my tongue in your mouth on the beach when we were twelve?* That would've gone over really well."

"At least you asked first, like the perfect gentleman." Her face softens. "That moment we shared as kids, under the stars, was magical. It's the story I'll tell my children, if I have any." She glances away, as if she's reliving it. "I came back every summer, hoping to run into you again. Your grandparents weren't here either. It had felt like a dream, something I'd imagined."

"I'm sorry. When my mom learned my dad was a cheating bastard, I became the thing they fought over having ownership of. My grandparents became obsessed with cruises and started only visiting in the spring. Because I loved this house so much, it was left to me when my grandfather's estate was settled. My grandmother was convinced I'd find love here. I guess she was right," I admit.

Billie steps forward, wrapping her arms around my waist. "I didn't recognize you. I automatically hated you because I felt something when I looked into your eyes. Maybe it was familiarity. I was so worried that if I met the love of my life at eighteen as a freshman in college, I'd give up everything. I'd be forced to work for my father, and I wanted to experience life. Hating you has always been easier than loving you."

I wrap my arms around her. "I understand and don't fault you. Being a Calloway comes with a lot of pressure. You did what was best, just as I did."

Her lips gently brush mine.

"I always dreamed of what I'd say to Max Holly if I ever saw him again."

I laugh, pulling away from her. "Yeah? Tell me. Please."

"Thank you. After you kissed me that summer, I felt pretty. No one had ever made me feel that way before. Just you. It gave me the confidence I needed to fuck up little teenage boys in boarding school." She smirks. "I was a terror because of you."

Laughter roars out of me. "Glad I could help. But, if it's any consolation, you're not pretty, Billie. You're fucking gorgeous."

"It was always you," she whispers loud enough for me to hear. "Un-fucking-believable. Just wait until I tell Harper."

AFTER WE EAT, WE GO ONTO THE BALCONY AND WATCH THE SUNSET and the storm rolling in. Her eyes shine, and I see the past unfolding behind them—the girl she once was and the woman she's fought so fiercely to become.

"I'm proud of you," I tell her. "No bullshit."

"Thank you," she says just as the sun sets below the horizon. "That means a lot to me."

"It's official. We've spent the entire day together," I say.

"From sunrise to sunset," she whispers. "I've spent so long running from this."

"Fuck, me too," I admit.

Darkness is upon us, but so is a storm.

"I'm so used to building walls and putting distance between me and anyone who tries to get too close. It's safer, easier." Billie pauses, her voice trembling slightly. "But I'm so fucking lonely."

"I am too," I say, my voice barely above a whisper. My chest tightens.

She exhales, and the warmth of her breath grazes against my skin. "Can we be lonely together?"

"When I'm around, you're never alone. Anytime we're together, it always feels like it's just you and me," I admit.

Slowly, I reach up, gently cupping her cheek and tilting her face toward mine. Our eyes lock. Hers are vulnerable, searching; mine are steady, reassuring.

I know what I've always wanted. Her.

She slides her fingers gently through my hair as she stands in front of me. My hands rest on her ass.

"I'm done fighting this, fighting you," she admits.

Her confession resonates deep within me, unraveling something raw and intense. The energy between us shifts, growing more electric, more desperate. Need and want take over.

I pull away. "Wait a goddamn minute. Are you finally surrendering to me? Is that a white flag I see?"

"Call it what you want." Her plump lips part, and her voice comes out shaky. "You have no idea how hard I've tried to hate you. Fuck, I was so close. I'd almost convinced myself you really were my enemy."

"I was," I admit. "Purposely."

She chuckles. "I should kick your ass. The harder I pushed you away, the more I wanted you. Do you have any idea how frustrating that is?"

"Coincidentally, yes." A small, amused smile tugs at the corners of my mouth. "Funny how that works, isn't it? It's almost like we have no fucking control over what we want."

She laughs. It's bittersweet and beautiful. "Now that I think about it, you've always enjoyed tormenting me. Even when we were kids."

"You always started it. I just ended it," I tease.

Her thumb grazes my jawline. "This doesn't feel real."

"It doesn't," I say, my voice growing serious. "If it's a dream, I don't want to wake up."

"I don't either," she whispers.

Billie's lips paint against mine, testing the waters. A nervous energy bubbles beneath her touch. I deepen the kiss gently, encouragingly, feeling her body relax and melt into mine.

"I'm scared," she whispers against my lips.

"Don't be," I say, pulling away. "I'll catch you if you fall."

Lightning crashes and causes us both to jump, pulling us momentarily apart. We glance toward the sky as rain slams down on us. Dark clouds are overhead, and I watch Billie bite her bottom lip.

"Come on," I say, grabbing her hand and leading her inside.

Droplets of water are on our faces as we stand in my bedroom upstairs.

"I hate sea storms. They're always more violent." A wave of nervousness is in her voice.

"No matter how bad it gets, it always passes," I reassure her, taking her hand as lightning strikes again. This time closer. "Come on. Let's move away from the windows. I don't want Brody killing me."

The lights flicker as we move out of my room and down the stairs. Billie releases a sigh of relief, and immediately after, the house's power cuts, and we stand in darkness. The buzzing of appliances stops, and it's complete silence other than the gusting wind outside.

Billie inhales sharply, gripping my arm tightly. "Please don't leave me."

"I'm here. You're safe," I say calmly, pulling her closer. "The backup generator should come on at any second. I've got you."

We wait in the dark.

Lightning brightens the room for a few seconds as the thunder rolls. I impatiently wait for the electricity to click on, but nothing happens.

She breathes a little harder. "It isn't working."

I wrap an arm around her waist. "I guess not, but we'll make the best of it. I won't let you go. Come with me."

I carefully guide her through the living room and back into the kitchen, grabbing candles from the cabinets and drawers. I light the gas stove, and it brightens the room. Once I have a long candlestick lit, I catch the other wicks. Within moments, warmth flickers throughout the space, our shadows dancing across the walls.

We move to the living room, setting them around the room. Billie smiles at me, then kneels by the fireplace, arranging logs and kindling. The fire quickly sparks to life, casting a golden glow across her face.

"Girl Scout?" I ask.

"No, tactical survival courses," she says.

"Oh, it's like that?"

She nods. "I can take you down in ten seconds flat."

"Might have to test that out," I tell her. "When you told me you'd fuck me up, I didn't realize you meant literally kicking my ass."

"Stop flattering me."

Billie scoots back and leans against the couch, mesmerized by the fire, and I sit beside her. We settle together on the plush rug. The crackle of firewood fills the silence between us. Billie leans against me, her head resting comfortably on my shoulder, fingers tracing patterns on my thigh.

"Tell me about your relationship with Eden," she says, staring into the flames.

My heart clenches, as I know the two of them were friends. I hesitate only briefly before speaking, my voice thick with memories. "She was the best sister anyone could have. Brilliant. Honest. Happy. She wanted the best for me. And I loved how she made everyone around her feel special, like they could do anything. Eden was sunshine, wrapped in strength."

Billie's fingers pause. "I'm sorry you lost her, Asher. After it happened, I wanted to talk to you, but ..."

"I know. I was in a bad place. There are days when I still blame myself," I admit quietly. "She called me that night and asked me to meet her, but I was too caught up in work and my own shit. I thought it could wait. I thought we'd have tomorrow. I didn't know ..." My voice trails off, heavy with regret.

Billie gently turns my face to meet hers. "You didn't know. That's not your fault."

"I could've answered the call," I say. "If I had, maybe she'd still be here. Maybe that fuck who was driving drunk would've crashed into a building instead of the car she was in. My decision could've changed *everything*."

Her eyes fill with empathy. "Ash, I'm so sorry."

I nod. "It's why it's so important for us to cherish every minute. The now is all we have."

Thunder roars overhead.

"I'm so grateful you're with me right now," she whispers.

We stare back at the wood.

"Sometimes, I feel her. Like she's pushing me to do things. Or I'll ask myself in certain situations, *What would Eden do?* I miss her a lot. I don't know if I'll ever be the same," I whisper, my words raw and painful.

She threads her fingers through mine, gripping tightly. "You honor her every day by living your best life. That's what she would want for you. She'd be so proud."

Emotion thickens my throat, and I nod silently, breathing in her comfort. This wasn't a conversation I expected to have, but it's healing to talk about Eden. Usually, everyone avoids the conversation. Everyone except Nick. He misses her as much as I do.

We sit quietly for several moments, leaning against the couch, stretching our legs before us.

"Who was your first love?" I ask.

Billie laughs gently, and her cheeks transform into a rosy pink. "Besides Max Holly?"

I smirk. "Besides that nerd."

She hesitates, sighing. "I'd say Josh was my first real love. My fling with Louis was never serious. Neither of us saw one another that way. With Josh, I almost imagined a future with him. I don't think I was ever truly in love though. It felt like a business relationship with mediocre sex." Her voice lowers. "It *never* felt like this. It never felt like kissing Max Holly."

Her gaze is vulnerable and honest.

My pulse quickens. I tilt her chin upward, our lips nearly touching.

"Fuck, princess."

Our mouths meet, and tenderness bleeds into something far more passionate. My hands roam down her body, and I memorize every curve of hers as her fingers slide under my T-shirt. The firelight flickers warmly across her face, illuminating the desire in her eyes.

"If we cross this line, we can never take it back," I warn.

"I don't want to." Her eyes meet mine with certainty. "You're who I want."

Billie's soft lips trace my jaw, the sweet torture of her touch making my heart pound wildly.

The storm outside grows louder, rain hammering against the windows, matching the fierce rhythm of my heartbeat.

My hands cup her face as I claim her mouth deeply, possessively. "You're sure?"

"I *chose* you, Asher. I told The Wolf to go get fucked for you." She clings to me, her body warm, surrendering completely.

I rub my nose against hers, laughing. "You're so damn stubborn."

"You love it," she whispers.

"I do. In the worst possible way," I admit, my mouth crashing onto hers.

The storm rages outside, the kind that makes the world feel like it's ending. Thunder cracks like a whip, like it's desperate to break in. The electricity's been out for half an hour. The fire illuminates Billie's face like a fucking masterpiece, painted in shadows and desperation.

An undeniable tension hangs between us. It's thick and electric, just like the air is right before a lightning strike. Billie sits beside me, her legs folded under her, her eyes locked on mine, like she's daring me to make a move.

Her hair's messy, and I think it's the first time I've seen it out of place since we were adults. Her lips—fuck, her plump lips—are swollen from the random kisses I've stolen from her. I can see the pulse in her neck, quick and erratic, and I want to put my mouth there, to feel it jump under my tongue.

"Asher," she says, desperately like she's been screaming, crying, or both. "What in the fuck are you waiting for?"

"I don't want to forget or rush this," I admit, reaching for her.

My fingers trail against the bare skin of her arm, and she shivers —not from the cool draft in the big house. Her eyes flutter closed for a second, and when they open again, they're darker, hungrier. I lean toward her, closing the space between us, and her breath hitches against my cheek. I can smell her—sugar and salt and something else, something fucking intoxicating that makes my cock twitch.

I kiss her like I've been waiting for this, for her, my whole damn life.

I have.

Her lips part under mine, and I plunge my tongue into her

mouth, tasting her, claiming her. She releases throaty moans. Her hands fist in my shirt, pulling me closer until there's no space left between us. I can feel every curve of her body pressed against mine as she climbs onto my lap and straddles me.

It's still not enough.

I need more. I need *all* of her.

I break the kiss long enough to carefully pull her shirt over her head. She gasps as goose bumps trail over her bare skin. Her tits are perfect—full and soft, with nipples already hard and begging for my mouth. I don't hesitate. I take one, sucking hard, and she arches into me with a whimper, her fingers tangling in my hair.

I flick my tongue over her peak, teasing it, and she whispers my name like a prayer.

"Asher," she breathes, her voice trembling. "Feels so good."

I move to the other breast, giving it the same attention, and her hips jerk against me, searching for friction. I can feel the heat radiating from her pussy through her pants, and I groan against her skin, my cock so fucking hard that it hurts. I slide my hand down her body, over the curve of her hip, and she gasps when I reach the button of her pants.

"Is this what you want?" I growl, my fingers pausing.

"Yes," she whispers, her voice full of need. "God, yes."

I undo the button and pull down the zipper; my heart pounds rapidly.

I shimmy her pants down her legs, and she stands to kick them off impatiently. I leave her in nothing but a pair of black lace panties that are soaked through. I can smell her arousal and it takes every ounce of self-control I have not to bury my face between her legs right fucking now as she stands before me.

Instead, I hook my fingers in the waistband of her panties and pull them down slowly, revealing her slick, delicate pussy. She's beautiful—swollen and wet, her clit hard and begging for attention. I press a finger against her entrance, and she moans, lifting her hips into my hand.

She whimpers, "Please don't tease me."

I slide one finger inside her, and she's so fucking tight, so wet; it's all I can do not to come in my pants. I move my finger in and out of her slowly, watching her face as she takes me. Her eyes squeeze shut, and her lips part in silent pleasure. I add a second finger, stretching her, and she cries out.

"More," she begs, her voice breaking. "I need more of you."

Fuck, I want to give her everything, but not yet.

I pull my fingers out of her and bring them to my mouth, tasting her. "Mmm. I've missed that."

She watches me with wide eyes, her chest heaving as she tries to catch her breath.

"So fucking good," I murmur, and she blushes, but there's no shyness in her eyes.

Only hunger.

I pull her onto the floor and lay her back against the rug as I kneel between her legs, spreading them wide. She's fully exposed now, completely open to me, and I can see every inch of her pussy glistening with arousal. I'm responsible for this.

"Fuck," I growl.

Slowly, I lean down and lick a stripe from her entrance to her clit, and she jerks like she's been electrocuted.

"Oh my God," she moans, her hands flying to my hair. "Asher—"

I don't let her finish her sentence. I fully bury my face between her legs, licking, sucking, and fucking her with my tongue like it's the only thing keeping me alive. She tastes even better now that I fully have my mouth on her, sweet and salty and so fucking addictive.

Billie, my buffet.

I focus on her clit, flicking it with my tongue as I slide two fingers back inside her, and she writhes beneath me, her hips bucking uncontrollably.

"Asher," she gasps, her voice high and desperate. "I'm gonna—oh God—"

She comes with a cry, her pussy clenching around my fingers as she rides out the wave of pleasure. I don't stop—I can't—and soon, she's coming again, harder this time, her whole body trembling as she screams my name and gasps for air. I pull my fingers out of her and lick them clean. She watches me with hooded eyes, and a lazy smile spreads.

"I don't think I've ever come so fast in my life."

"Really?"

She's breathless. "A Guinness record."

"Can't wait for my trophy," I mutter.

Billie gazes down at my bulge that's thick for her, straining against the cotton pants.

"Wow. I've—" She gulps. "I've won the cock lottery."

I try to hold back laughter but fail miserably. "Congrats. Now, what will you do with your prize?"

Every secret kiss, every stolen glance, every agonizing moment we've shared culminates here in this perfect collision of passion and truth.

"Treasure it," she confesses.

Thunder shakes the walls, but we barely hear it. Our connection is louder, stronger, and unbreakable.

I'll surrender to her, knowing exactly how high the stakes are, but no longer afraid of the fall because she'll catch me.

Billie might have chosen me, but I chose her first. In this game, we both win.

22

BILLIE

The house is dark, except for the flicker of candlelight. Our shadows are tall on the walls. My heart pounds so damn hard that I can hear blood pumping in my ears. Asher's hand brushes against mine, and my entire body tingles with anticipation. I've wanted this for so long, and now that it's happening, I'm ready to make his brain explode.

He leans his back against the couch, legs spread. Asher's inviting me into his orbit, a place I've not been welcome until now. His eyes are heavy, and those perfect fucking lips part just enough to make me want to devour them. But no, not yet. This isn't about me. This is about him. About making him feel so good that he forgets his name. I want him to know how it feels to be vulnerable with me.

It was always him.

My knees sink into the fluffy rug, and I focus on the bulge in his joggers, straining against the fabric. My mouth waters as I look at it —hard, long, thick. I press my hands against his thighs, feeling the heat of him through the cotton, and lean in close enough to feel his breath hitch.

"Surrender."

"Only because you did first," he says, his voice full of want.

My fingers work at his waistband, slow and deliberate. His cock springs free, already leaking at the tip. I lick my lips, my tongue darting out to taste the salty pre-cum before I even wrap my mouth around him.

The first touch of my lips to his dick sends a shiver through both of us. He groans, low and guttural, causing my pussy to clench at the raw sound. It's encouragement. I start slow, letting my tongue swirl around the head, teasing the slit, savoring the way his hips twitch beneath me. My hand wraps around the base, pumping him in time with my mouth. His fingers grip my hair, not pulling yet, but holding on like he's afraid I'll disappear.

"Ready to surrender yet?"

I take him deeper, inch by inch, until I feel him hit the back of my throat. My eyes water, but I don't stop. I fucking love the way he fills me, the way he throbs against my tongue. His cock is a dream, and I can't get enough of it. I suck harder, bobbing my head faster now, and his grip tightens in my hair.

"Yes." His voice cracks. "You're trying to break me."

"Returning the favor," I moan around him, the vibration making him curse even louder.

His hips start to buck as he fucks my mouth, and I let him. I let him take control, let him use me until he's panting and shaking below me. I can feel him getting closer, his cock twitching in my mouth, and I double down, sucking him deeper, harder.

"Fuck, Billie," he hisses. "I'm ..."

"Mmm." I nod, slowing down to a snail's pace.

His body trembles as I teeter him on the edge for minutes as he holds my hair tightly. I pull away, smirking, denying him his orgasm.

"Not in my mouth," I say.

His eyes darken, swirling with something I can't describe.

"I want you inside of me. Claim me, Ash," I whisper.

He shakes his head. "I wasn't prepared."

"I'm on birth control. I want to feel you with nothing between us. Just me and you, Ash."

He nods, giving me the permission I need.

The room is alive with the flicker of firelight, and the rain taps against the windows. It's dreamy and warm. Wax has begun pooling around the candles, and the air smells like sex and sin.

My breath is ragged, my chest heaving as I press him down onto his back on the rug. My knees dig into the plush fibers as I straddle him. His body is a fucking masterpiece under me: broad shoulders, a chest carved from granite, and that cock—Christ, his cock—thick and straining against my thigh, already leaking pre-cum like a goddamn faucet. I don't let him enter me yet.

My hand dips between my legs and wraps around him, squeezing just enough to make him hiss, his hips bucking up into my grip.

"I want you buried so deep inside me that I can feel you in the back of my fucking throat."

"Fuck, you're a goddamn tease," he groans.

His hands grab my hips, fingers digging into my skin like he's trying to mark me, to claim me. I don't let up, stroking him slow and deliberate against my pussy, randomly swiping my thumb over the sensitive tip, spreading that slick wetness down his shaft. He trembles underneath me, muscles strained, his veins bulging, and I can feel every inch of him suspended. He's already so damn close that I can see him fighting for control.

"Don't you fucking come," I whisper, leaning down. My lips brush his ear. "But you want to, don't you? Want to spill yourself all over me? Inside me? Too fucking bad. You're mine tonight—every inch of you—and I decide when you get to feel good after how you teased me for years."

I bite his earlobe hard enough to make him curse, and his hips jerk again, his cock twitching in my hand.

"I'm in control, Asher Maxwell Banks," I state.

His eyes are wild, pupils blown wide with need, defiance, and pure desperation. He's exactly where I want him.

I straddle him, my thighs framing his hips, and I grind myself against him, letting him feel how wet I am. The friction against my clit is electric, and I moan, my head falling back as I rub against him shamelessly.

"Bad fucking girl," he mutters, his hands moving to my ass, pulling me harder against him. "You're so fucking wet."

"You turn me on." I reach behind me, grabbing his wrists and pinning them above his head. He's strong—stronger than me—but he doesn't fight it. He lies there, watching me with hooded eyes, his chest rising and falling, like he's halfway to losing his mind.

I dip down, kissing the tattoos across his chest, then capture one of his nipples in my mouth. I hear him groan, like he's drowning in pleasure.

"It's never felt like this before," he whispers.

I pause, hovering above him.

"Not for me either," I admit.

Our bodies are so close, but not quite touching.

"I need you," he confesses.

"Beg," I mutter. "Beg me."

"Fuck," he whispers, his voice wrecked. "I need to feel you around me, need to be inside you so bad that it fucking hurts. Please, let me stretch your cute little cunt wide so you can feel me tomorrow." He lifts his brow, his tone changing. "Princess, your cunt is dripping wet for me. You're basically quivering—you want me so goddamn bad. This is torture for you. Maybe you should be the one begging, babe." He sits up on his elbows, pulling my bottom lip into his mouth, tugging hard and sucking. "I haven't fucking come since the night I kissed you at Weston's, and I'm going to fill you so fucking full that it leaks down your leg, you greedy fucking brat."

I gasp at how turned on it makes me. My breasts rise and fall.

"Mmm. I felt that pussy wink." He smirks. "You like being treated like my equal. Not a porcelain princess."

I lean down and kiss him, losing myself as he teases my entrance.

"You've been saving yourself for me?" I ask.

"Yes," he admits, casually putting his arm behind his head. Biceps flexing. He's relaxed—we both are. "Now, let me fucking break you how you deserve."

"Please do," I mutter, the mood morphing into something else completely as I sink onto him inch by agonizing inch. I moan out, needing this.

He's so large that he stretches me open in the best way possible. I take my time, savoring how he feels as he fills me, adjusting my hips as needed. When our ends meet, I lean forward, my hands on his chest for balance, and I feel like he might crack me in half.

"Are you okay?" he gently asks, his hands on my thighs.

I nod. "Yes. You just …" I take in ragged breaths. "It's so much."

"Take it as slow as you need," he says. "Let me know when it's in the back of your throat."

I burst into laughter, and Asher grabs my thighs.

"Fuck, you're squeezing me so tight."

At first, I start with just a lazy roll of my hips, our gazes locked. I find myself getting used to him and move harder and faster until I'm slamming onto him with utter desperation. The sound of our moans echoes through the room, mingling with the crackling fire and the storm outside. His hands are on my hips again, guiding me, helping me take him deeper, harder, until we're both gasping for air.

"You feel so fucking good. Like you were made for me." He moans, his voice barely recognizable. "So tight, so wet."

His fingers dig into my hips hard enough to leave bruises, and I love it—love the way he's so desperate for me.

I lean forward again, my lips brushing his as I whisper, "Come for me, Asher. Come inside me."

That's all it takes.

With a guttural groan, he spills himself inside me, his cock pulsing as he finishes deep in my core. I can feel every fucking twitch of him as he comes undone beneath me, and it's enough to push me over the edge too. My body clenches around him, waves of pleasure crashing over me as I ride out my own orgasm, milking every last drop from him until we're both trembling with satisfaction.

I collapse on top of him on the rug, our bodies intertwined, our breathing heavy. He's still inside me, still connected to me in the most intimate way possible. The storm rages outside, but here, at this moment, there's nothing but us—our bodies, our heat, our love.

I smile softly, running my fingers through his hair. "I want to do that again."

"Fuck, you're obsessed," he says against my neck, his voice more tender now.

"You say it like it's a bad thing," I say.

"It's not, babe. It's mutual," he tells me.

"I don't want this to end," I whisper.

And just like that, the desperation fades into something softer—something real.

I pull back, admiring his swollen lips and flushed cheeks. Asher looks at me like I'm the most beautiful thing he's ever seen.

"It doesn't have to," he rasps.

"Just promise me you have this all figured out," I tell him, and he holds me tighter to his chest.

"I promise." He grins. "You're my endgame, Ice Queen."

I'M A CHANGED WOMAN AFTER SPENDING FOUR DAYS WITH ASHER. I roll over, his arm wrapped around me as the sunshine beams through the windows. We stayed up most of the night talking and enjoying one another's company, knowing that this ease and comfort would disappear as soon as we left.

"Good morning, princess," he whispers in my ear.

I roll over onto my back as his fingers slide into my panties. I grab his wrist, gasping as he gently brushes over my clit.

"I was wrong about you," I confess as his circles on my clit grow more deliberate.

"I'm aware. Glad we're finally on the same page," he says, kissing my neck, pulling away, leaving my pussy throbbing for attention. "We should go."

"We have five minutes," I whimper, squeezing my thighs together, needing him more than I need air.

He shifts, his lips brushing my shoulder, and laughs. "I should leave your pussy begging for me."

"You wouldn't dare," I mutter.

"I wouldn't. Can't get enough of you," he coos, his voice rough from sleep.

His hand slides down my stomach, slow and possessive, and I bite my lip when his fingers dip between my legs, stroking the slick heat he left there.

"You're still wet," he says, and the rasp in his tone makes my hips roll, and I want more of him.

"You're still hard," I shoot back, my voice trembling as his fingers curl inside me, stretching me in that way that makes my breath catch.

He chuckles, and I can feel his cock swell against my leg, eager and thick.

"Always around you," he growls, and then he's rolling me onto my back, his body hovering above mine.

Asher claims me with a desperate and hungry kiss. His tongue fucks my mouth as his cock slides between my thighs, teasing my clit with each thrust. I moan against him, pulling him closer, needing him deeper.

"Break me." I breathe against his lips, my voice shaking with want. "Fuck me so hard that I feel you for a week."

He doesn't hesitate. He grabs my hips, lifting them so he can slide into me with one brutal thrust that punches the air from my lungs. I gasp, my nails digging into his skin as he stretches me open in the best fucking way. He pauses for a moment, his forehead pressed to mine, our breaths mingling as we both adjust to the feeling of him inside me.

"Billie," he whispers, his voice raw with emotion, and I can see it in his eyes—the vulnerability, the fear. "I think I'm falling for you," he confesses, and it's like the room tilts.

My heart squeezes in my chest, but before I can respond, he's moving, his hips pounding against mine in a rhythm that's relentless and delicious.

"I feel the same," I whimper and repeat myself to make sure he heard me. "I feel exactly the same."

Every thrust hits that sweet spot inside me, and I'm already close, my body tightening around him like a vise. He groans, his fingertips dig into my hips as he fucks me harder, his cock sliding in and out with a wet, filthy sound that only makes me hotter.

"You're mine." His voice is rough.

"I'm yours." I moan, as if giving the final words to a spell to complete it.

I arch into him as the pleasure builds. The orgasm puts me in a choke hold, my body tensing tighter and tighter until my control snaps. The orgasm rushes through me, and my body shudders as I come hard around his cock. My cries are muffled against his chest.

Asher follows me over the edge with a groan, his cock pulsing inside me as he spills himself deep, filling me with his warmth.

We collapse together, a tangle of limbs and sweat, and for a moment, it's perfect. But then reality creeps back in, and I can feel the ache in my chest grow as he pulls away, his body leaving me cold.

Asher helps me clean up and then sits on the bed's edge.

"Before this, you made a promise," he reminds me, his voice soft but firm. He runs a hand through his messy hair. "You have to hate me. I know it's hard as hell. Try your very best."

I nod, swallowing the lump in my throat as I sit up, too, the sheet pooling around my waist. "I will."

He searches my eyes. "Billie, I will have to do and say things that will not make sense to you. I will be an asshole. I will be rude. Please know that I don't mean anything I say unless it's just us, okay? Everything else is bullshit."

"Okay," I tell him.

"To make it up to you, I will make another promise. Anytime I cause you any amount of pain or frustration, I will replace it with pleasure."

"How? We won't be able to see each other." I search his face.

He nods. "I've decided I'm moving back into my loft. I'll meet you at sunset each day, unless I absolutely can't."

My brow lifts. "Okay, so back to this pain-payback plan. Should I keep a tally? I mean, at your current rate, you'll keep me coming until the end of next year."

He smirks. "That's the point, princess. One day, it will all make sense. I promise, one day, I'll tell you everything. But right now, I have to protect you. Everything I say or do is for that reason."

My heart skips a beat at his words, and I can't stop myself from reaching for him, my fingers brushing his cheek.

"I trust you," I whisper.

He leans in, capturing my lips in a kiss that's soft and sweet and full of promises I know he'll keep.

"Now, how about you make it look like you're trying to save your company?"

I roll my eyes. "You have no idea what I'm working on."

Asher smirks. "I can't wait for you to tell me."

When we finally pull away, the room feels too quiet. He gets up first, pulling on his clothes.

"Who wins this?" I ask, getting dressed too. My hands tremble as I button my shirt.

"The queen. She's the most powerful piece in this game." He takes two steps toward me, removing the space, and kisses me.

We don't speak as we leave the room, the silence heavy between us, but when we reach the door, he pauses, his hand on the knob. I slide on my riding gear, stuff my clothes into my backpack, and pop on my helmet.

"Fuck, you look sexy," Asher says.

I give him a smirk and climb onto the bike, cranking it. He walks to his car.

"Banks," I yell out to him.

He turns and glances at me. "Yes?"

"Fuck off."

He smiles, crossing his arms over his chest, easily turning on the asshole version of himself. "Nice to see you again, *Ice Queen*. Enjoy your ride back to hell."

We share a silent moment, and then I shut my visor. As I drive away, I already miss him. Us. And everything we shared.

23

ASHER

My heart pounds steadily in my chest as my driver stops outside the Frick Museum on the Upper East Side, where the benefit is being held. This location is tradition. I'd be lying if I said I wasn't nervous about seeing Billie tonight. It's all I've thought about since I left the Hamptons earlier today. She's always on my mind though.

I adjust my tie, trying to calm my racing heart as I watch the paparazzi line the sidewalk, snapping photos of the elite guests who enter the building. It's invite-only, as usual, and the wealthiest people in the world will be attending tonight.

Calloway Diamonds has hosted the luxurious black-tie fundraiser for eighty-seven years. There will be curated diamond exhibits, showcasing rare and priceless stones—all for sale in a private auction. The one-of-a-kind diamond pieces, exclusively designed for the event, are worth millions, and the proceeds help support underprivileged youth and aspiring entrepreneurs—something the Calloways are genuinely passionate about. The event raises nearly half a billion to be redistributed yearly, and it's something my family has *always* supported, one that I believe in and am committed to.

While much of my wealth has come from my great-great-grandfather's legacy, I always give back to make it possible for others to rise. My sister believed in that mission too.

My driver glances at me in the rearview mirror. "Would you like me to take you somewhere else?"

"No. I just need another minute. Apologies," I reply, and he nods.

I can't help but wonder if Billie has already arrived. I'd text her, but we didn't exchange numbers. It's best if we have no written communication. Considering my profession, it's not unreasonable to assume my phone might get confiscated and conversations sorted through if Josh Lustre decides to move forward with a lawsuit. I personally don't believe it will come to that, but Nick is very concerned. I'm playing it safe, even if it pains me.

Knowing I can't avoid this any longer, I exit the car. I'm blinded by flashes—something I should be used to by now, but I'm not. I walk up the steps and enter through one set of double doors that lead to a foyer with a stunning skylight. Hanging lights illuminate the space with a warm, inviting glow. Classical music plays softly in the background. I'm stopped for a photograph as soon as I enter—something that will surely be displayed on the foundation's website later.

The room is full of beautiful people, dressed in elegant evening wear. I spot several celebrities, billionaires, two editors from major publications, and a prime minister. It sounds like the start of a dumb joke, and it makes me grin.

Not getting an invite to this event would be an absolute embarrassment, and Weston is directly in charge of the guest list. Because of that, I know Josh Lustre will not be here tonight, which is a relief. One less person to deal with.

A server glides by and offers me a glass of champagne, and I happily accept it. The museum is one I've enjoyed since I was a kid.

I take my time studying a few oil paintings on the wall. This mansion, which was once a single-family home, was designed with the intent of becoming a museum. It's brimming with Western art history, and it features everything from mesmerizing paintings to intricate sculptures and furniture. I can never get enough of this place, and I take my time with the art as if I were catching up with an old friend.

While many guests tour the museum, most congregate in the reception hall. I see so many familiar faces, and I stop to give quick hellos to several of my clients.

"Asher Banks," Phillip says with a hearty laugh, holding out his hand.

I take his rough grip, feeling the calluses on his hand. While he might be a billionaire and his family owns one of the most successful cattle ranches in the country, he works his ass off. Phillip and his three brothers are in the trenches with the ranch hands, ruling their cattle kingdom.

"Hey! Wow, I didn't expect to see you here," I tell him just as his aunt, Martha Chambers, approaches.

She grins widely at me. "Asher! So lovely to see you again," she says in that thick Southern accent.

I smirk, taking her hand and placing a soft kiss on her knuckles. By the twinkle in her eye, I can tell she approves.

"Mrs. Chambers, it's always a pleasure," I reply, hoping—nearly praying—that she doesn't bring up Billie and me. I find that flattering her works best. "You should start seeing more of me now that I'm finally occupying my loft."

"Mm-hmm," she responds with a raised brow.

Words are clearly on the tip of her tongue, and I know she wants to say something.

"Okay,"—Phillip turns to his aunt—"what did I miss?"

"Nothing at all," I say, and she shoots me a wink.

It's our little secret—well, aside from the photo I posted for the entire world to see. It was painful, archiving it this morning. All that exists now are screenshots.

My eyes scan the room, searching for Billie. I'm calm and calculated.

"She's not here yet," Mrs. Chambers says.

I play dumb. "Who?"

"Billie Calloway," she replies.

I give her a laugh. "Oh, I'm not looking for her. Have either of you seen my brother, Nick?"

"Yes. He was at the bar," Phillip tells me, pointing at the glowing area with a line wrapped around it.

The lights are low, and the ambiance is pure perfection. Liquor flows endlessly because when inhibitions are lowered, wallets are opened.

"Thanks. Hope to see you around," I say, excusing myself.

As I find my way through the crowd, sipping my champagne, I run into Weston.

"Asher! Happy you could make it," he says, offering me a firm handshake.

Our eyes meet, and for a moment, it feels like he's sorting through my thoughts, trying to read my mind.

"I'm very honored to be here. This year's turnout is incredible," I say.

"The best we've ever had," he admits with pride. This event is his baby—something he's spearheaded for the past twenty years. Weston Calloway knows how to throw a party and tends to be the life of it. "I wanted to ask why—"

Heads turn, and that's when I see her, looking gorgeous as ever in a strapless black dress that splits at her breasts. It's outlined in diamonds that sparkle under the low lights.

Billie is so beautiful; she takes my fucking breath away.

"She made it," Weston says.

Across the room, Harper bursts into applause, and everyone follows her lead. Billie licks her dark red lips and glances over at Louis. He spins her around and then gently kisses her. The event photographers capture the moment as her arms wrap around his neck.

Make the crowd believe an engagement is on the horizon.

She smiles up at him, and my jaw tightens.

Macro, not micro. Big picture.

While they're acting, my jealousy festers. I remind myself that this is necessary and part of the plan.

They pull away from one another, and Weston turns to me. He studies me intently, like he's searching for a reaction. He doesn't say anything. He doesn't have to.

"Good seeing you," I tell him with a grin, giving him a friendly pat on the back before turning in the opposite direction.

Brody stares at me with his brow lifted.

Fuck. There are too many people here who know things they shouldn't, which is dangerous for my mission.

I find Nick drinking with Patterson at a circular high-top table. A candle flickers in the middle as they laugh about something.

"Hey, man. Didn't think I'd see you again so soon," I say, offering him a firm handshake.

He chuckles. "When a Calloway sends you an invite to anything, you go. Always. It's the rule."

"Is it? Hmm. Never heard that one before," I reply, finishing my current glass of champagne and grabbing another. I take a sip, letting the bubbles tickle my senses.

"It's unspoken," he says.

Nick watches me, searching for chinks in my armor. He won't find any. No one will.

"I think I'd like to meet with Josh on Monday morning in my office," I say, trying to sound casual.

He gives me a look like I've lost my mind.

"Make it happen," I say, and by my tone, he knows it isn't an option.

"And I thought your vacation would do you some good," he retorts.

"It did wonders. And I'm ready to move forward," I insist, but I'm firm.

Nick studies me, weighing his options. "I'll contact him first thing in the morning. He'll be there."

"And did you do what I asked?" I ask, still acting pissed at him. I'm not really.

I had the best week of my life because of his decisions, and I owe him for that. But I must protect everyone in my life. I will be the only one who sinks with the ship if it goes down; I will make sure of that.

"It's been done," he confirms, a hint of relief in his voice.

"Thank you," I tell him, breathing out as Billie and Louis approach us.

The atmosphere shifts.

She narrows her eyes at me, and when she's close, I slowly clap.

"What a fucking entrance, Ice Queen and Your Highness." I roll my eyes, pretending to be bored and unamused.

"Fuck off before I have my brothers escort you out of here," Billie warns, venom dripping from her tone, not caring who hears.

I almost believe her, but I also know my tongue was buried deep inside her just this morning.

"You think I'm scared of you?" I give her a sarcastic laugh and grit out, "Try *harder*."

She gets the hint and looks me up and down, sliding her arm from Louis. Billie approaches Easton, and his face twists in confusion. Lexi's mouth falls open in shock. The prince and I stand beside each other, watching it go down. I casually sip my champagne.

Louis glances at me, shaking his head. "You're fucked," he says.

Billie hugs her brother, and then they approach us. She watches Easton, waiting for her scary big brother to attack. Unfortunately, I'm still not intimidated. He knows it.

"Can I speak with you, please?" Easton asks, his tone serious.

I glare at Billie and shake my head, but a smirk plays on my lips.

"Sure," I tell him, and we move away from them so we can privately talk.

"Can you please stop being so fucking rude to her?" he snaps, crossing his arms over his chest like a protective barrier.

I open my mouth to say something, but Easton holds up his hand to stop me.

"Listen. Leave her alone. Right now, she wants you escorted out of the event, but I don't want to do that because I respect you. However, I cannot deal with this petty argument bullshit that's been going on between you two for years. Not during this event, please. If it happens again, I will ask you to leave. I will choose my sister every time, okay?" He studies me.

"Okay." I nod in understanding.

"Great," Easton says as we stroll back to Billie.

She grins, seemingly appeased, assuming he kicked me out. But when he tells her it's been settled and that I'm staying, her expression darkens. My girl loses her cool. Easton grabs her wrist and pulls her to him to whisper something in her ear, trying to calm her down. He's losing his patience, and I can't help but notice the wandering eyes of other guests taking in the drama. When she glances back at me, I give her a smirk, knowing we're playing on the same team.

To show respect to Easton and his request and to play the hand we've been dealt, I stroll out of the reception hall, wearing a cocky grin. I make my way up the grand staircase that leads to the second floor, which is full of exhibits that have been in this house since the 1800s. Museum staff stroll through the area to watch over the artwork and furniture, ready to share the history of each piece if asked. The silent auction items are also on display in each room.

"Sir, would you like a bid sheet?" a woman asks.

I take it with a grin, grateful for the distraction away from Billie. She looks so damn gorgeous, and I know I'll need to avoid her for the rest of the night so I'm not tempted to touch or kiss her.

I enter the first room and notice an opal ring and earrings, surrounded by diamonds, on display, bursting with colors, like a kaleidoscope. The stones were handpicked by Lexi Calloway, and they radiate a magical allure. I smile, loving how Easton included Lexi in this project now that they're married. Every member of the family designed a piece, showcasing their unique styles.

As I move into the hallway, I spot the woman who spoke to me minutes earlier.

"Can you tell me which room has the jewelry Billie Calloway designed?" I ask, eager to see what she created.

"The diamond princess?" Her brows rise. "It's at the end of the hallway. Good luck! That's the one that everyone fights for each year."

"Thanks," I tell her, passing several people perusing a diamond bracelet. *Only one can win*, I think to myself.

As I stroll to the end of the hall, I peek inside the room, noticing a gentleman studying the display case. He eventually leaves, and I enter, wanting to take my time with her creation. In the center of the room is a glass case, lit from below. I lean over and see diamond cuff links surrounded in platinum metal in the shape of a five-point crown. She named the set *King of My Heart*.

I roll my eyes, knowing everyone will think they're for Louis. From different angles, the diamonds almost morph into different colors, and it's beautiful. I write my bid on the paper and fold it in half, tucking it in my pocket.

When I turn to leave, Billie is standing in the doorway, wearing a soft gaze, and I can't believe she's looking at me that way. I focus on her, my eyes sliding from her pretty mouth, down her perfect body, and back up to her ice-cold eyes. Right now, it's just me and her.

"Ash," she whispers.

I shake my head as she approaches me. "We can't be seen together."

"We'll be quick," she says, wrapping her arms around my neck. "Also, I don't care."

"You should," I say, my hands resting on her waist. "Please return to Louis before people notice you're not attached to him."

"You say one thing, but your body says another. Guess that won't change." Billie captures my mouth with fervor.

Her mouth is soft—so fucking soft—like she was born just to ruin me. Her lips part wider under mine, and I can't help how my tongue slips in, exploring her like I'm claiming my territory. She tastes like champagne and bad decisions, and I'm drunk on it, on her, on the way her body melts against me in the shadowed room of the museum.

Her perky tits are pressed against my chest, her nipples hard enough to make me ache. My hands wander, sliding down her back to cup her ass, squeezing the roundness of her through the thin fabric of her dress that fits like a second skin. She moans into my mouth, and the sound goes straight to my cock, which is straining against my suit pants, nearly begging for freedom.

"I've missed you," she whispers, but her voice is shaky, breathless.

"We have to stop," I urge.

She doesn't listen, her tongue tangling with mine in a way that makes me want to lose control. I can feel her pulse racing as I kiss down her throat, sucking little marks that I know I shouldn't be leaving. But, fuck it, I crave her.

She's too hot, too willing, too damn perfect.

Her hands are tangled in my hair, pulling like she's trying to keep me there forever, and honestly, I'm not complaining. I push her against me, my hand resting in the curve of her waist, wanting her to feel how hard I am for her. Billie's breath hitches, and I inhale the sweetness of her skin. Everything about her drives me wild. It always has.

"*Go.* Walk away from me," I tell her in a strained whisper.

"I can't. I have no willpower with you." She gasps, but she's not stopping, not pulling away.

Our lips crash together, and at that moment, we're completely lost in one another.

"What the fuck?" I hear a deep voice from the doorway.

We freeze, and I turn my head just enough to see Easton, his face a mask of disbelief and rage. I can feel her heart pounding against my chest, her breath caught in her throat, and for a split second, everything freezes in time.

"What is it?" Weston asks from behind him, fully entering.

He stops and stares at us tangled together, lips swollen, a desperate mess, and I know we're screwed. Even as their eyes burn holes into me, I can't stop thinking about how fucking good she feels in my arms.

"This has to end right now," Easton demands, glaring at Weston.

"Agreed," Weston admits, annoyance creeping into his tone. "I sure would love a fucking explanation."

Seconds later, Brody enters. His eyes widen when he sees the scene unfolding before him.

I reluctantly remove my hold on Billie, ready to face the consequences of my actions as adrenaline floods my veins.

I exhale, trying to steady myself.

"Can I help you?" Billie's smile fades into a scowl as she steps forward, fiery determination in her eyes. "Choose your words wisely, brothers, because I will leave this venue right now and not look back. The optics of that would be terrible for both of you, and we know how much you care about image. What will you tell everyone when they ask where the diamond princess has gone?"

The silence stretches on for an eternity, the tension heavy in the air.

Weston would not take that risk, considering Billie is *the diamond* of the evening. Because of her position in the fashion industry, her jewelry designs sell for ten times more than anyone else's. It's the only time their two industries cross paths. The resale market for her pieces is ridiculous, and only true collectors dare to bid.

"Your boyfriend is searching for you," Brody mutters, frustrated.

"Tell Louis I'm *busy* and I'll meet up with him in twenty minutes," she demands.

He leaves the room, escaping the four of us. I don't blame him; I'd leave too. I want to.

Easton's livid, staring me down before shifting his gaze to his sister. "This stops now. It's too reckless. Both of you need to be logical. Bigger things are at risk."

"You don't get to tell me what I can do. Do you understand?" She glares at them, refusing to back down.

"Leave us, or I'm leaving," she threatens, but it's more of a promise.

"This isn't over," Weston says, grabbing Easton's sleeve.

After a moment, they concede and walk away.

I turn to her, smoothing her hair down and placing a soft kiss on her forehead. "Being with you like this *is* reckless."

She smirks, grabbing my tie playfully. "Reckless is my middle name."

"You're stubborn as fuck," I whisper against her lips.

"I just need a little more time with you. Please." She grabs my hand and leads me through another room that's connected. She opens a side door, glancing both ways, and we slip out into another long hallway. I glance behind me and see Weston and Easton arguing. She shushes me with a smirk, leading me down a narrow flight of stairs that looks like they were once used by staff. It's low-lit, almost dark, and gives us the privacy we need.

Billie pushes me against the wall and kisses me fiercely. "I need you."

"You have to go back to Louis right now," I say, my hand firm on the small of her back.

Her silky dress whispers against my fingertips; the fabric barely contains the curve of her ass. My fingers trail lower down her body, teasing the seam that splits open at her thigh.

"You're so fucking bad," I murmur into her ear, my voice rough and commanding.

She grabs my hand, forcing it under the slit and against the outside of her panties.

"The more you deny me, the more I want you." Billie lets out a whimper as I add more pressure.

"You need to be quiet, princess. Don't want everyone to hear how much of a fucking slut you are for me."

"More."

Her hips buck into my hand as I slide my fingers into the lace, finding her soaked cunt with practiced ease. She's hot and swollen, her clit throbbing under my thumb as I circle it slowly, deliberately. She bites her bottom lip, which is swollen from our roughness, but it's not enough to stifle the moan that escapes when I plunge two fingers inside her, curling them just how she likes.

"This pretty little pussy is mine. Who do you belong to, princess?" I ask, my cock straining against my suit pants.

"You," she whispers.

Her nails dig into my shoulder, her body trembling as I fuck her with my fingers. The sounds of her slickness, combined with her ragged moans, are too loud in the confined space. Her tits raise with each breath, her dress slipping just enough to give me a glimpse of her hard nipples, begging for my mouth. But, no, this is about her, about watching her lose control, about making her come so hard that she forgets where the hell she is.

"You're close, aren't you?" I taunt, my breath hot against her ear. "I can feel you clenching around my fingers like a greedy little whore. Come for me. And you're gonna do it quietly."

She nods frantically, her eyes wide and desperate as she bounces on my fingers. It's all the permission I need. I increase the pace, my thumb pressing down hard on her clit as I pump my fingers in and out. Her body tightens, her back arching as she fucking explodes. Her orgasm rips through her with a force that makes her legs give out. I catch her, holding her up as she convulses, her cunt milking my fingers.

"That's my bad girl," I mutter, my voice thick with pride and lust. "You came so fucking hard and fast for me."

"A record, I think." She wears an expression of defiance, and it mixes with the afterglow of her climax.

I pull my fingers out slowly, seeing them glisten under the dim stairwell light. I bring them to her lips, letting her taste herself—salty and sweet, fucking perfect. She looks into my eyes as she sucks my fingers dry, causing my cock to throb.

"Now, go back to your prince," I say, my tone harsh now.

I want to escape with her and bury myself deep inside her. I want to be back at the Hamptons with her in my arms.

"You've ruined me," she whispers. "I hope you know that I'll never be the same."

"And to think, it only took hardly any time," I mutter in her ear.

"Twenty years," she reminds me.

I take a step forward, pressing her back against the opposite wall. She looks like sin itself as she reaches forward, rubbing her palm down my cock. It takes everything I have not to push her to her knees and make her choke on my cock.

"Go." I grab her face, meeting her eyes.

It's just me and her. The world around us quiets. We hold a silent conversation as I gently slide my lips against hers.

"This is much harder than I thought it'd be," she admits, a hint of vulnerability in her voice.

"You promised me, Billie. And Calloways *never* break those."

I try to walk away, but she pulls me back to her, desperation in her grip.

"And you promised me you'd turn my pain into pleasure," she reminds me, her eyes sparkling with defiance.

"I did, didn't I?" I kiss her again and again and again, losing myself in the taste of her. "You're playing with fire."

"And you're burning me to ash." She looks up into my eyes, a mixture of longing and challenge. "I'm going to hell with you."

"Perfect," I say. "As long as we're there together, that's all that matters, Ice Queen."

I wish I could linger for just a moment longer.

"When will I see you again?" Her voice is barely above a breath.

"Soon." I straighten my tie and adjust my cock, the reality of our situation crashing back down. "Fix your crown, princess. The night isn't over."

I force space between us, taking one last look at her flushed cheeks and swollen lips before I walk away. It pleases me, knowing I'm the one who leaves her breathless and dripping wet in the shadows. Not anyone else. Just me.

As I take the stairs to the main reception hall, I know Easton is right.

This is reckless. But, damn, I'd do it again.

24

BILLIE

Asher still lingers on my skin, and my body buzzes from his touch.

How am I already so weak for him? This was *never* supposed to happen.

I try to recompose myself, wanting my heart to stop thumping so hard. I squeeze my thighs tight and can't help the smile that spreads across my face. I've never done anything so … risqué. Or in public. My heart races, and I feel myself growing obsessed with him. That scares me.

I make my way to the main floor and glance down the hallway, spotting my brothers still arguing with one another. They're heated, and I can't tell who's winning, but they both look furious. I can't face them right now, so I slip away. Quietly, I take a different hallway, walking as fast as I can to the elevator. Just as I step in and the doors are about to close, Brody enters, glaring at me.

"I didn't tell them," he says.

"I know. Thank you. I'm sick of it. I would've never told Easton to stay away from Lexi. I wouldn't have dared to tell Weston not to pursue Carlee. But they don't respect me in the same manner."

"It's not that," he replies.

I swear this elevator is being hand-cranked; it's going so slow.

"Asher's in a dangerous situation with Lustre. Being around Asher publicly could be unsafe for him. Do you understand? You're putting him at risk. And if anything happens to you, I wouldn't be able to live with myself. That's not what you want." He shakes his head, frustration etched across his face. "Let Asher do his job. Don't distract him."

My brows knit tightly together. "I—I didn't—"

"Yeah, I know you didn't think about that. Stop being a selfish brat for once and listen. *Fuck.*"

The door jolts open, and Brody storms out. I can't remember the last time he snapped at me, but it's not the first. Sometimes, he's the only one who can get through to me.

I hold my head high, forcing myself to keep performing for the public. I set my shoulders back and raise my chin. This event is now my runway as I walk through the foyer to the reception hall.

I scan the room and find Louis laughing with a large group of people. I grab a glass of champagne, downing half of it in one gulp, and Harper walks up to me, looping her arm in mine.

"Everything okay?" she whispers.

"It will be," I tell her. "One day."

She takes a step back, her head tilted. A small smile meets her lips, and then it grows wide. "Oh my God."

"Don't."

She searches my face. "You're in love with him."

I breathe out, knowing I can't deny it.

"How can I help?" she asks.

Harper has always had my best interest in mind. It goes both ways.

"Please help me avoid Asher publicly. We can't be around each other."

"Why?" she asks.

"It's bad for business," I tell her, repeating what Banks said to me in the Hamptons. "It's very important that everyone believes Louis and I are together."

"I'm on it," she says, turning me around toward the crowd. "Go to your prince. He's over there."

"Thank you," I tell her.

She gently pushes me forward. "You've got this, Ice Queen."

I move forward, joining Louis with a grin. He interlocks his fingers with mine, and everyone around us notices the affection.

"I missed you," Louis says genuinely as I finish my glass of champagne and grab another one.

"I missed you too," I repeat back.

I meet his eyes, remembering what Brody said and what Asher asked of me. I lean in closer, and he tries to steal a kiss, but it lands on my cheek. I *must* do this.

"Aw," one of the women says. "The two of you are absolutely stunning together."

"Thank you," Louis states, his green eyes shining with pride. "She's my diamond."

Easton and Weston appear on the opposite side of the room. Their eyes meet mine, and I look away, focusing back on Louis, but I'm not really listening to the conversation. I laugh when I'm supposed to, offering yeses where appropriate, but my mind is somewhere else.

Mrs. Easley, an editor at one of the major newspaper publications in attendance, asks Louis about his father. As he speaks fondly of the king, I glance over her shoulder and see Asher chatting with a cute redhead. Her hand brushes his shoulder, and she steps closer to whisper something in his ear.

Our eyes meet, and with a cocky grin, he barely flicks his brow at me. Asher rubs his nose with his finger and laughs at whatever the woman is saying. I can't help but notice it was the same finger he had buried deep inside me thirty minutes ago.

"Don't you agree, Billie?" Louis asks, pulling me back to the conversation.

"Of course," I reply with a laugh, clueless about what they were discussing.

"When can we expect a royal wedding?" Mrs. Easley asks, her eyes sparkling with excitement.

I chuckle nervously and say, "The Crown must approve everything. You know that."

"Not always," she counters, leaning in with a conspiratorial whisper. "Sometimes, love is more important than anything else. In the past, some royals have simply given up their crown to be with their person."

"That's not a traditional method though. I'd want the Crown's approval for marriage, considering I know how faithful His Royal Highness is to his country. It's important that whoever he makes his queen is suitable for everything that he is."

He proudly grins, pulling me just a little closer to him.

Mrs. Easley nods, understanding. "And that's why you two are the perfect pair."

I nervously chuckle and turn toward Louis, wanting to escape this conversation or at least segue it to something else. "If you had to choose between love or power, which would it be? Only one though," I ask him, curious about his answer.

"Is it true love? One that lasts until my last breath?" he asks.

"Yes," I confirm.

"True love is worth losing everything," he admits softly, then winks at me.

Something flickers behind his eyes, and I wonder if he's thinking about his secret girl, the one he has continued to keep hidden.

"I agree. True love is what I'd choose too." I take those words and hold on to them tightly.

Louis knows how I feel about Asher; I explained everything that had happened in the Hamptons on the way here. He's happy to keep playing pretend. It benefits us both.

Mrs. Easley eats up the conversation. "I'm very happy for you.

When there is a wedding announcement, please allow me to interview you."

"Absolutely," I say, knowing it won't happen. "Thank you for the opportunity."

Someone walks up, laughing, and she gets pulled away, leaving Louis and me to ourselves.

"That was entertaining. Where did you go?"

"Ah, well, let me just say, my brothers are pissed at me right now. They caught us together," I whisper.

"That explains their attitude." He watches Weston and Easton take the stage, and his eyes meet mine. "You should get ready for your speech."

"Shit, I almost forgot," I tell him, finishing my glass of champagne in a hurried gulp. "I'll be right back."

I glide across the room, catching a glimpse of Asher, who's flirting hard with that woman. Jealousy creeps over my body like a shadow, but I push it away, reminding myself that he must do this, especially after he archived the posts of us.

Earlier today, he uploaded a single photo of his feet in the sand. Mine were just out of view.

He titled it *New beginnings*.

It's our secret.

Just like how this relationship must be—for now. This has become a total mess, and it's my fault. I was selfish tonight, using Asher's greatest weakness against him—me.

I step onto the stage, joining my brothers. The crowd gives the three of us a warm applause as Weston takes a moment to thank everyone for attending.

"Also, a very big thank you to everyone at the museum who has helped make this night flawless. And a special thanks to my dad for continuing this tradition so that we can continue to do the same."

Easton takes the microphone next. He goes on for a few minutes, then wraps it up. "The jewelry is spread throughout the museum, so you can enjoy art while also being a part of something bigger than us. Good luck."

Applause fills the room, and then I'm handed the microphone. "Hi! Wow, welcome to the eighty-seventh annual Calloway Carat Gala. I speak for my entire family when I say we are truly honored that you have graced us with your presence tonight. In this room, we have people from all different walks of life and countries. Each year, I give a speech about the importance of entrepreneurship and striving for greatness. And every year, I can see some of you staring at me with glazed-over eyes, so I thought we might skip that part this time."

Easton stares at me, nearly begging me not to go off the rails. Weston wears the same expression of worry.

"I created a special set of cufflinks that I've named King of My Heart, and it was designed with lots of care and precision. At first glance, these pieces may look like regular diamonds, but they change colors. I used chameleon diamonds—some of the rarest in the world, each weighing in at three carats. Now, some might wonder why I chose that specific diamond for this setting. Well, it's to remind everyone that there are times when you don't fully understand someone or something at first glance. It's easy to get it wrong. Sometimes, a diamond just needs a change of environment to show you just how beautiful it really is."

I swallow hard, feeling Asher's eyes on me. When I look up, he's smiling, and it gives me a little boost. I quickly glance away, knowing I can't get lost in him right now.

"Thank you so much for being here. My grandfather would be so proud. Good luck, everyone."

I hand the microphone back to Weston and then walk off the stage. Louis waits for me with open arms, pulling me in for a hug.

He leans in and whispers in my ear, "Amazing speech."

"Thank you," I say as Weston continues to work the crowd.

If being the COO hadn't worked out for him, he'd have found a way to shine as a public speaker—or perhaps even become president. I guess that could still happen.

Pulling away from Louis, I scan the crowd for Asher again, but he's nowhere to be found.

It's better this way. No temptation.

For the rest of the night, Louis and I play the part of the perfect couple, entertaining various groups of people. We dance and laugh, sipping champagne like we're the quintessential duo. My brothers watch me from across the room, their expressions a mix of curiosity and concern, but I ignore them.

By the time the night ends, I'm pleasantly tipsy.

Louis and I leave hand in hand, still laughing. Once we're in the car, he gives me a high five.

"I think we did it," he says, leaning back against the seat with a satisfied grin. "My team will be thrilled. A scandal is the last thing they want."

"I know. We need an exit plan that doesn't tarnish either of our images," I explain.

"A nondramatic breakup is totally doable. We just tell them the truth—we're much better as friends than lovers. It's respectable," he says.

I can see right now that he's on top of the world.

Having everyone believe in our charade gives him more privacy with his secret girlfriend, and honestly, I want that for him.

The car slows as we approach my building, and we continue our little act. Photographers capture the simple good-night kiss we share, and then I slip inside. As I move into the elevator alone, a smile spreads across my lips. I can do this.

The doors slide open, and I step off the elevator, my heels clicking on the floor. Just as I turn my head, Asher's door cracks open, and his eyes rake over me. I swear I can feel his gaze like a physical touch. He doesn't say a word as I move closer.

Suddenly, he reaches out and grabs my wrist, pulling me into his place with a force that sends butterflies fluttering in my stomach. The door slams shut behind us, and just like that, we're alone. Just us—finally.

I wrap my arms around his neck. "I'm so sorry," I whisper against his mouth. "I lost control tonight. It won't happen again."

"Please don't apologize." His lips trail across mine, down my neck, and over my chest. His hands and fingers explore me. "You'll be the fucking end of me, Billie."

"Ash," I whisper, thrusting my fingers through his hair.

My heart pounds so hard that I can feel it in my throat. The air is thick with anticipation as the room glows softly from the lamp in the living room. I look up into his eyes, and they sparkle like diamonds. I love the way he makes me feel like I'm all he's ever wanted.

Am I?

When I'm with him, it feels like I'm exactly where I should be. It feels *right*. It's never felt like this with anyone else.

"You wrecked me tonight." I breathe out, my voice shaky as his lips crash into mine.

His kiss is savage, his tongue forcing its way into my mouth, claiming me, owning me. I whimper, my hands brushing over his skin, sending goose bumps trailing across my body. He touches me everywhere, reading me like Braille, like he's trying to memorize every inch of me.

"I could say the same about you. Your speech was brilliant," he compliments.

In one fluid motion, he's got me in his arms, carrying me to the bedroom like I weigh nothing at all. I'm so turned on that I can barely think straight. He sets me on my feet and takes a step back.

"Now, this is picture-perfect," he mutters, drinking me in.

I barely have time to catch my breath. His hot and relentless mouth kisses down my body, biting and sucking at every inch of bare skin he can access. Asher carefully unzips my dress, and it falls into a puddle around my feet on the floor. My breasts are fully exposed, my panties soaked through. The rush of cool air hits my skin, and I stand in front of him, completely vulnerable. My breathing is ragged, heat pooling low in my belly as I realize how he's looking at me. It's possessive and hot and greedy. I can hardly believe how my body reacts to him.

"The way you look at me makes me weak," I whisper.

He kisses me. "You're like a dream, Billie."

Asher drops to his knees before me, as if he's worshipping me. And he is.

Carefully, he unbuckles the high heels strapped to my ankles, kissing up my legs before guiding me back onto the bed. He slides my panties down, kissing and sucking my thighs like he's savoring every inch of me.

"Spread your legs for me, princess," he commands, his voice rough and undeniably sexy.

It's a simple request, but the way he says it makes my pulse quicken. I obey without hesitation, trembling with need.

I watch him, loving how his eyes darken as they roam over my naked body. I nearly beg for his touch, for him. Asher leans forward, and I can feel his hot breath against my clit. Anticipation curls in my stomach as he moves closer. I gasp as his hot tongue glides up my slit, teasing me, taunting me, claiming me. A cry escapes my lips, my hands fisting the comforter as he circles my clit with precision.

"You know exactly what I want," I whimper, my hips instinctively lifting off the bed to meet him.

The way he sucks on my sensitive bud sends shock waves through me; each flick of his tongue takes me higher. The pleasure builds to an unbearable peak as he works me expertly with his mouth and fingers, curling them inside just right.

I take it all in—how he makes me feel, my breathlessness, my insatiable need for him. It seems too good to be true.

How has this man always been in my life and I've never really noticed him until now?

Asher buries his face deeper, and I tighten around his fingers.

The pleasure intensifies with every stroke of his tongue and thrust of his digits.

How has he memorized my body and every sensitive spot? I'm drowning in the sensation of him, of us, of this.

"Ash," I gasp, my voice barely above a whisper, but it's enough.

I'm lost in the moment, spiraling into a blissful haze, where nothing else exists except for him and the pleasure he's giving me. My thoughts scatter like leaves in the wind, rustling across the sidewalk on a nice autumn day.

I'm completely consumed by the need to feel more of him.

It's intoxicating, overwhelming.

I can't think straight; every nerve ending is on fire as he brings me closer to the edge.

How can the man I've hated for so long make me feel so alive?

Just when I think I'm about to break, he pulls back slightly, a devilish grin on his lips.

"Flip over for me and arch that pretty pussy for me," he demands.

I instantly do as I'm told. My body trembles with need as he kisses and palms my ass, diving into me from behind.

Moans echo off the walls, and I've never heard the noises that release from my throat. I'm completely under his spell.

Asher's tongue fucks me from behind, and I want more of him. His tongue and mouth return to my sensitive bud as he fully devours me, and I can barely take it. He's relentless, working me so fucking good that I see whole galaxies.

"I'm gonna come," I whisper, my voice breaking as the orgasm crashes over me, wave after wave of pleasure ripping through my body.

He doesn't stop, working me through it until I'm a trembling mess, begging for mercy.

But he's not done with me yet. Before I can catch my breath, he's sliding down his pajama pants. My heart hammers in my chest as his thick cock springs free. Asher slowly pushes into me, inch by glorious inch. He's so fucking big, stretching me in the best way possible as he fills me.

"You were made for me," he mutters, his fingers digging into my hips as he pounds into me.

I scream his name with every thrust, wanting more, wanting all of him. He fucks me like he's claiming me, like he's trying to make sure I'll never forget him. And, God, I don't ever want to forget. He flips me over and gently slides deeper into me. The way he feels inside me, the way he looks at me—like I'm the only fucking thing that matters in the world—it's intoxicating.

"I'm yours, Ash," I whisper, my nails digging into his back as he drives into me again and again.

"Say it like you mean it, princess," he says.

"I'm yours," I scream out. "And you're mine, Ash. You fucking belong to me now."

"Fuck yes," he growls in response, his hips slamming into mine as we both lose ourselves in the heat of it.

When he comes, it's with a roar, his cock pulsing inside me as he spills himself deep. I can feel him everywhere—in my body, in my fucking soul—and I know there's no going back from this.

I crumble again, clinging to him as the waves of pleasure crash over us both, our bodies trembling together in the aftermath. We stay like that for what feels like forever, wrapped up in each other, neither of us willing to let go.

The warmth of his body next to mine and the soft rhythm of his breathing make everything else fade away. And as we drift to sleep, legs tangled in the sheets, I know I'm falling for him. Hard.

I just hope I can survive him.

25

ASHER

TWO DAYS LATER

The early sunrise floods through my window, waking me before my alarm sounds. I stretch my arm out, feeling the cool sheets where she was just hours ago. I'm already missing Billie, wishing her warm body was pressed against mine. I love how perfectly she molds to me when we lie together. She snuck out after I fell asleep, per usual—which I appreciate because I hate watching her go.

After showering and getting dressed, I move to my home office and open the bottom drawer. Inside is a black leather folio with worn edges, and I pull it out, taking it to the kitchen with me. As I brew a cup of coffee, I open it.

I flip past the cover page after scanning over the words—*Project Glass Slipper*.

What started as a quiet mission has morphed into something else entirely. Maybe Easton and Weston suspected it would the entire time. Maybe they saw something I didn't.

Once the caffeine hits, I pull eggs and bacon from the fridge.

Just as I grab a skillet, there's a soft tap at my door. I hurry to grab the folio, slide it into a cabinet, and then rush over.

Billie stands before me in a sleek black pantsuit. Her hair is slicked back, and her lips are a bold, dark red. She holds a box of doughnuts. "Breakfast?"

I appreciate the view of her. "Are you on the menu?"

"I wish. I have to be at the office in thirty minutes for a meeting about London Fashion Week. Dreading it, honestly."

I lean against the door as she hands me the box. "You do look good enough to eat."

This earns me her perfect smile.

She grabs my tie, stealing a quick kiss. "Navy blue looks good on you."

"You'd look better on me," I mutter, unable to resist the tease.

"Stop. You'll make me late, and I cannot be," she says, sounding stressed, but she shakes her head with a laugh. "Have a great day, Banks."

"So far, it's the best, Ice Queen."

Billie slides away from me and moves to the elevator. She steps inside and gives me a seductive smirk. I capture the moment in my memory and retreat into my loft, grinning like an idiot.

"She's mine," I say out loud, then throw my fist into the air. "Billie Calloway is mine."

It's then that I realize I'm in love with her. I think I've always been.

I place the box on the counter, and when I open it, I find two chocolate-covered doughnuts and a pair of lace panties. I hook them with my finger and smile, noticing the crotch is soaked with her juices. *"Bad, bad girl."*

I bring them to my face and inhale her sweet scent, knowing she was thinking about me this morning while she was touching herself. My girl is insatiable for me, and I will never be able to get enough of her. My breaking through Billie's barriers in the

Hamptons was exactly what we both needed. I'll forever be grateful to Nick for that.

My cock springs to life, but I ignore it, saving every drop of myself for her, just as I promised. I stuff the panties in my pocket with a smirk. It's already shaping up to be one of the best Mondays I've ever had.

I bite one of the chocolate-covered, cream-filled doughnuts, looking forward to when we'll wake up and fall asleep together. For once, I don't think I'll drift through this life alone because, for the first time in years, someone feels the same way as I do. I've never experienced anything like Billie. Fuck, she's glorious.

I grab the folio and flip it open to the notepad, where I've kept extensive notes over the years. I scribble something about today.

Wearing black pantsuit. Hair slicked back. Total fucking smokeshow. Brought me breakfast and panties. She's a walking dream.

Billie Calloway might have been the purpose, but now she's the entire plot, the only woman I want.

As I scan over the things I've written about her over the years, I realize that this—us falling in love—has been inevitable. Maybe that was Weston and Easton's plan when they approached me about watching their sister.

Has Weston been playing matchmaker this entire time?

Apparently, he's known for that.

Josh enters my office, wearing a snarl. I pull the USB drive from my computer and give him a smile.

"Please, sit," I offer, being disgustingly nice, imagining how sweet it will be when I gain enough access to his systems to be able to prove that Lustre Fashion is nothing more than a money laundering scheme. That's all it's ever been.

Josh plops down and crosses his arms over his chest like a literal child. Billie was right when she once called him a man-child.

"What do you want? I told Nick I no longer wanted you on my contract," he states.

"I owe you an apology," I reply sincerely, knowing I have to be the one to hack into his system and gain the proof I need. No one else can, not even Nick.

His brows crease in surprise. He didn't expect that.

"You're *apologizing?*" he asks incredulously.

"Yes. The only reason I got together with Billie was to figure out how I could better help you." I give him an evil grin, trying to show him we're the same. Far from it, but assholes like him enjoy other assholes—birds of a feather and all of that. "Come on. I know you dated her to get information about the industry," I say, keeping it light and just toxic enough so he knows I'm not fucking around.

He's intimidated by me, which he should be.

"At first, yes. But I fell in love with her. Her heart. Her tight ass."

My stomach turns, but I keep up the act. "I realized that, and I ended things once I got the information I needed to help Lustre Fashion take over the world. Now, if you want to work with me, I'm willing to do whatever it takes to earn your trust. I will take you to the top, Josh."

"Is that revenge I sense?" he asks, a smirk playing at the corners of his mouth. "Did the curse get you?"

"Actually, it is revenge." I chuckle, knowing he doesn't know it's directed at him. "I'm *her* karma and curse. Now, what do you say? Ready to make the rest of our time together count?"

He cracks his neck, then stares at me. "I want you working in my office, at my headquarters, and working exclusively for me. I need help with my public image."

"I can absolutely help the public see you for who you are," I say without hesitation and without lying. "They should know who's behind Lustre Fashion and the hard work you've put into increasing your cash flow and bottom line over the past six years."

That's when the money laundering began. How do I know? My sister figured it out and started a file on the people she wanted to expose. After I hacked into her locked folders, I extracted the information and found everything. In a way, I'm doing this for Billie, Eden, and just because I've never fucking liked the guy.

"I want her back, Asher," he whispers.

I give him a knowing smile, my brow lifting. "You don't need her, Josh. There are so many oth—"

"You're forbidden to be around her for the rest of my contract."

"No issue at all," I reply with a confident nod. "However, there may be times when we are at the same location. For example, London Fashion Week. I'd want to join you at that event. It's going to be a huge night for you. Also, I work with Weston and Easton, so we may cross paths."

"You are absolutely joining me for London Fashion Week. I want you to be my shadow. Make my company the best there is. When I'm better than her, she'll want me back. I always get what I want, Asher," he tells me.

"Me too," I say. "Are you giving me another chance?"

He grins widely, extending his hand. "Yes."

I grab it firmly, shaking it, knowing I can't trust him.

"Don't let me down, or I'll fucking kill you."

I grip his hand harder, ready to break every bone. "Threaten me again and see what happens to you and your entire family," I warn him.

When we pull away, I see real fear in his eyes, but it doesn't make him any less dangerous.

Josh's methods and the way he deals with those who cross him aren't exactly legal. He needs to be put behind bars because he is a danger to anyone close to him.

"I look forward to earning your trust again, Josh," I say, keeping my tone steady. "Know, in any situation, I will always do the *right* thing."

It's a promise. One that I will keep.

"Thanks," he offers as he walks away, rubbing his palm with his opposite hand.

My grip might have been too firm earlier, but oh, well. The door closes behind him, and I let out a breath, realizing that was so much easier than I thought it would be.

Fuck. Josh. Lustre.

I roll my shoulders back, relieved that it's over, but also hoping I don't lose myself in the process. I'm worried I might become as ruthless as the men I despise—men like my father. These methods aren't traditional by any means, and hacking is inherently dangerous, but no one has the guts or knowledge to put a stop to Lustre. Only me.

Before I get too caught up in work, I grab my phone and call my brother. "Please come see me."

A few minutes later, Nick sits across from me at my desk, his eyes filled with curiosity. "What have you done?"

"Starting tomorrow, I'll be working at Lustre Fashion, exclusively for Josh, for the next month."

"He has two months left on his contract," Nick points out.

"It won't last that long. Because of this change of events, this will be over much sooner than I anticipated. One month. Once I have access to his database, he's *cooked*," I say, picturing it in my mind.

"Asher"—Nick shakes his head—"you said you were stopping with the boogeyman stuff."

"Yeah, well, I changed my mind," I reply with a shrug. "I only help ethical businesses, Nick. I destroy the others because they're poison. Everyone knows that. Josh invited the vampire into his home, and now he'll have to deal with the consequences of being so fucking stupid. He asked for my help because he sees me as a threat." An evil grin spreads across my lips. "He should."

"Why are you so determined?"

"For Eden," I say, knowing Lustre was on her takedown list. My sister may have been sunshine, but she was also a wraith, the real

Batman of business. This was her Gotham City. "I've almost finished everything on her dream list, Nick."

He studies me. "And then what will you do? Leave the city?"

I lean back and smile. "I'm going to ask Billie to marry me."

"Asher, it's still really new," he says.

"This has been going on for twenty years, Nick. She's always been my dream girl, and I finally have the chance to make her my wife."

He chuckles. "Too bad she doesn't have a sister."

"No, but she does have a best friend who just happens to be your brand-new step-sis," I say.

Nick laughs. "Harper has always basically been my little sister because of Zane. A relationship with her will *never* happen."

"That's too bad. She seems like a lot of fun," I say.

BILLIE SITS BESIDE ME ON THE COUCH IN HER LOFT.

"Today, I told Josh I'd never see you again. I'm breaking a contract right now."

She snorts. "He believed you?"

"Yeah," I tell her, and she leans in and kisses me, pushing me onto my back. "I'm still trying to understand what you saw in him."

She sucks in a deep breath. "I had his attention, and he understood my world. He's attractive. Small penis. Could barely get me off. I usually had to finish myself, but he tried. And he still had the audacity to cheat on me. He broke my trust, and once that's lost, it's over."

"I'm sorry," I whisper, knowing she deserved so much fucking better than that.

"The sick part is, had he not cheated, I probably would've settled for him," she says. "No one wants me."

I grab her hand, pulling her closer to me. "Please shut the actual fuck up. Everyone wants you, trust me."

"No, they don't. I'm not approachable." She grins widely, flames dancing in her eyes.

"You just need a strong man," I say. "Someone who isn't intimidated by you. Most are."

"You're not?" she asks.

"No, princess. I like that you don't back down in what you believe in or how you feel. You're authentically you in whatever situation you're in," I tell her, stealing a kiss, wondering if she knows what she's done to me. "It's admirable."

Flickering candles burn on the coffee table, casting a warm glow around us as she lies on my chest.

"I have a confession to make," I say, rubbing my thumb gently on her bottom lip.

"Okay," she says.

"I applied to Stanford because I'd read that was your dream college and I wanted the chance to see you again."

"Really?" she questions. "That's actually kind of cute."

"I made sure I was the best version of myself when I found you again."

"And then I instantly hated you," she whispers, her voice softer now. "I'm sorry. To be fair, I was really intimidated because I literally would've given you my virginity. When our eyes met, I was … pissed. The first cute guy I ran into gave me butterflies … *weak ass*."

I chuckle. "I'm kind of glad, to be honest. I think I would've had a different life had we found each other sooner. Not a bad one, just a different one." I imagine us, married, working for our parents at jobs we hated and going through the motions of life. "I don't regret it."

"I don't either," she says, grinning. "I'd probably have ten kids by now."

"Do you want children?" I ask, knowing this isn't something we've talked about.

"I don't know. Right now, I'm happy with my life. And Lexi is due in a few months. I'm going to see how I feel about motherhood after their triplets are born because I promised Lexi I would help her as much as possible ..."

"I forgot it was triplets. Wow."

She kisses me. "Did you really hate me?"

"I hated and blamed you for not ever giving me a chance when I knew I could make you so fucking happy," I admit.

"Cocky. Love that."

"But I did enjoy pushing you to your limits. Playing pranks on you because you'd get so mad that your face would turn red. Watching you act like a little brat, trying to make me jealous with other guys. The tension was always there in college. Fuck, I wanted you so bad."

"Didn't notice," she says playfully, a teasing smile tugging at her lips. "So, was this your plan all along? Make sure I got addicted to you?"

"No, but things change. Environments change."

She nods. "Chameleons."

"Speaking of, do you know who won your cuff links? Have the bids been finalized?"

"Not yet, but whoever wins will keep it anonymous," she says. "I've tried to figure out who it was for years, but the auction house will not budge. I even tried to bribe them."

I interlock my fingers with hers, kissing her knuckles softly. "Probably some rich asshole."

"Obviously. I think it's Easton and Weston because I've never seen the pieces worn. I think they're just being nice and funneling money into the foundation with an anonymous purchase. Plus, it's always outrageous amounts," she says. "Are you attending London Fashion Week?"

"Actually, yes," I tell her.

"Perfect." Her eyes trail all over my face, as if trying to memorize every detail.

She's admiring me, and I love being under her gaze.

"Can't wait to sneak away with you," I admit.

"I need to tell you something," she says, swallowing hard, her voice a little shaky.

"Okay," I encourage her, wanting her to spill it because the anticipation feels too heavy.

"There was this one time." She pauses, then continues, "Okay, it was *several* times. But ..." She swallows hard again. "I don't know how to say it, so I'm just going to blurt it out."

I laugh, finding it adorable that she's so flustered. "Mm-hmm."

"There were times when Josh and I were having sex and I said *your* name."

My mouth falls open, and then a grin spreads. "You fantasized about having sex with me?"

"It was the only time I could, you know ..." she admits as she tucks her lips into her mouth.

"*Bad fucking girl,*" I mutter, leaning in to steal a kiss, savoring the taste of her. "No wonder he hates me."

"He was convinced I was with you when he and I were together," she says, a hint of mischief in her voice. "Only in my mind."

"I fucking love hearing this. Ah, sweet victory. Winning without even trying is the best." I lean in and kiss her again, feeling our electric connection. "I used to have wet dreams about you in college."

"Really?" she asks, her eyes widening in surprise. "*Hot.*"

"And now I get to live those dreams with you," I say, my voice teasing.

"But in secret," she adds, a slight frown crossing her face.

"Does it bother you?" I ask, wanting to know how she feels.

"Kinda. I read several articles today talking about how in love I am—but with Louis. It's not right that he gets credit for it," she tells me, a hint of frustration in her voice. "I want the world to know about us."

"They will," I promise, trying to reassure her. "And our love story will be one of the greatest ones ever told."

She has no idea how deep this really runs.

"It already is," she whispers across my mouth, leaning in for a kiss.

26

BILLIE

My phone buzzes against the bedside table, jolting me awake. My heart sinks the moment I read the text from an unknown number.

UNKNOWN
Soon, the world will see you for the whore you are.

Anxiety snakes through my chest and wraps around me until I can barely breathe. I quickly read the message again, but the threat lingers in my mind, a poison that seeps deep under my skin.

This must be Josh. I remember him saying something similar when I called him out for cheating.

I've never been unfaithful to him or anyone else. It's just not how I operate.

I don't want this beautiful thing that Asher and I have built over the past few weeks to shatter like glass. I don't want things to change between us. While I wish Asher and I could be public, I enjoy keeping him to myself, away from the pressure and permission of the outside world. Anytime I'm in a relationship, the media jumps straight to marriage and kids—something that's been happening since my early twenties. Imagine seeing your face on the front of every raunchy tabloid just because you held someone's hand in public. Because of how cruel the public can be, I'm savoring every private moment we share, knowing that, one day, we won't have to hide.

I just have to wait for Asher to finish whatever he's so determined to do.

Josh has been working Asher ragged, making him pull eighteen-hour days, and I haven't seen him in four days. The last time we were together, he kissed me softly and promised me it was almost over.

I lock my phone, trying not to spiral. I don't want this to set the tone for my day.

I dress quickly and mechanically, my mind racing. My fingers tremble as I smooth down my black silk blouse, then button my suit jacket with a quick flick of my wrist.

I wondered how long it would take for Josh to threaten me. I anticipated it, almost expecting the worst.

When I climb into my car, I stop my driver from pulling away and text Brody.

A minute later, he's sliding into the back seat with me. "What's up?"

I unlock my phone and hand it to him.

He reads the text message, his brow furrowing. "Whose number is this?"

"I don't know. It's probably a burner phone. But I think it's Josh," I tell him, my voice barely above a whisper.

My cousin meets my eyes, and his jaw locks firmly in place. "What does he have on you?"

"I have no idea," I whisper, my heart thumping hard. "This is my worst nightmare."

Brody's eyes soften. "Have you told Asher?"

I shake my head. "Not yet."

"I'll talk to him," Brody tells me.

"Please discuss this in person. Do not text him, okay?"

"I can do that," he says.

"Nothing regarding this or us can be put into writing," I confirm.

"Little cousin, what have you gotten yourself into?" Brody asks, concern etched in his features.

"I don't know," I admit, not liking how any of this makes me feel. It's like a weight pressing down on my chest.

I'm let out in front of Bellamore headquarters. On my way to my office, my assistant hands me a double shot of espresso. I thank her and move into the waiting room, glancing over my sculptures.

"Do you think these resemble dicks?" I ask, raising an eyebrow. "The truth, please."

Her brows pop upward, and she swallows hard. "Are you going to fire me?"

"No," I tell her.

"Yes, they do," she says with a small smile.

"Please have these moved out and donated to the Calloway Fine Art Museum by the end of the day. My brothers can decide where they'll be displayed." I wave my hand dismissively, as if that will make the sculptures disappear faster.

"Yes, right away," she says.

I move into my office, sinking into my chair behind the desk.

I glance over my shoulder, catching sight of Asher's building with blinds erected to block my view. It's okay because I know he's not there—he hasn't been since we returned from the Hamptons.

Things are changing so fast that my head is spinning. I won't complain though, because I don't feel as lost as I did a month ago. Thanks to Asher, I'm hopeful for the first time in years.

The day drags on, filled with grueling hours of meetings with designers. Harper and I are pushing forward with our plan to fake out Josh with our designs. Did he figure it out?

Conference rooms and calls blur together, voices fade into the background, and I randomly remember the threat that was texted to me this morning. It haunts me, lurking like a shadow.

"You okay?" Harper asks, leaning against my office doorway, her expression filled with concern. "You've looked rattled all day."

"I'm fine," I lie, forcing a smile that feels more like a grimace.

She sighs knowingly, stepping in and gently closing the door behind her. "Billie, you can't pretend with me. What's going on?"

I close my eyes briefly, then admit quietly, "I got a threatening text message this morning. I know it's from Josh, Harp. I don't know what dirt he has on me, but—"

Her jaw tightens. "Don't let him do this. Don't give him that power. You're Billie Calloway. He can threaten all he fucking wants."

"You don't know what he's capable of," I whisper, gathering strength from her words.

"I do." Harper squeezes my shoulder reassuringly. "You've got Asher on your side. He won't let anything happen, babe. Now, show me what you've been working on."

I unlock my iPad and hand it to her. She swipes through the different outfits I've designed. It's how I've kept my mind busy, pouring my feelings into fabric and sketches.

"Wow," she says, and wiggles as if trying to shake off the goose bumps covering her arms. "This gave me chills. This is it. This is what we showcase in London."

"Harp," I whisper, anxiety creeping in, "we have a little over three weeks. There's no way I can get it all together."

"Listen to me. You're Billie fucking Calloway. Make it happen," she insists, her tone fierce. "I'll compile a team of our very best seamstresses. Do you have a model in mind?"

"Of course I don't. I was messing around with this," I say. "It wasn't serious."

"It's incredible," she tells me, pointing emphatically. "You walk this design on the runway."

I shake my head vehemently. "Harp, I haven't done a show since I was a teenager."

She licks her lips and smiles. "Guess that's changing."

"Please don't pull rank," I whisper, half joking, half serious.

"You are the right height and build. You're confident and commanding. Shine like a diamond," she says.

I swallow hard, doubt creeping back in. "You can't be serious. This is impossible."

"Nothing is impossible unless you believe it is. You are our showstopper, babe." She giggles with excitement, her energy infectious. "We keep it a secret. No one can know what we're working on." Harper darts her pinkie toward me. "Swear it."

"But..."

"Lock it in," she demands, and I know she won't let me wiggle out of this one.

We hook our pinkies together and lock them, a promise sealed.

"I have a good feeling. It's one I never ignore," she says, a radiant smile lighting up her face. Harper claps her hands together and laughs. "This is our comeback."

"I don't have a name for it," I say, feeling a mix of excitement and apprehension.

"You'll think of something," she encourages, her belief in me unwavering.

"And what about our original lineup?" I ask, still trying to grasp the situation.

"We'll keep what we have with one addition." She points down to the dress. "This one."

I sigh. "It's risky."

"It's unexpected. A risk I'm willing to take," Harper confirms with a bright smile. "Looks like you have work to do."

"Harp," I whisper.

"I'll contact Lucia, the head of product development, and we can work on getting a pattern cut by the end of the day tomorrow," she says, her voice steady and confident. "No more playing small, Billie. Show them why Bellamore is the best."

My emotions flood in. "What if I can't?"

"You can. You *will*. I believe in you."

"This isn't our brand," I say.

"*We* are our brand," she confirms, her eyes sparkling with conviction. "Just be you. That's what everyone wants."

"Asking you to be my partner was one of the best decisions I ever made," I tell her. "I'm proud of you, Harp."

"I'm proud of you, Little Miss CEO. Now let's fuck them up. Show the world what we're made of instead of lying down for these shitty men who think they understand women's fashion. This is *our* industry, not theirs."

Harper looks at me, fire igniting behind her eyes, like she's ready for us to burn down the whole damn place to prove a point.

After my pep talk, Harper leaves me to gather my thoughts.

The pressure on my shoulders feels almost unbearable. I haven't designed like this or walked a runway in over a decade, and I've never created a runway-worthy concept in this amount of time.

I glance down at the ball gown I sketched last week. It fades from burnt orange to red, a fiery masterpiece that seems to pulse with life. When I close my eyes, I can vividly imagine it fluttering at the hem. The fabrics and fit are so clear in my mind. Sparkling embellishments will line the bust; the painstaking task of hand-beading will take hours.

Dread tightens its grip around me, but I push through it the best I can as I contact Fallon, our design director, who works directly under Harper.

I leave work the moment the sky melts into shades of orange and pink. I sneak out the back exit of the building and slide into my car, eager to shield myself from the paparazzi and return to my elusive self. When I make it to my building, I let out a relieved sigh.

Once I walk inside my loft, I head straight to the couch, setting my satchel on the floor. I lean my head back against the cushion, staring up at the ceiling, letting my mind drift for a moment. My phone buzzes in my bag, and I dig inside to pull it out.

> BRODY
> He's been made aware.

I hurry to respond.

> BILLIE
> Thank you.

My cousin sends me a thumbs-up emoji, and I lock my phone, returning to my racing thoughts. I don't know how long I sit on the couch, lost in my own head. The only thing that pulls me away is a knock.

Our secret knock. *Knock, knock, pause, knock.*

I open the door to find Asher standing there, his eyes full of concern.

I pull him inside with me, needing his presence like air.

"Brody told me, and I rushed here," he mutters before capturing my lips in a kiss.

I melt into him, missing him so damn much. He pulls me into a hug, holding me tight against him. I inhale his cologne—a scent that feels like home, wishing I could bottle it up and keep it with me always.

"I've missed you," I admit, my voice barely above a whisper.

"Fuck, I've missed you too," he replies, and I can see the exhaustion etched across his face. "Have you received any other threatening messages?"

"No." I force myself to smile, but it's weak, fractured, like a cracked mirror.

He shakes his head, cupping my face gently in his hands. "What could he have on you?"

I let out a shaky breath, trying to steady my thoughts. "I don't know. Text messages? We were together for four years, Ash. He could release every conversation we'd ever had."

Anger flashes through Asher's eyes. "I won't let this happen."

"It's not me I'm worried about," I whisper, gripping his shirt and pulling him closer. "It's you, Ash. I can't lose you."

"There is nothing Josh could ever say that would make me give you up." His expression softens instantly, protectiveness mixing with raw vulnerability. "You won't lose me. Ever. This love isn't fragile, Billie. It's fucking bulletproof. No matter what happens, it's you and me against the world."

Emotion wells in my chest, relief mixing with determination. "You promise?"

"I swear it," he murmurs, pressing a soft kiss to my lips, grounding me in this moment. "You're mine. Nothing changes that."

I breathe out, surrendering completely to the warmth of his embrace. His touch ignites something deep within me, melting away the lingering fears that have held me captive. He kisses me slowly, deeply, his mouth tasting of promises and forever. His hands slide gently down my body, stripping away the layers, both physical and emotional. My heart races, my breath catches, and my entire world narrows to just him.

The fading light casts shadows across our bodies as we kiss. It's tender yet possessive, each movement echoing the depth of our commitment—a silent vow that we'll face whatever comes our way together.

"You're mine, princess." His whispered words against my skin send shivers down my spine. His hands thread through my hair as he kisses my forehead, eyelashes, and cheeks. It feels like worship.

"You're everything," I whisper against his lips. "Everything I've ever wanted."

Tears prick my eyes as I cling to him, overwhelmed by the emotions surging through me. He presses his forehead against mine, our breaths mingling as we spiral together. This—us—is worth every risk, every sacrifice.

Asher Banks is my future, my heart, my home.

And I'll fight anyone who dares to threaten that.

"I'll go to war for you," he confesses, pressing his lips gently against mine. "Fuck, I already have."

I WAKE UP TO ASHER'S LEGS TANGLED AROUND MINE, A WARM WEIGHT that anchors me to this moment. His strong arm is like a fortress over my body, and I feel the steady rhythm of his breath against my neck.

"Good morning," he whispers, his voice rough, pulling me closer, as if he's afraid to let go.

I turn to face him, our noses almost brushing, morning breath and all. A grin breaks across my face, and I feel like I'm dreaming. I always do when it's just us and the fluttering of our hearts.

"Ash, I want to wake up like this every day. I know it's a tall order, but I can't stand the thought of going days without you," I confess, my heart racing. "And I miss your smart-ass mouth."

He stirs, blinking against the sunlight spilling through the curtains. The golden light dances across the floor, making his messy hair shine like a halo. A smile grows on his perfect lips, and, damn, he looks like a Greek god with his chiseled jaw and the stubble that lines it perfectly.

"Will sleeping next to me make you happy?" he asks, brushing his fingertips softly against my cheek, sending a jolt of electricity through me.

Goose bumps cover my arms.

"The happiest." I breathe out, wishing I could freeze this moment forever, where everything feels right and uncomplicated. Nothing can bother us when we're alone like this.

"Then consider it done," he replies, a smirk playing at the corners of his mouth.

"Really?" Laughter bursts from me, light and carefree.

"It's always a yes if I get that reaction," he says, his expression softening as he leans in closer, lightly brushing his lips across mine.

"You always know how to steal my breath away."

He smiles. "It's because it's right. Inevitable."

The word hangs between us, heavy with meaning. Inevitable—like gravity, like sunrise and sunset, like how my body has always responded to his touch or the way he looks at me with those deep, searching eyes.

"I don't regret much in life, but—"

"Don't say it," he interrupts, pressing a finger to my lips. "Regret nothing. Without it, we wouldn't be here now. And don't assume we would be because there are no guarantees." His gaze, so serious now, holds mine with an intensity that makes my heart race. "Remember the past, but don't relive it. We have an entire future to plan."

"I hope you mean that," I whisper, realizing that I've fallen in love with him with a ferocity that scares me. "I don't think I can live without you."

My words hang in the air between us, heavy and sweet, like the promise of something beautiful.

"Then don't," he says simply, as if it were the easiest solution in the world.

A thrill runs through me, a mix of excitement and vulnerability, because I know this man is mine if I want him. Even though my life is chaotic, this feels like the beginning of something life-changing. I can't tell if I'm terrified or exhilarated at the thought, but either way, I want to dive in headfirst.

Asher's lips find my neck and slide up to my mouth. He kisses me like he's committed, and I know he is. The certainty of it makes my chest ache in a way that's both thrilling and terrifying. This feeling has me so fucking scared that I nearly tremble.

Carefully, Asher slides his hands down my body, his touch leaving a trail of fire on my skin. His fingers slip into my panties, and he swallows hard, feeling how wet I am for him. My body has always been honest, even when my words and actions weren't.

"Fuck, princess." He moans against my neck, his breath hot against my skin. "Insatiable for me."

"Always," I whisper with a moan as he gently rubs circles on my clit.

My eyes nearly roll into the back of my head when he slides two fingers inside, curling exactly where I like.

I sink into him as he kisses my neck and whispers in my ear, his voice a seductive rumble, "I fucking love that sound."

"Ash," I whisper, my voice thick with need, "I want to feel you." The words spill out, both a plea and a demand.

He chews on his lip as he slides out of his boxers, hovering above me, and our eyes meet—my sea blue against his sunset brown. At that moment, I see everything I've been afraid to hope for.

He slides deep inside of me, and it's a promise. We're in this together.

Asher and I float into the abyss, into nothingness—just us, sharing a moment that catapults us to a different universe. It's always been him, this man who so patiently waited until I was ready for him, for *this*.

"More," I groan out, arching my back off the bed, my body craving more of him. "You feel so good."

He stretches me so wide and slams into me so deep that I nearly see stars. His breath in my ear is intoxicating, nearly undoing me.

"One day," he whispers, placing soft kisses on my lips, "I'm going to marry you, Billie."

I smile against him, then pull away, meeting his gaze. In his eyes, I see our entire future unfolding. "I hope you do."

Butterflies flutter in my stomach, and his words feel like a promise. Asher Banks never breaks those. And as he moves inside me, claiming me completely, I realize I've never felt more alive, more seen, more loved. I've fallen in love with him completely and irrevocably, and there's no going back. I don't want to.

This is true love. I've been searching for it my entire life, and I've found it in him.

I was always the problem, not Asher. He's always believed we were destined and was just waiting for me to finally wake up. My eyes are wide open.

27

ASHER

ONE WEEK LATER

I glance at the clock in the corner of my computer screen, watching the minutes tick down.

Twenty minutes later, Josh Lustre enters the office I'm occupying while working at his headquarters. He carries a tablet in his hand, then slides it across the desk to me.

A Royal Wedding Is in the Works: The Diamond Princess and Her Prince.

He glares at me. "How did this happen? They're moving too fast."

I shrug, knowing this is a losing argument. It always is when it comes to Billie. After working this closely with him, I understand why she left. He's okay in small doses, but in large ones? Annoying as hell.

"My job isn't to stalk Billie Calloway. You know how I feel about her. She's *boring*. You can do much better," I tell him.

"They cannot get married, Asher. They cannot! I will not allow this to happen!" he screams in my face.

I smile, understanding his frustration, but knowing this lie is a very large piece of a puzzle.

"Please sit," I say calmly, and he does.

Once he's settled down and is no longer having a toddler fit, I breathe out slowly. Somehow, I've become one of the few people who can calm him down when he's having a meltdown like this. Always pathetic, consistently over Billie.

"Okay. Now listen to me. If she does marry the prince, she'll acquire royal duties and no longer have time for Bellamore. That benefits you directly."

"But if I lose her, I'll lose her forever. I can't bear it," he says, his fist clenched.

The way he's acting makes me want to bash his fucking face in. I want to shake him and ask him why he didn't treasure her while he had her. What's sad is, had he not cheated, she probably would have never left him. Even if she wasn't in love, she was happy. Comfortable. They were comfortable.

"Then what?" I ask. "What will you do?"

"I have a plan," he tells me. "One that will guarantee the palace will not approve of this marriage."

My heart rate upticks slightly, but I remain calm. "Which includes?"

"Sex tapes," he says. "Lots of them."

My nostrils slightly flare. "What are you talking about?"

He grins mischievously. "I used to secretly film us having sex in my house. Maybe a few of those videos should find their way onto the internet somehow. No way the palace would let a whore like her be a queen—not with her pussy and tits all over the web. They want a princess, not Billie Calloway."

The fact that he would take their intimate moments and weaponize them against her has me cracking my knuckles. "That's also very illegal."

"So? No one will care. They'll just remember what she did and how she begged for my cock. It's career-ruining." He stands, agitation radiating off him. "I swear to fucking God, Asher. I can't have her with Prince Louis any longer. I must end this before I lose my damn mind. After what I share, no one will want her. She'll be reduced to a whore."

"Let it go, Josh. You'll destroy your family's company if you don't. Be logical," I tell him, trying to snap him back to reality. "This is a felony. Jail time. She'll know it was you, and she has the money to prove it. She's a Calloway. You really don't want to do this."

"The consequences can get fucked," he shoots back defiantly. "I love her. After what I show the world, I'll be the only one who will want her."

"What does that even mean?" I ask, feeling my mask begin to slip.

He's crawling under my skin. I picture myself slamming my fist into his nose, imagining him crying like a little bitch afterward.

He laughs, and I join in, but for a different reason—my amusement is laced with irritation.

I want to ask him if he sent her that text message. The way he's acting feels like a confirmation. He's oozing jealousy and anger, upset that it's Louis instead of him. If only he knew the truth.

"My best friend and I used to share her," he tells me. "Every other weekend."

"Too bad I wasn't your bestie back then," I reply with a shit-eating grin.

He buys it, smiling widely and giving me a high five. "She was such a whore for the cock. Loves it in her ass."

"Hmm. You should've told me that before. Would've been great info to have," I say, and while the locker-room talk makes me sick, I know it's just part of the game we're playing.

It encourages Josh and makes him overly comfortable when he's surrounded by people who are as crude as he is. So, I mirror his personality, giving him what he gives.

"If she takes me back, consider it done. We'll fuck her until she can't stand, and then we'll keep going," he says with a laugh.

It takes every last drop of control I have not to knock the hell out of him. With that, he's officially pushed me to the very edge.

"Appreciate the offer, but I'm good. Sick of sluts, to be honest. I want a good girl next. One who knows how to follow the rules and do *exactly* what I say," I tell him with a laugh, knowing Billie is that girl. "You can keep the Ice Queen. Not really my type."

"The way she used to look up into my eyes and whimper when I shoved my cock down her throat—seeing spit run down her chin and hearing her choke on me—it was music to my fucking ears. Makes me miss her," he says, pulling his phone out. "Let me show you."

Josh shows me a video of Billie masturbating—a FaceTime call he recorded. She shoves the toy deep inside her, and my face stays neutral until I realize what's in her hand.

"Oh my fucking God," I say, shaking my head before I burst into laughter. "That toy. Do you know what it is?"

"No," he says, turning it toward himself and zooming in on the golden cock.

"It's a mold of Prince Louis's dick. There was a huge scandal a few years ago. You don't remember the slogan, *Wear the crown and ride the prince*? Look at the emblem on the end. Each toy came with a crown ring. Women around the world kept talking about how it felt to fuck a royal." I breathe out. "If I were you, I wouldn't post that one. It would only help Prince Louis's second chance at romance, especially with her masturbating with his dick. For you, that's such a bitch move. It's like she did it for him."

Josh growls with rage, shoving his phone in his pocket. "She will pay for this."

"Choose your next move carefully," I warn. "Let me take care of this for you."

"Please," he states. "But I doubt she'd listen to you. She fucking hates you."

I smirk. "Yeah, well, maybe a dose of reality will be helpful for her. You have to change your rule about me not seeing her. I want it in writing."

He pulls his phone from his pocket and seconds later, I receive an email from him recanting that I never see Billie again.

"Good enough for you?"

I grin. "Yep. I'll do my best."

"It's about time you helped me," he says, before he storms out of my office, acting like a brat.

I close my laptop, lean back in my chair, and stifle my laughter. Billie always held the upper hand with him. She was also so much more intelligent than those she dated. Even though I can't help but feel the jealousy creep up my neck.

While these manipulative conversations make my stomach twist and do bother me at times, I love looking him in the face, knowing my name is the one released from her lips every night. Billie has fallen asleep in my arms since she told me she wanted to wake up to me every day. Sure, there are mornings when I sneak away, but our nights are spent holding each other like the other might disappear.

Billie Calloway is mine, and I *will* make her my wife.

Once we're official, Josh won't dare mess with her. One phone call and a suitcase full of cash is all it would take for me to end him. But after what he's done, I'd rather play with him a little before I *legally* end it. I want his entire fleet of battleships to be sunk, not just one, which means infiltrating from the inside.

Lustre Fashion is just the beginning. When I finish with him, his personal and professional life will be a living hell. I'm called the Boogeyman of Business for a reason. Everyone was warned. Josh fucked around, and now he's finding out.

I am his worst nightmare.

I pick up my lucky ball and throw it in the air, catching it, knowing I need to slightly reroute my plan. I toss it higher and lower, watching a loose thread in the leather dangle.

This ball reminds me I can make anything happen, even a bases-loaded, out-of-the-park home run. I watched a star fall before I went to bat, then made a wish that's currently coming true.

That was the summer my parents finally stopped arguing over me and decided to file for divorce. My mom let me stay with Nick and his mom, Silvia. I was fourteen, and my big brother spent the summer with me while he was home from college. My dad insisted that I sign up for an extracurricular activity, so I joined a summer baseball league. There were only a few times when I felt like a normal kid; that was definitely one of them.

Nick lived on a cul-de-sac in a small town just outside of New York. His mom always had grape Kool-Aid in the fridge and fresh oatmeal cookies on the counter. I understood why my dad had cheated on my mom with her; she was everything my mother wasn't, right down to being genuinely nice. I got high for the first time in his backyard, kissed a girl four years older than me, and spent countless nights dreaming about seeing Billie Calloway again as I stargazed on my back in the grass.

Now I smirk as I realize I'm completely in love with her, to the point of wanting to ruin the life of the last guy who hurt her. Nothing Josh could expose would ever change how I've always felt about my diamond princess. What we have has been building for a long time, and now that it's finally here, I won't give her up for anything or anyone.

I check the inner pocket of my laptop bag to make sure my USB drive is safely tucked away. I grab my lucky baseball from my desk and flick off the lights in my office at Lustre.

On the way to my firm, I text Harper. We have our own little code.

I text her a simple, *Hi.*

She replies with, *How are you?*

I send her a thumbs-up emoji. Until this whole thing with Lustre is over, I can't text Billie directly. This little exchange tells

Billie to meet me on the top floor of Banks's Advertising and Marketing Firm.

As soon as I arrive, I take the elevator to the top floor. It's a space for remote workers visiting the city, but right now, it's completely empty. I find myself staring out the expansive windows while I wait for her.

Fifteen minutes later, the door to the conference room swings open and then clicks shut. I hear the sharp sound of high heels tapping against the floor, and I turn my head to see her. It feels surreal when our eyes finally meet, and she beams at me, looking stunning in a white pantsuit.

"Wow," I whisper, taken aback.

I left before she woke up this morning, and seeing her now is just … breathtaking.

"Thank you," she replies shyly, making her way toward me.

When she's close enough, I rest my hand on her hip, feeling a rush of warmth.

"No more black?" I ask, intrigued.

"I'm ready to play my own game," she tells me, perching on the edge of the desk, exuding confidence.

"I need to tell you something," I say, crossing my arms over my chest, my tone turning serious.

Her brows knit together in concern. "I don't like that look on your face."

"Josh is losing his mind over the potential engagement between you and princy. You need a scandal to break you two apart that will make you look like an angel," I explain, watching her reaction closely.

Billie shakes her head vehemently. "No. I can't do that."

"Listen to me. Josh has recorded videos of your and his sexcapades. He had hidden cameras set up at his place."

The color drains from her face. "What?"

I nod gravely. "A sex scandal never really disappears, princess. It will follow you for the rest of your life, even if it's fake. It's not worth the fight. Trust me, it's not something you ever want to deal with," I tell her firmly. "Just play his game for a few more weeks for me, *please*."

"He's lying," she whispers, tears spilling down her cheeks. She looks utterly horrified.

"He showed me a recorded FaceTime call. I'm curious why you used the Prince Louie," I mutter against her mouth, pulling away just enough to lift my brow in question.

Her cheeks flush, and she buries her face against my chest. "I thought it was hilarious."

"I want it thrown away immediately," I state firmly. "No way his cock is going inside of you ever again. Mold or not."

She grabs my tie and pulls me closer, her eyes fierce. "I haven't needed to touch myself since we've been together. I always save myself for you, Ash. All of me. That's yours. Just like yours is mine."

I steal a kiss, melting into her, wanting to stay hidden with her at the top of my building until the sun sets.

"What else did he say?" she asks.

I open and close my mouth, my jaw setting. "He said he and his best friend railed you."

Now she looks pissed. "Does that bother you?" she asks, her voice sharp.

"I don't know. I haven't been the best boy either, if you know what I mean," I admit, not wanting to have this conversation.

Jealousy overtakes her, and I love seeing her worked up over me.

"Tell me about it," she says, blinking up into my eyes.

"I dated two best friends. The three of us used to spend our weekends together. I also fucked both their moms," I say, smirking a little.

"Wow," she says, and I see something flicker behind her eyes. It's rage. "I didn't realize you had it like that. I mean, the swagger it must take."

"Billie," I whisper, trying to hold back a smile, "the man I was ten years ago is not who I am now. Okay?"

"I don't want to talk about it."

I see her putting up a wall, and I grab her hand, pulling her back to me.

"How do I stop him?" she finally asks, desperation creeping into her voice.

"You and Louis must break it off very soon. Pretend, behind the scenes, that you want to get back with Josh and hold him off until the fashion show. Afterward, it won't matter. I need you to call him and use your Calloway acting skills. For me, pretty please."

"When?" she asks, raising an eyebrow.

"Right now," I tell her, my tone serious.

She sighs. "Do you know what you're asking of me?"

"Yes. And it's why I'm begging you. I know how this ends, Billie. It's not good," I whisper, grabbing her hand and forcing her to stand as I drop to my knees. "Pretty please. I'm so fucking sorry it's come to this, but trust me. I will *never* lead you astray. Ever. I promise," I say, looking up into her eyes, drowning in them, as usual.

She runs her fingers through my hair, and I lean into her hand, feeling the warmth radiate from her touch.

"You're so strong. You can do this," I offer, my voice soft.

She pulls her phone from her pocket, unlocking it with trembling fingers. She swallows hard, determination slowly replacing her uncertainty.

"Your brothers said you weren't cutthroat enough," I say as I unbutton her suit pants. They fall to the floor and pool around her feet. I lean forward, inhaling her scent. "I told them they were wrong. *Call him.*"

"Asher," she whispers.

I encourage gently, "Say everything you think he'll want to hear."

I hook her panties with my fingers, peeling them off her. I wrap my arms around her, kissing her stomach and sliding my mouth down, peppering kisses around her soft skin. I guide her back onto the desk, spreading her thighs wide and moving closer. "I'll turn pain into pleasure, as promised."

"Asher," she moans out as I swipe my tongue up her wet slit. One of her palms slams against the desk, the sound echoing in the quiet room.

"Mmm. My favorite fucking flavor," I mutter against her sensitive little bud as I suck.

Billie puts the phone on speaker, and it rings and rings. When Josh picks up, I dart my tongue inside her wet hole, slurping her up eagerly.

"Josh," she says breathlessly.

"Billie?" he replies, genuinely surprised.

"I just …" she mutters as I shove a finger inside her and curl it just right. "I just ran into Banks. He's a fucking bastard," she groans out, riding me as I plunge as deep as I can inside her. "He told me I was a bitch for leaving you and …" She sighs, her body trembling with pleasure. "He's right. I was thinking about you, just like old times."

A moan escapes her lips, and I can see her pulse quickening in her neck. I didn't even have to tell her what to say; she just knew.

Josh has severely underestimated Billie Calloway. So have her brothers. This woman is ruthless.

I twirl my tongue around her clit, her cunt glistening for me—a sight I can't get enough of.

"Are you touching yourself?" Josh asks.

"Mm-hmm. Remember when I used to need you so bad?" She grunts, and I want her to remember who's giving it to her now and forever. "We should start over. Be my best-kept secret."

Her eyes meet mine; she's talking directly to me, and the connection is electric.

"Can I see you now? Finish you off?" he begs, sounding desperate.

It's pathetic.

"No. I can't see you until after Fashion Week in London. I'm seeing Louis then, and I want to tell him to his face that it's over. It's the least I can do for the future king."

"FaceTime me," Josh tells her as her eyes roll into the back of her head.

"I can't," she whispers, already teetering on the edge for me. "I'm in my office. Touching myself. So fucking horny," she whimpers as I drive her even closer to the brink. Her muscles tense, and her pussy squeezes my finger so tight.

"Come for me, princess," I whisper across her pussy, just loud enough for her to hear. "Let him listen to what I do to you. What I've always done to you. How I make you desperate."

That's all it takes, and her pussy convulses as she rides out her orgasm. I stand up, spinning her around. I carefully place my hand around her waist, holding her steady as I undo my pants, then slam my cock deep into her. She screams out, dropping her phone on the desk so she has both hands free for better leverage.

"I wish I could see the look on your face," Josh says.

"I wish you could too," Billie replies, and I hear the smirk on her lips. "I wish you could see me right now."

Billie continues to cry out as I fuck her so hard that we both see constellations. Seconds later, she's squirting and coming again on my cock as I empty inside of her, holding back my grunts. I bite her shoulder, and she sighs as my cum slides down her leg.

"Did you hear what you did to me? How I lost control?" she asks.

I nod, my scruff brushing against her back as I hold her steady.

"I heard you, baby," Josh says. "I'll be your secret."

"Okay," Billie whispers and then ends the call.

She turns to look at me, her legs spread open.

We hold a silent conversation, knowing there's nowhere else for us to go from here. We're wild and desperate and dangerous together—an utter fucking mess.

Her mouth crashes into mine, as if she can read my mind, read the words of my heart in my eyes.

Our tongues swirl together, and she captures my heart and soul.

"How did we end up as secret lovers?" she eventually asks.

"I don't know," I admit.

"We won, Asher," she confirms. "We found what we'd always been searching for."

"I know," I say matter-of-factly, and we're on the same team without me even having to tell her the plan.

We clean ourselves up, and Billie turns to me.

"I never slept with Josh and his best friend. They begged me to one weekend when we were drunk in the Hamptons, and I said no."

I laugh. "I never dated two best friends and banged their moms. But kudos to me because you thought I could pull it off," I say, and she steals a quick kiss.

"You're an asshole."

"And you're my dream girl."

"When were you going to tell me you were lying?" she asks, raising an eyebrow.

"I planned to tell you right now. I just wanted you to squirm a little," I admit with a smirk.

She chuckles, shaking her head. "I don't want to think about anyone touching you."

"Same," I mutter, feeling a little defensive. "But unfortunately, your exes are shoved in my face nonstop."

"You're better than both of them combined," she encourages, leaning in for another kiss before leaving. "Yes, even better than a future king. He doesn't understand me in the ways you do. No one does. I think that's why I'm so scared of losing you."

I wrap my arm around her waist, smiling against her lips. "I'm not going anywhere, I promise."

"Thank you," she says, pulling away from me. "Have you had a good day so far?"

"It's much better now," I tell her, feeling a warmth in my chest.

Billie shoots me a wink. "Love the way you look at me."

She disappears, and I try my best to come down from my high. I sit in the desk chair and check my phone, seeing that Josh texted me.

> **JOSH**
> Thanks, man. Thanks for always coming through and having my back.

I smell Billie on my fingers, and I can't help but smile as I reply.

> **ASHER**
> She knows who she belongs to.

Me.

> **JOSH**
> Yes, she does.

> **ASHER**
> I have some meetings to attend at the firm. I'll return soon. Good luck. I wish you the best.

Josh has no idea what's coming.

28
BILLIE

TWO DAYS LATER

Knock. Knock. Knock.

"Did you hear something?" Asher's voice rumbles against my ear.

"No," I whisper, rolling onto my back, the sheets tangled around me, and strain to listen.

Everything is a sleepy haze, and I'm too exhausted to care. Eighteen-hour shifts over the last two days have drained every ounce of energy I had left.

I've spent every waking second hunting for the perfect fabrics and overseeing the fit tests my designers have been running for the dress I'm revealing at the fashion show. The bodice—everything hinges on how it fits and flows, and time is slipping away. In less than three weeks, my entire team will be on a plane, flying across the ocean to give the fashion world an unpredictable surprise. I just hope I can pull it off.

My mind drifts, surrendering to the pull of sleep again.

Knock. Knock. Knock.

My eyes bolt open, irritation bubbling up.

"Okay, I heard it that time," I whisper, frustrated.

"What time is it?" Asher asks drowsily.

I reach for my phone on the nightstand, and the screen's brightness blinds me like a spotlight. "It's just past midnight."

He groans, but his breathing steadies.

Josh has been working Asher hard in preparation for the same fashion show. Right now, my days consist of having dinner, a shower, incredible sex, and then sleep. Rinse and repeat, but I wouldn't want it any other way. It doesn't feel so monotonous with Asher by my side. We've also been taking turns sleeping at each other's loft. I have a key to his place, and he has a key to mine. We just have to sneak in, hoping Mrs. Chambers doesn't catch us. So far, we've managed.

"Billie!"

The familiar muffled voice has me groaning.

"Ugh!" I grumble, pushing the blanket from me.

"Who is it?" Asher asks in a deep rasp.

"It's Harper. I'll be right back." I press soft kisses across the tattoos on his chest, catching a glimpse of his tired eyes before swinging my leg over him. I feel the heat of his body against mine as I lean down to capture his lips. "You're so sexy."

"Hurry back to me," he mutters, his grip tightening on my ass before I slide off him.

I quickly throw on a T-shirt and some shorts that were on the floor. It's what I had on earlier before Asher peeled them off and unwrapped me like a present.

I shuffle down the hallway, yawning and blinking away my tiredness. Peering through the peephole, I see Harper's grinning face and blushed cheeks—a telltale sign that she's had entirely too much to drink.

I swing the door open and freeze at the sight of Brody leaning against the wall behind her. His jaw is set tight, and I see a storm swirling in his eyes. The tension is thick, and his demeanor pricks at my instincts.

"Uh, hi?" My voice is hesitant, as I'm unsure of what's going on.

Harper wraps her arms around my neck, her breath warm and sweet with the scent of alcohol. "I'm in love."

I can't help but chuckle, holding her steady as she sways slightly. "Really? Or are you just drunk?"

She giggles, pulling away to stumble inside. I lead her further in and glance back at Brody, his cold, angry eyes piercing through the moment.

Something's off.

Harper twirls dramatically in my living room before flopping onto the couch like she owns the place. "I'm madly in love!"

I sit beside her, grinning despite Brody's reaction.

"Give me the details," I urge, trying to be supportive. This feels like a page out of our old playbook—sharing stories of our crushes and dates right afterward.

"Last weekend at the gala, I met this gorgeous man," she gushes, her voice bubbling with excitement. "Micah Rhodes. He's an entertainment lawyer. Do you know him?"

I shake my head. "The name doesn't sound familiar. But I can ask Weston since he helped compile the guest list."

"Please do! I'm crushing so hard. I feel like a teenager again." She leans closer, lowering her voice. "You know what he said the first time he saw me?"

"Did he ask if you fell from heaven?" I glance at the stacks of fabric littering my living room—a reminder of how much work I have to do.

"No. He said he'd waited his entire life to find me." She beams, lost in the memory.

"That's sweet," I reply, understanding that emotion deeply. It's what I searched for and found in Asher. "And how did you feel?" I ask, genuinely curious.

Her grin widens. "Flattered! We walked through the gallery together and shared things about ourselves for hours. At the end of the night, he kissed me and then asked me out. Tonight was a dream, Billie. I'm floating on cloud nine."

"I'm so happy for you, Harp," I assure her, sincerity filling my chest. It's been ages since I've seen her this alive—years, possibly a decade.

"I might invite him to London for the show. Be my plus-one!" A giddy smile spreads across her face.

"Let's discuss it when you're not toasted," I tease. "Tipsy Harper sometimes makes questionable decisions."

She leans forward and pulls me into a tight hug. She smells like cotton candy. "I make smart ones too! Oh shit! What time is it?"

"Close to one in the morning." I yawn, stretching as fatigue threatens to pull me under.

"Oh no. It's late! I should go." She pulls away. "Can we meet up soon? I've missed you."

I roll my eyes playfully. "Oh, hush. You see me nearly every day."

"Okay, but seeing CEO you and hanging with my best friend are two totally different things," she insists.

"We'll plan something when we're back from London."

Harper stands, still glowing with excitement about her latest crush, and I can't help but feel hope for her. I hope he's the one. No man has been worthy of her heart before—at least none that I've met. She deserves someone who sees her brilliance and beauty, who will protect her kind soul.

She gives me another tight squeeze, and her warmth seeps into my bones like sunshine.

"I love you, sister," she says.

"I love you too," I reply, opening the door to find Brody still where I left him.

He's like a gargoyle, a silent guardian standing watch.

Harper glances at him as she heads toward the elevator.

I move closer to Brody, lowering my voice like we're sharing a secret. "What's going on?"

"I don't trust Micah," he says, tension lacing his words, his brow furrowed.

"Is he dangerous?" My heart races as a knot forms in my stomach.

Brody doesn't answer, but his silence speaks volumes.

"Don't let her out of your sight," I demand, urgency rising within me. "That's an order. I'll talk to Easton and Weston tomorrow about it. I'll call Zane."

"You're my responsibility. Not Harper," he says firmly, his voice steady, but his expression is concerned.

"Please," I nearly beg, my voice softening as vulnerability creeps in. "I need you to keep her safe. I'll be at work for another eighteen hours tomorrow and then home. Asher will be with me."

"Okay." Brody nods and walks away, leaving me leaning against the door, trying to regain my composure.

I move back to my bedroom, where Asher sits at the edge of the bed. His presence grounds me as my mind tangles with thoughts. As I approach him, he wraps his arms around me, pulling me close, as if he can shield me from it all. When we're alone like this, it's easy for me to believe.

"What's going on?" he asks.

"Harper's dating someone new," I say, trying to keep my tone light.

"That's great," he says into my hair.

"Do you know Micah Rhodes?" I ask, searching his face for any clues that might ease my mind.

His jaw tightens at the name, a flicker of something dark crossing his features.

"What is it?"

"He's older—mid-forties at least—and he's weird. Very uppity and particular about things. I dealt with him at conferences when I worked for my father."

"Brody doesn't trust him," I add quickly. "I told him to follow her."

"Good," he says, capturing my lips in a reassuring kiss before folding down the blankets for me to climb in. "He'll make sure she's safe. Now, come on. You need your rest."

I climb under the covers and nestle into him as he scoots behind me, wrapping his warmth around me like a shield. He protects me from it all.

"You're the perfect big spoon," I say over my shoulder.

He leans in and kisses my cheek. "You're the perfect spork," he replies, nuzzling into me.

"Spork?" I laugh, caught off guard by his choice of words.

"You may be smooth in some places, but you still have sharp edges. Love that about you."

"I love a lot about you, Ash," I mutter.

I let out a contented sigh as my breathing slows. I feel so lucky to have him here with me.

"Good night, princess." He kisses me again, lingering this time.

"Night," I whisper, wanting to say those three words, wanting him to know how I feel.

THE NEXT MORNING, I WALK INTO WORK, CARRYING A BOX OF Harper's favorite pink doughnuts. My heels click against the polished floor, echoing in the otherwise quiet office. I push Harper's office door open, half expecting to find her buried under a mountain of sketchbooks and loose drawings now that we're finalizing next season's designs.

True to my request, Harper hasn't sent anything digitally regarding our upcoming launch. Whispers have spread around the office, but I don't care. I'll do whatever it takes to protect my company. Right now, the only ones we trust are our directors, who have been given closed-door meetings about what we're doing.

If anything gets leaked, I'll be able to confirm it's management who's responsible for double-crossing us and feeding Josh our designs. I'm convinced it's them.

As soon as I take two steps inside, I notice the room is overflowing with vases of dark red roses.

Harper stands with a smile stretching across her pretty face, tears shimmering in her blue eyes as she reads a card. "He's so sweet."

"Harp, wow," I say, setting the box of doughnuts I brought for her on the edge of her desk. The sweet fragrance of roses fills the space. It's intoxicating, but for some reason, it makes me uneasy. "These are gorgeous. Who sent them?"

"Micah." She beams as I set the doughnuts on her desk.

Micah.

His name drips from her lips like honey, but my mind flashes back to Brody's intense gaze when I asked about him. I haven't been able to shake off that look on his face, but I also can't place it. Something isn't right, but he's not one to speculate.

I force a smile, knowing exactly how this story could unfold. I've been down this road before—Josh and his charm had me quickly wrapped around his finger too.

Anxiety floods the back of my mind, but I shove it down until I can get Weston's and Easton's take on this guy. Maybe Brody's wrong.

Brody's never wrong.

I lean closer to the flowers, inhaling them. "Tell me all about him."

She glides over to me, her excitement contagious as she unlocks her phone. Within moments, she's showing off photos of them together from last night. He's handsome—dark hair, light-green eyes that glint with something more. I can see the allure, the spark that has her captivated. I swipe through their pictures, and genuine happiness radiates from her, but there's something more sinister lurking in his expression.

"He seems familiar," I say, tilting my head.

"I thought so too. But I think it's because we're invited to the same events."

I try to tell myself I'm overreacting. I'm just overprotective of my bestie. That's it.

"He's forty-four," she continues, her voice rising with enthusiasm. "Never been married. And it seems like we both want the same things in life. I think you'll like him. He's smart. Business savvy. One of the best entertainment lawyers in the country," she adds with a dreamy sigh. "As soon as things settle down, can we do a double date?"

"With the prince?" I quip, arching an eyebrow.

"With *your* prince, not *the* prince." She grins wider, clearly envisioning a double date with Asher and me alongside her and Micah.

Asher and I are still very much a secret. Louis and I are playing the power-couple role, but it won't last much longer at this rate. Now, I'm toying with Josh, something I hate to do, but it is necessary to save my ass. I've instructed Josh that I will call him, not the other way around. He'll listen to me for a little while, until his mask slips. I can handle him for three more weeks. I don't know what Asher is up to, but I trust him. He's given me no reason not to.

"I would like that. Once we return from London, consider it done," I reply, nodding, but internally, I'm hoping this is just one of those quick flings she tends to have.

"So, Brody was with you last night..." I say, trying to decode her expression when I mention his name.

"We just happened to be at the same bar," she explains, a hint of nervous laughter escaping her lips. "After Micah left, he walked with me to your place. I talked the entire time—God only knows what I said to him. I barely remember seeing you."

I study her, searching for signs of doubt. "Do you feel safe with him?"

"Of course. Brody is—"

"I wasn't talking about my cousin," I say sharply, my voice slicing through the air. "Micah. What did it feel like the first time you two spoke?"

It takes every bit of strength I have not to overanalyze her next words. Not that I'm an expert, but there's a specific feeling when you meet *the one*. Her expression softens, almost as if memories are flooding back.

"I didn't pay him any attention at first," she whispers, "but the conversation flowed. It almost felt like talking to an old friend because he knew so much about me."

My stomach tightens at her words—a flutter of unease dances in my chest.

What if Micah isn't the Prince Charming he appears to be? I envision a giant red flag, but I push it away.

"You're popular," I say, aware that millions of people I don't personally know, know things about me. With who we are, it happens. "I don't know if I have a good feeling about this," I finally admit.

"Once you meet him, you'll love him, trust me." Her eyes tell me that she's infatuated. "He agreed to join me in London."

"Wow. I can't wait," I say, knowing we will barely have any time to ourselves between the fashion shows and meetings.

I glance around her office, searching for answers hidden among the extravagant arrangements. My instincts tell me that I need to dig into Micah's past before he becomes a permanent fixture in Harper's life.

I'm caught between wanting to protect Harper and needing to know more about this man who's so quickly captivated her.

"Have a beautiful day. You deserve it." I tap the box of doughnuts and open the lid. "I was thinking about you this morning."

"Thank you! My favorite," she replies, her entire face lighting up like the sky at a fireworks show.

"Anything for my BFF," I say, my voice steady despite how I feel.

"I'm proud of you," she offers as I leave her office. "Oh, I've also seen the mockup of your dress. You're going to shine like a diamond."

"Thanks, Harp." I smile widely, and my heart squeezes as I leave her office.

The weight of uncertainty lingers in the air, and I can't shake the feeling that something is off. The office buzzes around me, and I have five million other things I need to do, but all I can focus on is finding out who Micah Rhodes is.

"Billie. Wow. This is a surprise," Carlee says as I step inside the penthouse at Park Towers.

Once inside, I glance at the spot where Asher claimed and kissed me in front of everyone. That moment changed my life.

"How can I help you, sis?" she asks.

"I need to speak to LadyLux," I reply matter-of-factly, blinking at her.

We haven't talked since I discovered who she truly was.

She smirks, a playful glint in her eyes. "I don't know what you're referring to."

I sigh. "What do you know about Micah Rhodes?"

Her brows crease in thought. "The entertainment lawyer?"

"Yes," I confirm.

"Is everything okay?" Carlee asks as she notices my unease.

I've been wound tight ever since I left the office.

"Harper's seeing him, and I have a terrible feeling about this guy. Brody couldn't tell me if he was dangerous or not, but he doesn't trust him. I really need LadyLux's investigative skills to help me figure him out. It's not a favor I'd typically ask, but she owes me at least one."

Carlee studies me intently, knowing I stole her laptop and posted her journal entries on the internet for everyone to read about how she really felt about my brother. I'd do it again without regret—because now they're happily married.

"What else aren't you telling me?" Carlee asks.

"He looks familiar, like I've seen him somewhere before, but I can't pinpoint it," I explain. "He's also in his mid-forties, and he isn't married. *Huge* red flag."

Carlee reaches for the notepad and pen on her coffee table, scribbling something down before tearing the paper off the pad. "I'll tell LadyLux you stopped by. She may or may not be able to help."

"Thank you," I say, meeting her eyes sincerely, knowing she will never admit it's her. "I appreciate it."

I turn toward the door, seeing myself out.

"I never got to properly thank you for helping me and Weston. Even if it took a little petty theft," she says, raising her brow with a teasing smile.

"My brother needed you, Carlee, and I'd do anything for my family. That includes you," I reply, giving her a warm smile before I leave.

When I step onto the elevator, she flashes me a smile that I return just before the doors close.

Easton and Weston picked two of the best women in the world to be their partners.

I want them to feel the same about Asher. I want them to know how he makes me feel safe and even makes me a better woman. I'm not the same because of Asher. I'm better because I want to be for him.

That's the true Asher Effect.

29

ASHER

ONE WEEK LATER

Billie left before sunrise this morning. Before slipping out of bed, she gave me a sweet kiss on the cheek and told me how much she already missed me. I didn't imagine it, even though it felt unreal to be on the receiving end of her affection. My girl has always looked at me that way.

I pull fresh strawberries from the fridge for my oatmeal. As I eat, I unlock my phone, search for Billie's name online, and scroll through the headlines until one catches my eye. I shake my head, smirking.

With all the drama that has gone down in the past few weeks, LadyLux slipped off my radar. With this post, she's back on it.

Who the fuck are you?

The Ice Queen and Her Future King

I brace myself to read the article, claiming Billie is destined to be with Louis. Surprisingly, the article isn't about him at all, but rather about Billie and the shitty relationships she has had over the years, focusing on Louis and Josh Lustre. I quickly read it to the end.

I don't believe this relationship is real, but do I think Billie Calloway is in love? Yes. Absolutely.

(But also, allegedly.)

With whom? That's the question of the hour. She's so secretive, but I can tell Prince Louis isn't the king of her heart. Maybe her real Prince Charming will finally step up and claim her once she's done playing games with a royal. Until then, let me remind him what she deserves.

Billie Calloway needs a man who will claim her, who will love her for more than just being a Calloway. She needs someone strong who will protect her and, above all, who will be honest. That woman has dealt with so many snakes and liars over the years. If she can't be the center of your universe, move on. Strong women need strong men. I understand being careful, but love is all you need. It can conquer anything. Believe in that.

That's all for this week, LuxBabies. I'll see you next time as I dive headfirst into a brand-new billionaire who's caught my eye. Don't worry, Asher Banks ... I'm still watching you. There will be a part 2. Stay tuned.

LadyLux

I scoff, rolling my eyes. The nerve. I wonder if she needs help marketing her blog.

An evil smirk crosses my lips as I search her website for her contact information. I find her email address and type a message.

Subject: Well, well, well ...

You officially have my attention, Ms. LadyLux. I will find out who you are. It's just a matter of time. I look forward to part 2.

Asher Banks

I press Send and hear the notification that my email was sent. *Your move, gossip queen.*

Once I finish eating and set my empty bowl in the sink, I grab a towel to dry my hands and notice a sheet of paper folded in half with my name scribbled on the front. Leaning against the counter, I open it and scan Billie's neat handwriting.

Asher,

Go visit her. It's a new day, a new chance at something incredible. Change starts when you decide to do something different. Break out of the cycle.

I'm thinking about you.

Always,
-B

P.S. Eden would tell you to stop being an Ash-hole. You can do this. :)

Laughter escapes me because she would. Eden always believed in tough love. She was a member of the Build a Bridge and Get Over It Club.

Below her words is a pair of red lips, and I imagine her kissing the paper with her eyes closed. I rub my finger across it, wondering if she wrote *I love you* in invisible ink.

Damn, I'm in love with her. So truly, madly, deeply, and insanely in love that I can barely handle it.

I take a deep breath, knowing today is one of the few times I want to hide from the world. It's officially been five years since my sister passed away. I'll never forget how I fell to my knees when Dyson arrived at my door in the middle of the night to tell me what happened. I'll never forget the pain of knowing I'd never get to talk to my sister again. She was *stolen* from me, ripped away from my family because someone had *chosen* to drink and drive. *It was a choice.*

I will never get to hug my sister again or tell her about Billie. She'll never see me fall in love with my person. We'll never have that dance I promised her at her wedding, and I'll never get to see her become a mom. No one can understand how much I miss her. Now she only lives in my heart and mind, and as each day passes, the details grow fuzzier —her voice, her laugh, her encouraging words... all distant memories.

I squeeze my eyes shut, already feeling numb. I rub my palms on my eyes, needing to pull myself together.

I told Josh I wouldn't be at the office today, and Nick knows it's a personal day for me. Instead of staying cooped up in my house from sunrise to sunset, I decide to venture out into the world.

Maybe Billie is right.

I pick up the pen next to the paper and write a return message on the back for her to find later.

You're my everything, Ice Queen.

I leave the loft and stop by a flower shop to grab a bouquet of bright purple forget-me-nots. My driver meets me on the curb and I slip into the backseat of the car. An hour later, I arrive at Sleepy Hollow Cemetery, feeling a weight on my shoulders that's almost too heavy to carry.

When I learned this was where my sister wanted to be laid to rest, I laughed. She had always loved *The Legend of Sleepy Hollow*, and now she's forever a part of it.

Walking through the gate, the path leads me toward a meadow filled with soft grass and wildflowers. I've only visited this place in my nightmares. The cemetery is peaceful but haunting.

I slow down as I approach my sister's headstone. Her name sparkles in golden letters, just like on the side of the firm building. Sunshine blankets the area, and I notice fresh, bright yellow daffodils on her grave. I bend down and touch the soft petals, setting the purple flowers next to them. Eden loved spring and summer, along with colorful flowers. Every Monday, she had a fresh bouquet on her desk, even if she bought them herself.

Close by is a tree, and under it is a bench with one of her favorite quotes engraved on the back—*Be the change you want to see in the world.*

I sit on the bench, interlock my fingers, and close my eyes. I wander down the deep hallways of my mind, searching for the forgiveness I never gave myself. A cool breeze travels through the trees from the Hudson River and brushes against my cheeks. It grounds me in the moment, pulling me back to the present. I exhale, and it feels like Eden is surrounding me.

Since she died, I've become much softer. Her death broke me. It was the wake-up call that made me realize how precious time was and how it was slipping through my fingers.

"You were right about Billie," I whisper, squeezing my eyes shut. "She is my perfect match."

I grow more emotional as I sit in silence. Eventually, leaves rustle across the sidewalk, and I feel that familiar cool breeze brush against my skin again. When I open my eyes, the brightest blue jay I've ever seen is perched on the corner of my sister's gravestone. We stare at one another for a moment, and it feels like a sign—a confirmation. I watch it fly away and wipe the tears that flood down my cheeks.

"Thanks, sis," I say, choking up, my vision blurring.

I know exactly what I have to do. Billie deserves to know the truth before we move forward. No half-truths or lies.

Clarity sweeps over me as I turn to see my brothers, Nick and Dyson, approaching in three-piece suits, wearing serious expressions. They sit on either side of me. It's comforting to be here with my brothers, even in silence.

Every year, they've visited together, and every year, I've declined.

"I'm sorry for hurting you," Dyson finally says, and the breeze carries his voice away. He's apologizing for going after someone I thought I loved.

"Don't worry about it," I tell him, realizing I have bigger issues to solve. "In the grand scheme of things, it doesn't matter. Just don't let it happen again."

"Finally," Nick says. "Now, can we go eat tacos? That's what Eden would have wanted."

I burst into laughter.

Nick sets his flowers next to mine and then talks to the grass.

"Right, Eden?" Nick asks, putting his ear close to the ground. He raises his voice. *"Right. Listen to my favorite brother, even if he's only half."*

She used to tease him about being my father's love child, but I think she liked him better than us. Since he lived with his mom, Nick didn't have the chance to annoy us as much as we annoyed each other.

"Taco time," Nick says, blowing a kiss toward Eden's grave. "Love you, sister."

As we walk toward the car, I know I have to tell Billie about Project Glass Slipper.

No more fucking secrets.

30

BILLIE

I tuck the box under my arm and unlock Asher's loft with the key he gave me. Our schedules are hectic, and we're constantly working weekends with no time off, but we're making the best of it.

When I walk in, I close the door and lock it behind me. After I drop this gift, I must return to Bellamore for a fitting.

"Ash?" I say loud enough for him to hear if he's inside.

I almost expect him to walk out of his bedroom, wearing that sexy grin he reserves just for me. I wait a few seconds, but it's complete silence. I hope he went and visited his sister's grave today. Harper mentioned in passing he'd never gone once. She also reminded me of the anniversary.

I set the box down on the counter, smiling at the big white ribbon placed on top.

He's going to love it.

Giggling, I wiggle out of my panties and take them off, hooking the red silk lace on my finger as I walk into his bedroom. This is one reason I love wearing skirts—easy access.

His bed is made, and sunlight shines through the sheer curtains. I place them on his pillow and smile, knowing today, he'll arrive home first. I imagine him walking through the door, removing his jacket, tie, and shirt, then stopping when he sees my lingerie on his pillow. A precursor to what will happen later. When I turn, I notice a leather folio sitting on his nightstand.

The edges are worn, and I vaguely remember him always carrying something like this at Stanford. I sit on the edge of the mattress, staring at it like it's a deadly cobra that will strike.

"This is ridiculous," I tell myself as I reach forward and flip it open.

My eyes dart toward the glass slipper icon and the words *Project Glass Slipper*.

Curiosity gets the best of me, and I turn the page, seeing Asher's neat handwriting that could be its own font.

> **Project Glass Slipper**
> **Never let her break.**
>
> **Phase 1**
> **Protect: shield her from harmful external threats.**
>
> **Phase 2**
> **Grow: empower her reputation and creativity.**
>
> **Phase 3**
> **Soar: no longer surviving but leading.**
>
> **Billie Calloway isn't the future. She's a revolution.**

My fingers fly through the pages. Asher wrote details dating back thirteen years, when we met at Stanford. Some of it's written in code, and I'm not sure what it means. Every conversation we've had, each time we've run into each other—it's all here, noted in journal entries.

I blink rapidly as disbelief travels through me like ice water in my veins. Asher's handwriting is immaculate, calculated. My fingers tremble as they trace over timelines. For thirteen years, he has meticulously documented every milestone in my life. Even my social media updates were dissected down to their subtext, which he got right.

This man knows me better than I know myself, and that scares the fuck out of me. Based on this, I'm convinced Asher can predict my every move, reply, and emotion before it even happens.

A bitter laugh escapes me, sharp and hollow, as I read how my brothers approached him to watch over me. The reason I went to Stanford was to escape them and their prying eyes. I was so naïve.

When I realize this project is just another one of Weston's obsessive strategies and Easton's relentless drive for control over me, I snap. Anger floods out of me, knowing my brothers have orchestrated every aspect of my existence, down to who I fell in love with.

I'm stunned, unable to read another word as tears sting my eyes.

Was I nothing more than a project? A to-do list with phases and bullet points?

I slam the folio shut, my jaw clenching tight. I tuck it under my arm and text my driver. I'm sick and tired of Weston and Easton interfering in my life. My rage takes over as I rush to Calloway headquarters. I'm let out in front of the building, and paparazzi wait for me and snap pictures as I step inside.

I give them *go to hell* looks, officially feeling like I'm watching my villain origin story play out.

Weston likes to think that he's Batman. Yeah, well, today, I'm the Joker, and I will be both of their worst fucking nightmares. I press my thumbprint against the keypad, and the elevator shoots me to their floor. My heart rapidly beats in my chest, and I try to suck in deep breaths, but it's no use.

"Ms. Calloway," their secretary says.

I walk past her, ignoring her every step with my hands squeezed tightly into fists.

"You can't go in there!"

"Fuck off," I tell her, moving into Easton's office.

He glares at me, livid, and then Weston turns to me. Beside him are familiar broad shoulders and messy hair.

Everything feels like it moves into half speed when Asher turns around, and his golden-brown eyes meet mine. Confusion and betrayal settle in my expression, and I'm hurt.

My jaw clenches tight as I look at the three of them. Asher sees the folio in my hand and tenses. My brothers see the rage swirling in my eyes. I'm ready to explode, a ticking time bomb full of rage.

"I told you not to interfere in my life. You refused to respect my wishes," I say, my voice steady.

I am the calm before the storm, the one where I decimate them entirely off the planet.

"Billie, what is your fucking problem?" Easton spits out just as Stormy enters behind me.

My nostrils flare, and I realize no matter how many times I've asked them to leave me alone and not meddle in my business, my brothers have never listened. They've always done whatever they want, playing by their own game.

"You've continued forward with controlling me and my business, whether I was on board or not," I say, whispering. "For the last fucking time, I don't want any of your help."

"Billie," Asher says behind me as angry tears stream down my face.

"Don't talk to me," I bark out, needing to escape the suffocating room.

I step onto the elevator, and he chases me inside. The doors slide closed, and when I look into his eyes, the elevator feels like it's free falling.

I need air. I need to breathe. I need to calm down.

"I can explain everything," he says, slapping his hand against the

Emergency Stop button. We're suspended by nothing more than wires and time. "You're in your head."

"I don't want to hear another one of your fucking lies," I say, acting cold, like the ice queen he believes I am.

He takes a step forward and smirks, like he's enjoying it.

"The very last thing you should be doing right now is looking at me like that. This isn't a joke."

He gives me a cocky grin, amused. It makes me angrier.

"On a scale from one to ten, how fucking enraged are you, Ice Queen?"

"One billion."

"Ah, luckily, I can work with billions," he says, cupping my cheeks in his hands and sliding his warm mouth against mine.

I instantly relax and melt into him; my body has always been a traitor when it comes to him. It still is.

He's a traitor.

I push away from him. "You can't just kiss me like that. You tricked me into falling in love with you."

He bursts into laughter. "Yeah, right. Give yourself more credit than that. Falling in love with me wasn't a trick, princess. It was a full-ass treat."

"You're enjoying this too much," I say between gritted teeth.

"Ah, you know I love seeing you at your limit. It's my kink. Your heart rate climbs, and your breasts rise and fall with each ragged breath. That, combined with the swirling disdain in your eyes that drown me each time I look into them, is almost too much. And that mouth. Mmm. Fuck, that smart-ass mouth of yours. You know, the other day, I was wondering if the ruthless Ice Queen still existed. Thanks for confirming she does. You'll need to let this version of you appear when we're in London." He shrugs, unbothered by me and my eternal anger.

"I am not seeing you in London."

"How many shit sandwiches do you want to eat? I'll see you in

London because you can't fucking resist me, Billie. The heart wants what it wants," he says, way too confidently.

"Yeah?" I step away from him, creating much-needed space. "And what does your heart want, Asher? More under-the-table favors from my brothers?"

His face softens. "You. Just you. *Always you.*"

"Because I'm your glass slipper."

"No." He shakes his head. "Because you're the only one it fits."

I reach over and press the button. The elevator jolts and continues its descent to the ground floor.

"I know you're upset with me, and you have every fucking right to be. But please give me a chance to explain. Afterward, if you never want to speak to me again, I'll make sure your wish comes true."

I meet his eyes, seeing the resolve behind his gaze.

"You'd pretend I didn't exist?" I ask.

"If that's what you want."

I hold up the folio. "Truly riveting information."

"Give it to me," he says, holding out his hand.

"Not a fucking chance. This is now mine. Hope you have your plan memorized," I sneer.

The elevator doors slide open, and as I move to walk away, he gently grabs my elbow, pulling me back to him. The smell of his cologne and the lingering taste of his lips on mine nearly do me in.

"I promise I had your best interest in mind," he whispers in my ear.

I don't know if I want to kiss or smack him. "Fuck off, Banks."

He laughs, and I hate that I love the sound of it. "Great. Am I still seeing you tonight at around eight for dinner?"

I glare at him, feeling hurt and pissed, and then walk away. As I glance over my shoulder to see if he's following me, I see the elevator doors slide closed. Asher is returning to my brothers, to the puppet masters of it all.

As I step out into blinding sunlight, paparazzi swarm me, like vultures circling fresh prey. Their cameras flash relentlessly, capturing every fractured emotion etched across my face—anger, heartbreak, determination. Everything I am has always been laid out for the public to scrutinize. Why would now be any different?

I slide into the car that's waiting for me and zoom toward Bellamore.

Right now, I don't know who to trust. Considering how my heart flutters when Asher's near, I can't even trust myself.

31

ASHER

Seeing Billie so upset with me has left a hole in my fucking heart. Over the years, we've been at each other's throat, tearing out the other's jugular, and had public blowups that were just short of gouging out one another's eyes.

But this is different. This time, it's so damn personal that it hurts deep inside.

Not telling her about Project Glass Slipper sooner might be one of my biggest mistakes. I understand what it's like to have trust issues and be betrayed.

I think back to where the folio was kept. I must've forgotten to put it away, which was careless, but so is keeping secrets from the person you love.

My anger steadily boils on the elevator ride to the top floor, and I'm upset with myself. I step into Easton's office and close the door more forcefully than intended.

"Did you know she would be here? Was this a setup?" I glare at them incredulously.

"No," Weston mutters. "We're masterminds, but that shit wasn't planned."

"What did you want to speak to me about?" I ask, checking my watch, needing to leave immediately.

Nick is still in the car, waiting for me. I've already been here for nearly ten minutes.

"Are you fucking my sister?" Easton bluntly asks, crossing his arms over his chest.

"That's none of your goddamn business," I tell him.

"Billie will always be my business, no matter what. If you hurt her …" he sneers and turns to Weston. "I thought you said they weren't together."

They stare at one another, and I can tell Easton isn't happy.

Weston tucks his hands into his pockets. "I haven't confirmed becau—" Easton opens his mouth to say something, but Weston continues speaking. "Let me finish. It wasn't my place to ask our adult sister if she was hooking up with our *friend*." How he stressed the word *friend* isn't lost on me. "I trust Asher will make the right decisions. I believe he cares deeply about Billie and won't hurt her."

"It will—"

"*Fuck, Easton*! Leave it alone, or I'll lose it. I don't have any patience left today after everything we've gone through this morning. Okay? Fucking drop it."

Stormy doesn't say anything. The office is so quiet that I could hear a pin drop.

I shake my head. "Please tell me you didn't call for an emergency meeting to ask me that, because if—"

"Actually, no," Weston says, waving his hand. He's calm, but he's also tense. "Can we all sit?"

My brows rise. "Actually, no. What do you want? I have a fucking mess to deal with and need to go."

Stormy opens her mouth, and I hold up my hand.

"Shut the fuck up. I don't even know why you're here. You're shady, and I don't like your tactics. I look forward to the day when I replace you."

She bursts into laughter. "I'm irreplaceable, babe. But, wow, still that cocky asshole, I see."

"You told Billie to stay away from me. You told her to forget I existed," I say.

She smirks. "Of course I did."

I stare at her, nostrils flaring.

"But I knew she'd never listen. She's too rebellious. A complete wild card. She enjoys going against the grain and doing what she shouldn't. It's why the two of you get along so damn well, isn't it?" She licks her lips. "Her career is now in your hands, Banks. Don't fuck it up. That woman chose you over her entire career."

I smirk. "Every person in this damn room, including me, already knows that. Anything else, or is more of my fucking time going to be wasted today?"

"Are you in love with her?" Easton asks.

He's never been the type to make subtle hints. It's something I appreciate about him.

"Yes," I say without any hesitation, meeting his eyes. "And she's in love with me. So, either you can both accept that or disrespectfully fuck off. I won't lose her."

I move to the door.

"What are you waiting for?" Easton asks.

I turn to him, and my brows crease. "Excuse me?"

"If you're in love with her, what the fuck are you waiting for? Someone else to swoop in and marry her?" His voice is stern.

I cross my arms over my chest. "I don't know if you've noticed, but your sister is currently fake dating Prince Louis while trying to pull off a fucking magic trick for the London fashion show in less time than what's needed. She's under a lot of stress and pressure from the public attention, and she can't handle anything else right now." I stare at each of them. "So, let me do my fucking job and stay out of my way."

"Are you aware that Josh is telling *everyone* that he's getting back with Billie?" Weston questions.

Stormy rolls her eyes as she picks at her nails. Everyone knows Josh is a trash human.

"Have you told her *I love you* yet?" Easton asks. "Has she said it back to you?"

"That's none of your fucking business. Don't ask me anything else about her. I won't tell you, Calloway."

Easton moves forward, stepping into my face, and Weston crosses his arms over his chest. "If you hurt my sister, I will ruin your life."

"I hope you fucking do." I smirk, wishing he would test me right now. I stare into his eyes, not intimidated, not backing down.

Weston pulls Easton away from me, and I move toward the door.

"Wait. The reason we called you here was to discuss LuxLeaks."

My eyes darken. "I will find her."

"You won't," Weston says. "I can guarantee that."

"I have people, Weston. Hackers. Men who laugh at the dark web. If I wanted to find LadyLux, I absolutely would," I say, my voice lowering to a near growl. It's not a threat, but a promise. "Unless you'd like to admit that she works for you."

"No." Weston shakes his head with a laugh. "Hilarious. LadyLux works for no one, which you can see by how she's chewed me up and spit me out over the last decade."

"She continues to," Easton says, and I think I see him almost smirk.

Weston's jaw clenches tight as he pins me in place. "Believe me when I say, you do not want to mess with her, Asher. What is wrong with you?"

"Ahh, did she call her watchdogs to take care of the *issue*? Is that how she gets into all the private parties and has insider information no one would have unless they were there? LadyLux may be doing her research on me, but trust me, I will do my research on her." I glare at him. "She should've left my name off her site. Mmm. Guess she fucked around and found out."

"Fine. Good luck," Weston says, his smile fading to a straight line. "You'll need it."

"Anything else?"

"You don't need to start a war with LuxLeaks while fighting battles with my sister and Josh Lustre. You have more than enough on your plate right now." Weston pats me on my back, squeezing my shoulder as he leads me to the door.

I reach for the doorknob. "I do what I want."

"That will be your downfall," he tells me as I leave the office with my heart in my throat.

I step into the elevator, almost wishing I'd have stayed cooped up inside today. So far, it's turning out to be an awful experience.

Paparazzi snap photos of me leaving Calloway headquarters, and I slide into the back of the waiting car.

Nick stares at me. "What the fuck happened? I saw Billie leave, and she was *furious*. Did they tell you to stay away from her?"

My face cracks into a smile. "Actually, no. Guess this clusterfuck does have a silver lining."

I ENTER MY LOFT, AND THE WEIGHT OF EVERYTHING THAT'S HAPPENED today settles heavy on my shoulders. My mind races with thoughts of Billie—her fighting spirit, her fiery temper that I both love and fear. I want to call her, apologize, and explain everything, but I know better. She needs space to cool off, and I need to own up to the mess I've made of things.

This is the consequence of my actions of saying hello. But I'm not giving up after how she kissed me back on the elevator.

As I move into the living room, something catches my eye, and I stop. A white box, tied with a ribbon, sits innocently on the counter. My heart skips a beat because Billie left this for me. I move closer, knowing this is how she found the folio. I slide the lid off, and inside is a letter, already torn open.

Billie's name stares back at me in my sister's familiar handwriting. A chill travels down my spine.

I can't read it now. My throat tightens, an unwelcome lump forming. Not yet. I'm already too emotionally drained. I set the letter to the side and dig deeper into the box, my fingers brushing against something rectangular. I pull it out, carefully unwrapping the tissue paper as curiosity tugs at me.

When I see a small painting of my sister smiling brightly, surrounded by flowers, my eyes water. I try to blink away my tears, but I fail. The colors explode on the canvas.

Below the painting, an inscription reads, *Don't be an Ash-hole.*

A smirk tugs at my lips despite the storm brewing inside me. I move to my bedroom and stop in the doorway when I see red lace panties on my pillow.

I've let Billie down, and there's no denying it. But as much as regret gnaws at me, I wouldn't change my choices regarding her. I hope she shows up at eight p.m., like we planned before. Either way, I try to prepare myself for whatever comes next.

She chose me once. Will she do it twice?

I PACE THE LENGTH OF MY LOFT WITH MY HANDS SHOVED DEEP INTO my pockets. It's well after eight, and I know Billie's home. I watched her enter the building from my window. Every step feels heavier; each second stretches into eternity. She's not coming over. Can I blame her?

Billie saw everything, the entire truth. Project Glass Slipper was a secret I'd carried for thirteen years, and it was exposed in the harshest light possible. She deserves answers, an honest, unfiltered explanation. I owe her that.

My phone buzzes, pulling me away from my racing thoughts.

NICK
Well?

ASHER
She didn't show.

On the way to my loft, I gave him the abridged version of what had happened.

NICK
I'm sorry. I'm sure she needs time to process it.

I glance at the chicken Alfredo and breadsticks I made for tonight, no longer feeling hungry. I toss the phone aside, trying to calculate my next move. I miss her.

My eyes glance at the painting she gifted me of my sister, and I scan over the words at the bottom.

I leave my loft and stand in front of Billie's door. Intimidation isn't something I typically experience, but right now, I feel it in the pit of my stomach. My palms grow sweaty, and I wipe them on my pants. My nerves take hold as I knock softly, using our secret knock.

A minute passes, and her not answering is an answer. As I turn to walk away, the door slides open. She's standing in sweatpants and an oversized hoodie with red eyes. She's been crying, and it hurts me, knowing I'm the cause of that.

"Princess," I whisper.

"Don't *princess* me," she says.

"Whatever you say, Ice Queen." I give her a small smile, but she doesn't return it. I lower my voice. "Billie, please."

"You have five minutes," she replies, stepping to the side to let me inside.

I enter, knowing we can't be seen talking to one another, just in case Mrs. Chambers catches us. Neither of us trusts her.

I face her. "I was wrong. Completely. No justifications, no excuses. I know I broke your trust, and I will spend the rest of my life proving that I've always had your very best interest in mind."

She shakes her head. "You don't get it. Neither do my brothers. I want to make my own mistakes. I don't need to be guided or *manipulated* to do things. You had every opportunity to tell me when we were in the Hamptons. You chose to say nothing, but you still took notes and wrote journal entries about our time together. I'm your passion project."

"Oh, you are much more than that to me," I say. "You're my person. And I'm sorry for hurting you. I'm so fucking sorry for not telling you how much you fucking meant to me all those years ago. However, I am not sorry for what I did for you. I am not sorry for making sure you were safe. I am not sorry for cleaning up bullshit articles about you online that should've never been posted. I'm not sorry that I protected you. I'm also not sorry for loving you. You. Just you. For exactly how you are."

She tucks her lips into her mouth, tears streaming down her face. "Did my brothers force you to be my friend in the Hamptons? And to kiss me that summer?"

"No," I whisper, tilting my head. "There was nothing fake about our relationship. Ever. We met at a charity golf tournament, and they learned I was heading to Stanford. They asked me to look after you. I promised I'd make sure you were safe, and they promised me guaranteed support. They didn't know we'd met as kids. No one ever knew other than Eden and you. No one tells your brothers no, especially not an eighteen-year-old kid."

She walks past me, moving into her kitchen. She grabs a bottle of water and drinks. "You continued this after college."

"You're my favorite hobby, babe. Everything I wrote, every thought I documented, every moment I tracked—it was because I cared. It's how I connected with you, knowing I'd never have you.

The more you hated me, the more I helped you, and I needed the reminder. Macro, not micro."

"Turning pain into pleasure," she whispers.

I nod. "I also continued to help you because of Eden. You were at the top of her list that she was working on behind the scenes."

"Then why did you work with Josh?" she asks.

"Because you'd never work *with* me," I explain.

"You know me too well and used it to your advantage, knowing I'd work against you."

Billie shakes her head, staring at me, and the awkward silence draws on.

"What happens after phase three? You move on and find another *project* to complete?"

"Absolutely not," I say, understanding she's hurt and upset. "You can't begin to understand how much you mean to me, how much you've always meant to me. I would burn the world to ash for you without apology—because the glass slipper only fits one princess. And that's you. It's always been you. It will always be you, Billie. I'm so sorry for hurting you. I hope, one day, you'll forgive me."

She stands there like a fucking goddess in a baggy hoodie that hangs off one shoulder, exposing the smooth curve of her collarbone, and a pair of sweatpants that clings to her hips like they're begging to be ripped off. Her hair's a wild mess, her lips—damn, her pouty lips—are slightly parted, like she's contemplating telling me to fuck off.

"Hmm," she says ruthlessly, but I see a mischievous sparkle in her eye. "I think you should beg. On your knees."

32

BILLIE

Asher strides forward like a Greek god in a dress shirt that clings to him in all the right places.

He closes the distance between us and drops to his knees before me. I look down into his golden-brown eyes, taking in the shimmering flecks at this angle. When our gazes lock, my body temperature increases.

"Is this what you want, princess? Me on my knees, begging for you, just like this?" His voice is a deep rumble in the back of his throat.

The raw need in his eyes is almost enough to make me forgive him.

The air is thick with tension, unspoken words, and emotions that I haven't fully processed yet. Time is what I need. But I also need Asher Banks.

His fingers trail up my thighs, making my skin prickle and making my breath hitch. We hold a silent conversation, but it's so fucking loud.

"Pretty, pretty please forgive me," he pleads, and it nearly undoes me. His face is a mess of regret and hunger, and I can see the way his cock is already straining against his pants, begging to be let out and put to work. "Please," he rasps, his voice rough. "Let me make it up to you, princess."

"Seems like you have thirteen years' worth of making up to do," I say.

His strong hands push up the soft fabric of my hoodie, and he leans forward, placing his warm lips on my stomach. I shiver, unable to stop him, wanting him to worship me as he grovels.

"I'll do anything," he whispers, his breath hot against my skin. "Anything you want."

I tilt my head, pretending to consider it, but really, I'm just savoring his desperate touch.

"Continue," I say, fully aware that I'm no longer playing defense with him. If this were still a game, it'd be one I was winning.

"Fuck," Asher groans low in his throat, holding me like I might disappear. "You're a dream."

My nipples are hard—because of him, because of this fucking tension, because I can feel his eyes on me, like he's already undressing me with his mind.

"Please," he mutters against my pussy, kneeling in front of me.

His hands move to my thighs, gripping me like I'm his anchor, his lifeline, his fucking salvation. And I *want* to be. His head is bowed, but I can see the tension in his jaw. The button-up shirt is rolled to his elbows, showing off those forearms that make me want to scream.

I drink in every inch of him, still upset that he didn't tell me, but I understand why. Asher never got the real me, not until recently. My life has been a whirlwind since the moment he kissed me at Weston's, and we've barely had time to slow down.

"I fucked up," he grovels, his voice a sexy rasp. "I know I fucked up. But you know you're mine, don't you?"

His hands slowly slide up my thighs like he's memorizing every inch of me, like this may be his last chance to ever touch me again. His fingers brush against my bare skin, sending shivers down my spine. The other hand grips my hip, his fingers digging in just enough to make me gasp. His breath is warm against my stomach, and I can feel his lips hovering over my skin—so close, but not close enough.

"Do you hear me?" he demands, his voice like a fucking command. "I'll make it right. I'm going to make you feel so fucking good that you'll forget you *ever* hated me."

His mouth finds my skin then, hot and wet and hungry. He kisses my stomach, his tongue darting out to taste me, and I swear I can feel it down to my clit. His hands are everywhere—my hips, my ass, my thighs—touching me like he's branding me as his.

"Please," he whispers, his voice broken. "Let me worship you the way you deserve, Ice Queen."

I chew on the corner of my lip, my heart fluttering. He looks at me like I'm the only thing that matters in the world. He's always looked at me that way.

He slides the waistband of my sweatpants down just enough to expose the curve of my ass, and his fingers slip under the fabric, teasing the edge of my panties. Asher's strong hands claim every inch of me as he pushes my joggers down. Those beautiful lips brush against the inside of my thigh, and I can feel his hot breath close to my pussy. He's teasing me, torturing me, and I can't help but whimper. My hands fist in his hair, tugging hard enough to make him groan, but he doesn't stop. If anything, he grows more desperate and more determined, as if that were even possible.

"You're so fucking perfect," he growls against my skin. "Every inch of you. And I'm going to spend the rest of my life proving that to you," he promises.

His fingers hook into my panties, pulling them down at a snail's pace, and it feels like actual torture.

His mouth is back on me, hot and wet and so fucking sinful that I can barely breathe. His tongue is relentless, licking and sucking and devouring me like I'm his last meal. He slides his tongue in deeper, lapping me up like he's completely addicted to the flavor of me.

Asher doesn't take his eyes off me as he devours me.

"Fuck," I finally moan, my hips rocking against his mouth, desperate for more.

"Mmm. I knew I'd get you to break your silence eventually," he growls against me, the vibration sending shocks of pleasure coursing through my body.

His tongue circles my clit before he takes me into his hot mouth. My eyes bolt shut, and I swear I see stars exploding behind my eyelids.

One of his fingers slides inside me, curling just right, and I'm fucking gone. My legs shake, my knees go weak, but he holds me steady with his strong arms as I surrender to his fingers and tongue.

"That's it," he growls, pulling back just enough to speak, his breath warm against my skin. "Come for me, princess. Let me hear you."

"No. I'm still mad at you," I whimper, feeling the build as my muscles tense.

His fingers are inside me, and I'm trying not to scream, but, fuck, it's hard when he's moving them like that—curled just right, brushing against that spot that makes my legs shake with anticipation. He's wearing that cocky-as-fuck smirk I've grown to adore, the one that says he knows exactly what he's doing to me. His other hand is on my thigh, steadying me.

"Oh, you're not gonna come yet, like a brat?" he whispers, his voice low.

His fingers move at a tortuous pace, and I whimper, squirming under him, but he doesn't fucking care. He's in control; he always has been, and he knows it.

"I haven't decided yet." I gasp, my voice cracking with need. I sound pathetic, but I don't care. I need him to keep going, to fuck me with his big fingers until I can't think straight.

"Mmm. I can do this all goddamn night, but I think I've just decided that you'll come when *I* say," he tells me, and his lips transform into that smirk again. "Just say please."

The way he moves his fingers—like he's trying to drive me wild—makes it impossible for me to think. His thumb circles my clit, and I arch my back, my nails digging into his shoulders.

"Fuck you," I hiss, but it comes out more like a moan than anything else.

"No, baby," he says, his voice dripping with the perfect amount of arrogance that I both hate and love. "Fuck you."

And then he pulls his fingers out, and I almost scream in frustration. Before I can say anything, he stands, lifting me in his arms and carrying me to the bedroom. Asher sets me on the bed, continuing to worship every inch of me as he fully undresses me.

He takes a step back, his gaze full of want and need. "Do you forgive me yet?"

"No," I say, watching him unbutton his shirt, seeing the fabric fall to the floor.

Muscles cascade down his stomach, and I try to memorize every inch of him as he strips away the last of his clothes. Then he moves to the bed, hovering above me, his body radiating heat.

His cock waits outside my entrance as we stare into one another's eyes. "I'm so fucking sorry."

"I know. I don't want to lose you," I confess, my heart racing. "You're one of my only constants."

Asher softly kisses me, his thumb brushing against my cheek. The mood grows serious, emotional, and too intense. This isn't just a kiss; it's war—with each other, with ourselves—and right now, we're fully surrendering. His tongue invades my mouth, hot and slick, twisting with mine. I can feel the heat of him pressing against me, his cock hard between my thighs, teasing the slickness he created. Asher hasn't entered me yet, but, fuck, he's so close.

Then he's inside me, stretching me open, filling me up in a way that makes my head spin. He's so damn gentle that it doesn't feel like two people fucking out their frustrations. I can feel every inch of him as he thrusts into me, deep and deliberate, like he's trying to erase every mistake he made.

He breaks the kiss, meeting my gaze with soft, hooded eyes, full of so much admiration that it nearly takes my breath away—"I love you. I always have."

My emotions tear through me, and it feels so overwhelming. "I love you too."

Our mouths crash together, and he kisses me as if he's trying to make me forget my name. Damn, the way his tongue slides against mine—deliberate and filthy—is like he's mapping every inch of my mouth. I can taste my arousal on his lips, and it makes my head spin. His groan vibrates against my lips, deep and guttural, and I swear I can feel it in my fucking soul.

"You're my religion," he mutters.

His mouth trails down my neck, biting and sucking at my skin like he's trying to leave a mark on me. I tilt my head back, moaning as his hands roam my body while his cock moves in and out of me.

"Fuck," I moan, my fingers clutching the sheets like they're the only thing keeping me on earth.

Each thrust hits that spot that makes me see stars, and I can feel myself getting closer and closer to the edge as he fills me completely. But he's not letting me fall yet. He slows down again, teasing me, driving me fucking insane with the way he moves inside me.

"Please," I beg, my voice shaking, and he laughs again, but it's softer this time, almost tender.

"Not yet," he says, and then he pulls out completely, leaving me empty and aching.

I turn to glare at him, but before I can say anything, he's sliding down me and spreading my legs wide. His mouth is back on my clit before I can even think, his tongue circling my sensitive bud, pushing me closer to the edge.

"Ash," I moan, my fingers tangling in his hair as he licks and sucks, insistently driving me closer.

"Are you ready to come for me yet? Or do you want to keep playing games?" he asks, his voice muffled against me, and that's all it takes.

I'm coming hard, my body shaking as wave after wave of pleasure crashes over me. He keeps going, his tongue relentless, until I come again. Seconds later, he's repositioned above me, his thick cock at my entrance. His eyes are dark with the kind of hunger that makes my stomach flip as he slams into me. He's hard and perfect.

I scream out his name, my pussy clenching around him so damn tight as my body continues to tremble.

This is ecstasy.

Asher is my drug, and I'm so damn addicted.

"You're my everything," he whispers into my ear as if he can read my thoughts, then presses his mouth against mine.

I lose myself in the kiss, wrapping my legs around him, allowing him to fill me as full as possible. We're in perfect sync, like we're anticipating each other's moves. The way he kisses me is passionate and raw, but also full of love—electricity courses through my veins as he softly moans in my ear.

"Do you hear that?" I whisper. "That's you surrendering to me."

"Always." His breathing increases, and his movements become more intentional.

The way he kisses me is passionate and raw, a fucking claim, but also full of something deeper as he thrusts inside me. I rake my nails down his back, and he groans.

"So close," he whispers, leading me to the edge, and as if someone snapped their fingers, we're falling together.

I cry out in pleasure as my pussy squeezes Asher's throbbing cock, continuing to milk him. We're breathless, sweaty, and tangled in each other's arms. I feel the undeniable shift between us. When our lips meet in a slow, lingering kiss, I know he feels it too. It's almost like a silent vow, a promise that he will always be there for me, always protect me.

After we clean up, Asher pulls me into his arms like he's afraid I'll vanish if he lets go. He kisses my forehead and holds me tight, inhaling the scent of my hair. Our legs are tangled together, and I never want this moment to end.

"We still have a lot to talk about," I say, feeling his fingers drawing circles on my skin.

"I'll tell you everything," he promises, his gaze steady as I get lost in his eyes. "No more secrets. No more lies. No more half-truths."

I lean in, sliding my lips gently across his. "You were never the villain."

He smirks, a playful glint in his eyes. "And you were never the damsel, Ice Queen."

A soft smile touches my lips.

"You have to break it off with Louis tomorrow," he tells me.

"Why?" I ask.

"Because you're mine, princess, and I don't share."

33

ASHER

"Shit," I hear Billie whisper beside me as she hops out of bed. I roll over, sunlight streaming in, and see her typing away on her phone.

"What's up?" I ask as she rushes around naked. I can't help but admire her.

"I overslept! I've got a meeting in five minutes about the fashion show, and we need to finalize our seasonal designs," she says. "Oh, and check this out."

Billie hands me her phone and heads to her closet to get ready for work.

I glance at the article headline from LuxLeaks—"Who Is the Other Woman?"

There are a few blurry pics of Louis with someone. It's clear it *wasn't* Billie he was kissing. The long, light-brown hair gives it away.

"When I said it needed to end, I didn't mean like this," I say loud enough for her to hear.

"This wasn't planned," she replies, and I hear clothes rustling.

I sit up and quickly read the article. "Who the fuck is this?"

"No idea. He won't tell me who he's seeing. I've asked several times."

"Not Louis's secret girlfriend. LadyLux."

I continue reading.

Not to say I told you so, but I knew His Royal Highness wasn't Billie Calloway's king.

Billie doesn't respond, but eventually, she steps out, wearing high heels, a short black skirt that shows off her long legs, and a black sheer shirt with a long split between her breasts. She leans against the doorway to her closet, looking like a snack.

"Wow," I say, blinking up at her. "Bringing back the black?"

"Until the fashion show," she says. "Everyone expected a royal wedding, so I wore a white pantsuit to play the game. With this scandal, it's back to black until Fashion Week. I'm in mourning for Josh Lustre's career."

My girl is a fucking firecracker.

"I'm going to find out who LadyLux is and stop her," I admit.

Billie tenses. "Don't."

I try to read her like a book as I slide on the slacks I wore yesterday. "You know who's behind it. Weston and Easton do as well. Yesterday, they called me into their office to threaten me to leave LadyLux alone."

She stares at me. "You weren't there to discuss me?"

I smirk. "Don't flatter yourself, princess. You weren't the topic of conversation until you bolted into the office, ready to burn the place down."

She playfully swats at me. "I needed to curse out my brothers for meddling. You being there and seeing Stormy set me off. It felt like a betrayal."

"I'm sorry. They wanted to meet with me because I emailed LuxLeaks and told her I'd find out who she was. And I will," I say as she nearly freezes in place. "If it's you..."

Billie shakes her head, moving toward me. "It's hilarious you believe I have time to run a billion-dollar fashion corporation and talk shit about my brothers and friends. Also, if it were me, I'd have written plenty of scathing articles about you over the years to destroy everything you were *without* apology."

A chuckle escapes me. "That's a good point. Almost forgot you throw every punch you can."

"Don't forget who my brothers are. I have to be this way to protect myself." Seriousness covers her expression. "I'm asking you to trust me and leave this alone. If LadyLux wants to reveal herself to you, she will. Just be patient."

Billie moves into her bathroom as she slides diamond earrings into her ears.

"You make her sound like the tooth fairy," I say, following her. "Is it Weston or Easton?"

"No." She gives me a dirty look in the mirror. "Please don't ask me anything else. I won't tell you. I can't."

I slide my arm around her waist. "Then I'll discover who it is and decide if it's worth exposing her afterward. I'm so fucking intrigued now."

"Don't piss me off, please."

I shoot her a wink, kissing softly on her neck. "At least you used your manners. Just tell LadyLux if she mentions me again, she will be my priority once I take down Lustre," I say.

"LadyLux doesn't listen to anyone. Not me. Not Easton. Not Weston. If I threaten her, she will make you the focus, and trust me when I say, you do not want to do that." Billie turns to me, tracing her fingers across the tattoos on my chest. "And if I remember correctly, you're supposed to be groveling still. So, you kind of have to do whatever makes me happy until the end of time."

I burst into laughter, running my fingers through her hair, admiring how pretty she always is. "You play so fucking dirty," I say, and she gently brushes her lips across mine.

"You have no idea." She outlines the bird on my chest. "Why this tattoo?"

I gently grab her wrist, holding her hand against my heart. "It's a phoenix. It represents resilience, strength, and rising from the pits of hell. I felt like I was dying when Eden passed away. I turned the pain into this. One day, I will have it colored in," I admit. "When I finish my sister's wish list."

She smiles. "That's so special. Did you read the letter Eden wrote me?"

"No. I couldn't. I will soon." I place my hand on her elbow, stealing a kiss.

"No rush," she tells me.

"I already miss you," I say.

She exhales. "We never have enough time together."

"We eventually will. Have the best day, princess."

Her face softens. "It usually is when I wake up next to you."

"Same. Thanks for giving me another chance," I tell her.

Billie interlocks her fingers with mine. "Please don't make me regret it."

"I won't," I promise as she walks away. "If I want LadyLux to help with a takedown, how do I get in touch with her directly?"

Billie turns to me. "Regarding?"

"Insider trading, stock manipulation, digital espionage, design theft, contract fraud, money laundering, and sexual harassment claims regarding Lustre Fashion."

Her mouth falls open. "You have proof?"

"I have the receipts. I need a trusted source to drop the story. She's trusted if your entire family is protecting her."

Billie shakes her head. "And what's in it for her?"

"I'd personally protect her brand for the rest of my life."

We hold a silent conversation, and she swallows hard. "I'll speak with her."

I close the distance between us, kissing her deeply, threading my fingers through her hair. Our tongues twist together, and she sinks into me.

Billie pulls away breathlessly. "What was that for?"

"I'm so fucking in love with you," I mutter.

Our lips crash together again. We have to force ourselves away from one another. Her hair is a mess, and her lips are swollen. My cock is rock hard.

"I think you're the one who's bad for business," she says, adjusting her clothes as I slide on my shirt.

"Oh, I absolutely am, but I'm so damn good for you too."

"The *only* one for me."

"The only one who can handle you."

She scoffs as she walks toward her door with a sassy smile. "*Barely.*"

I GO TO MY LOFT AND SHOWER. IT'S A BIT PAST SIX, AND I DON'T HAVE to arrive at Lustre's headquarters until eight, so I have plenty of time. Once I'm dressed, I quickly make a cup of coffee and a bowl of oatmeal, then grab the letter Billie gave me the day before.

I pick it up and smooth my fingers across my sister's handwriting. My heart lurches forward when I see she drew hearts over the *i*'s in Billie's name. Carefully, I unfold the letter.

> BILLIE,
> I WANT TO OFFER A HUGE CONGRATULATIONS ON WHAT YOU AND HARPER HAVE ACCOMPLISHED WITH BELLAMORE IN SUCH A SHORT TIME. YOU SHOULD BE VERY PROUD, CONSIDERING HOW COMPETITIVE THE MARKET IS. BECAUSE I KNOW YOU AND HOW INDEPENDENT YOU ARE, I DON'T IMAGINE YOU'D EVER ACCEPT ANYONE'S HELP REGARDING YOUR COMPANY, BUT I WANT YOU TO KNOW THAT BANKS'S ADVERTISING AND MARKETING FIRM IS ALWAYS WATCHING

out for you. However, that's not all I want to discuss.

I want you to know how dangerous Josh Lustre is. I know you two have just started dating, and it seems serious, but he's a scoundrel. He knows nothing about fashion. He chose you because you're a shining star and you have precisely what he needs to continue pushing his shady-as-fuck company forward.

For two weeks, I've contemplated whether I should warn you or not, and with good conscience, I can't ignore this. He needs you not as a life partner, but as a business partner. Never collaborate with him. Do not give him too many details about what you're working on. Protect your brand!

I know a piece-of-shit CEO when I see one, and not to mention, he's a known cheater. Once he's given the opportunity, he will do to you what he did to the other women he dated in the past. Refuse to sign an NDA with him.

Now, the next thing I want to discuss is my younger brother. I'm aware, along with the entire planet, that you and Asher don't get along and have disliked each other since college. He can be a total asshole and push things too far, especially when he's right. I know how much he gets under your skin, and trust me when I say, you do the same to him. However, the two of you could be great together. I promise this isn't me writing a letter to tell you to stop seeing Josh and date my brother, but you should.

Why? Because I see the way you two look at one another. I see how when you're together in the same

ROOM, EVERYONE ELSE DISAPPEARS. EVEN THOUGH YOU TWO GO BACK AND FORTH CONSTANTLY, YOU EACH ENJOY IT. PLEASE PROMISE THAT ONCE YOU'VE HEALED FROM JOSH, YOU'LL GIVE ASHER A CHANCE.

AS YOUR FRIEND, I WANT YOU TO BE HAPPY.

AS A SISTER, I WANT MY BROTHER TO BE HAPPY.

I'M CONFIDENT YOU COULD BE HAPPY TOGETHER.

THE TWO OF YOU ARE A MATCH MADE IN HEAVEN, AND MAYBE, SOME DAYS, YOU ARE MORE OF A MATCH MADE IN HELL, BUT REGARDLESS, YOU ARE STILL A MATCH. I'VE ALWAYS IMAGINED THE TWO OF YOU TOGETHER, AND THE THOUGHT BRINGS ME SO MUCH JOY THAT I CAN BARELY CONTAIN IT. I DON'T KNOW HOW TO GET THE TWO OF YOU FROM HATE TO LIKE TO LOVE, BUT I KNOW IT'S MEANT TO BE. DESTINED.

HARPER AND I HAVE DISCUSSED THIS HEAVILY, AND SHE MENTIONED THAT YOU DIDN'T WANT ANY OF HER LOVE PROPHECIES, BUT YOU DIDN'T TELL THAT TO ME.

ONE DAY, YOU **WILL** BE MY SISTER, AND I CAN'T WAIT TO DANCE AT YOUR WEDDING. ALSO, I KNOW YOU'RE ROLLING YOUR EYES AS YOU READ THIS, WHICH IS FINE. I CAN'T WAIT TO TELL YOU I TOLD YOU SO.

THE LAST THING I WANT TO DISCUSS IS HOW YOU CAUGHT ME AND BRODY TOGETHER. PLEASE DON'T TELL ANYONE ABOUT OUR RELATIONSHIP. WE'RE FALLING IN LOVE, AND I'D LIKE TO KEEP OUR SECRET SAFE FOR NOW.

THANK YOU FOR BEING A GREAT FRIEND.

EDEN

.

.

.

P.S. PLEASE DESTROY THIS LETTER WHEN YOU'RE

FINISHED READING IT. I DON'T WANT IT TO GET INTO THE WRONG HANDS.

My eyes blur with tears as I set the letter down, trying to process everything I read about Josh and me and her secret relationship with Brody. After her death, he avoided me, and things just weren't the same between us. For years, I thought I'd done something to him, but it never had anything to do with me. He was secretly in love with my sister, and no one knew it other than him, Eden, and Billie. Brody has been secretly mourning her, and knowing that nearly breaks me.

I wipe my eyes and cheeks and get myself together. I slide the paper back into the envelope and finish my coffee and oatmeal.

Right now, my sister is everywhere and nowhere, all at once.

As I leave my loft, my phone vibrates in my pocket.

> WESTON
> Dinner at my place tonight at eight sharp?

> ASHER
> Who's invited?

> WESTON
> The four of us.

He doesn't have to say anything else. I know that means him, Carlee, Billie, and me. I smile.

> ASHER
> I'll be there.

As soon as I enter my office at Lustre Fashion, Josh enters with a pep in his step. He sits in the chair in front of my desk, smirking.

"Billie and Louis are over," he says proudly.

"I hadn't heard," I say, playing coy.

"I had Louis followed," he replies.

My eyes widen. "You do not want to mess with the palace."

He laughs. "Oh, but I do. Anyway, will you be joining our monthly meeting? It starts in five minutes."

"Yes," I tell him. "I'd like to see the designs you're launching for the fall, along with the marketing plan your team has devised. I know our contract expires in five weeks; however, I want to ensure you're standing on a solid foundation for your launch."

"Hiring you was the best thing I ever did," he says, standing and adjusting his tie.

"Remember you said that."

I act as Josh's shadow for ten hours and am exhausted by him and how he speaks down to every person who comes in his vicinity. Sometimes, it's very hard to bite my tongue, but I remind myself that this will be over soon and Josh won't be able to continue down this path.

Eventually, the sun fades behind the horizon, and I yawn, checking the time. I can't be late to Weston's, so I grab my things and text my driver. As I slide my laptop into my bag, Josh bursts into my office in a panic.

His panic is a complete one-eighty from his cocky-as-hell attitude this morning.

"What's up?" I ask, used to his erratic behavior.

"There has been a major data breach. We've been hacked," Josh says. "I just got off a call with the chief security officer. This is very bad."

He's hyperventilating.

"Sit down," I tell him, returning behind my desk. "Explain."

"Someone breached our database and bypassed all security protocols. Scans indicated extensive downloads of financial records, private emails, contracts—everything. They're still investigating it, trying to determine when this started. Whoever did this was a professional and knew exactly what they were looking for. Right now, the website has been hacked, and we can't do anything."

My brows crease together. "Excuse me?"

"Come to my office," he says, and I follow behind him as he rushes. He sits behind his desk and pulls up the site.

I see a skull and crossbones with the words **GAME OVER**, along with a countdown.

A chill runs up my spine because I'm not responsible for this. It's next level.

"Who did you piss off?"

He rubs his hands over his face. "I don't know. I don't fucking know!"

I breathe in. "This is a PR nightmare."

"What do I do?"

"We need to release a statement, so employees know what's going on. You need to make the public aware as well. Announce that you are committed to transparency and accountability."

"Yes, that's really good," he says. "And then what?"

"You'll need media training, coaching on how to answer questions that you will inevitably be asked."

He slams his hand on his desk. "I just realized what the timer is counting down to."

I meet his eyes. "What?"

"My runway show at London Fashion Week."

I SOMEHOW ESCAPE LUSTRE AS HE HAS A MELTDOWN. I WONDERED how long it would take his cybersecurity team to notice there had been a major breach in their database. They should've realized it weeks ago. However, I'm not sure my breach and this one are related. I tend to fly under the radar. Whoever did this wanted him to know they were destroying him. But who?

I told him to make sure he always had security on him and to watch his back, and then I left him shaking like a leaf. If he weren't such a horrible person and didn't treat people so terribly, I might feel bad. Unfortunately, these are the consequences of his actions. He's finally reaping what he's sown, but it's obvious that I'm not the only person onto Josh. Someone else is too.

My car slows at Park Towers, and when I get out, I'm surprised cameras aren't waiting to take photographs. It's a weeknight though, when things are much slower. The weekends are different.

As soon as I walk into the lobby, I pass Harper, dressed in evening wear. "Hey, Harp."

She smiles widely and greets me, "Asher. Didn't expect to see you here."

"Having dinner with Weston and Carlee," I tell her.

"Tell them I said hello. I'm meeting Micah for dinner and drinks."

"Have fun," I say, and we go our separate ways.

There is something about Micah Rhodes that has always made my alarm bells go off. I make a mental note to do more digging on him as I take the elevator to Weston's.

I knock, and the door swings open.

Billie stands there with a grin. "Hi."

My eyes slide up and down her body. "Hi."

She grabs my hand and pulls me in. We move to the table, where a set of dice and a notepad sit.

"Gambling?" I ask.

"I'm teaching them how to play a game we love playing back in Texas. It's called Farkle," Carlee tells me.

"It's actually really fun," Billie says, moving closer to me, but I keep my hands to myself to respect Weston.

His eyes haven't left me since I entered.

"Thanks for inviting us to dinner," I say to him with a smile, though I don't fully trust his intentions, considering our last exchange at Calloway headquarters.

Carlee moves into the kitchen and pinches Weston's ass when she passes him.

"Woman," he says, squirming away from her.

She laughs. "Get out of my way."

He pulls her into his arms, bringing her back to him. "Never."

Billie's eyes meet mine, and I can't wait to be alone with her.

It's barely past eight, and I feel like I've lived one of the longest days of my life.

"I watched Louis's press conference," Weston offers from the kitchen.

"Really?" I ask. "I was in nonstop meetings today. It was awful."

Billie nods. "I watched it at double speed. He told everyone we broke it off days prior, but hadn't had a chance to make an announcement yet. He said we were much better as friends. Palace is pushing that there was no cheating involved and is trying to keep his crown polished."

"After the Prince Louie scandal, I can understand why," I say, meeting Billie's eyes, knowing she bought one of those toys.

A sly grin slides across her face. "Exactly. I think it will all be okay though. Everyone is buying it."

"That's great news," I tell her, knowing that if Louis hadn't dated Billie that summer, we probably would have become friends. Once they got together, he was immediately added to my shit list.

"What?" Billie asks, noticing I'm smiling at her, admiring her.

I think back to Eden's letter, knowing she's kept it safe all these years.

"Nothing," I tell her, utterly taken aback by how damn pretty she is.

I feel like I'm walking on the fucking moon when she's near, like nothing in the world matters. All it ever takes is one glance.

Carlee clears her throat. "I have to tell you something."

I glance at her, and she's staring directly at me. "Me?"

"You have to sign this first," she says, sliding an NDA toward me with a pen.

Billie and Weston say nothing.

"Is this where I get initiated into your cult?" I ask.

Weston bursts into laughter. "Fucking hilarious. But yes."

"He's lying," Billie says. "We're not in a cult."

"You're not being convincing," I say as I quickly scan the contract, knowing it's a standard NDA, nothing outrageous or out of the ordinary.

I've been presented with thousands of them in my lifetime, and I could probably write one verbatim at this point. I sign my name at the bottom, and it feels like minutes of silence pass. It stretches on.

"If you don't spit it out, I might die from anticipation," I say dryly.

Carlee glares at me. "I will help you take down Josh."

"*You?*" I ask, shocked.

She scoffs. "Yes, *me*." She sounds offended.

Then realization dawns on me, and a cheeky grin fills my face. "You're LadyLux."

"Are you shocked?" she asks.

"Yes, because you're nice, and LadyLux is a real bitch. And I honestly thought she was a middle-aged widow with a chip on her shoulder."

Weston howls with laughter.

"Hmm, you're just used to people bowing down to you because you're a nepo baby. LadyLux doesn't worship anyone. Reality checks are needed when you have as many zeros in your trust fund as you, Banks. I'm the only one brave enough to serve the truth on a silver platter," she says.

"It's an honor," I say sincerely.

"It's a deal," she says, holding out her hand.

We shake on it. Neither Weston nor Billie interrupts. This is official business between Carlee and me, no one else.

"I'll keep your brand safe," I promise.

"I know, and that alone is worth it," she says. "Now, can we please eat? I'm starving. I made spaghetti with fat meatballs and garlic knots. It's my mawmaw's recipe."

"Sounds amazing," I offer as we make our plates.

During dinner, the conversation flows easily. I steal glances at my Billie, and I love seeing her this relaxed. She's smiling and happy, and it's so easy to imagine a future with her.

"I need you to tell me everything," Carlee says, stealing my attention.

I smirk, sliding my hand into my pocket and pulling out the USB drive that's full of the information she needs to destroy Josh.

"You just carry this data around with you?" she asks.

"Yes," I say. "I figured after I made my offer, LadyLux would reveal herself to me because she knew I was a weapon. I wanted to be prepared."

Carlee grins. "I need time to go through this."

"I understand," I say, clearing my throat. "I do have more news."

All eyes are on me.

"Someone else hacked Josh's database. His website has been taken over. You have to witness this for yourselves," I tell them, pulling up my cell phone and going to the page. "He also admitted to being responsible for the photos of Louis being leaked."

"*Game over*," Weston whispers, his jaw clenched tight. "Do you know who would do this?"

"Not sure. But whoever it is seems fed the fuck up and has the resources to act from the outside," I say.

Billie exhales hard. "I should tell Louis what Josh did."

"You should text him now so he can let his people know," I tell her.

"Extra security is a must in London, sis," Weston instructs. "You'll travel with an entourage, you and Asher. It's an order."

Billie studies him. "Do you think I should cancel this trip?"

"No," Weston says. "It's important that you both go. You can't let him take this from you. You're the diamond of the show."

34
BILLIE

FASHION WEEK

The plane touches down in London, and my nerves take over. Harper grabs my hand and squeezes it as we deboard. Brody follows behind us, not saying a word. We climb inside the blacked-out SUV, and the extra security my brother hired follows in another vehicle.

We head toward the W, a luxurious hotel that only needs one letter. The London location is one of my favorites, with the best views of the city. Conveniently, the fashion shows are held in the venue next door and have private entrances from the hotel.

Our crew, designers, and models arrived a few days ago to organize everything, and I've been updated on timelines and clothing arrivals. We are ready for tomorrow, and I plan to do a walk-through a few hours before our show begins. Josh's feature is directly after mine, and I'm dreading it because I know I'll have to see him.

Exhaustion covers me, and I'm already suffering from jet lag. I've been working myself to the bone, but it's almost over. My stress level is at its max, and my anxiety is at an all-time high.

The vehicle zooms away, and Harper pulls out her phone as I stare at the fading sky.

Brody turns to me. "He's arrived."

I know he's referring to Asher.

A smile touches my lips, and butterflies swarm me. "Best news I've heard all day."

We're keeping up appearances throughout this event until the Lustre stuff is finalized. After my showcase tomorrow, we're running away together for two weeks. I'm looking forward to spending every waking and sleeping hour with him. It's a silver lining.

"What's the plan if Josh approaches me?" I ask Brody, somewhat concerned.

"I'll be ready to attack, if he has the balls."

We've worked through this scenario several times after Josh texted me yesterday. I swear, Brody has a hard-on for smashing in Josh's face.

I think everyone knows that we will never ever get back together, everyone except for Josh. I'm convinced he thinks he's smarter than me. He's not.

When I walked out of his penthouse, I knew I'd never return to him. Enough was enough; for once, I chose myself and my dignity.

Eden was right about Josh, even though I didn't want her to be. She was also right about Asher. I wish she were here so I could thank her. That letter has lived rent-free in my head for a little over five years. She wrote it to me a month before she passed away. I didn't listen. I was too stubborn and thought I knew best. Not many people like Josh, but now I know why. It was a hard lesson I had to learn, one I wish I'd have avoided.

The SUV slows outside the W. The hotel entrance is surrounded by people lined up, trying to catch a glimpse of those arriving for the event.

Brody jumps out first to clear a path for Harper and me. "Stay close to me. Both of you."

We're greeted by paparazzi shouting our names.

"Billie! Billie! Right here! Harper! Smile!"

Brody instructs those rushing us for photos to back up. Flashing lights and clicking cameras overwhelm me as I move toward the hotel entrance. Harper grabs my hand, and I concentrate on putting one designer heel in front of the other while I try to cover my face.

"You okay?" she asks.

"I will be," I explain.

She knows I hate big crowds of people.

We move to the front desk, where we are expedited. In less than a minute, penthouse keys are slid across the desk to Harper and me. I give Brody his, noticing the six buff guys in suits with earpieces, waiting off to the side.

"Do you think bringing the Secret Service was necessary?" I ask him.

"Yes," he says. "If some shit goes down, it'll ensure you and Harper are safe."

He escorts us toward the elevator. We're staying on the same floor so he can better monitor us. I don't plan on leaving my room unless I have to.

The elevator stops on our floor with a ding, and we enter the hallway with marbled floors and high ceilings. There are three doors on this floor, all penthouses.

Brody leads the way to mine. "If you leave, promise you'll tell me."

"I will," I say, and then I turn to Harper. "Do you have plans tonight?"

"Micah is supposed to arrive in a few hours. Might sit in the tub and wait for him," she says, and I notice how Brody tenses beside me.

"Okay." I smile at her. "The same rules apply for you. If you leave, let Brody know."

She gives me a nod, then disappears into her room.

My cousin and I stare at one another for a few seconds.

"I don't like him," I whisper.

"I fucking hate him," Brody says with a clenched jaw. "Anyway, have a good night."

"You too," I tell him, scanning my key.

The door swings open, only to reveal Asher waiting for me. He's wearing jeans and a T-shirt, which hugs him in all the right places. My breath catches in my throat at the sight of him, and swirling emotions hit me all at once.

He rushes to me; our lips find each other. The stress from traveling dissolves as his lips move over mine with urgency.

"I missed you so much." He pulls me into his arms. "Are you hungry?"

"Starving," I say, and then I notice he has dinner waiting for us on the table. Candles flicker, and a soft smile meets my lips as he kisses me, nearly stealing my breath away. "Why are you so perfect?"

"I'm hardly perfect." Asher chuckles, releasing me from our kiss. He takes my hand and leads me toward the table, pulling out a chair for me. "But I am pretty damn close."

I laugh and sit, admiring the food spread before us.

"This looks incredible," I say, my stomach rumbling in anticipation. "What is all this?"

"I'm not sure exactly," Asher replies as he uncorks a bottle of red wine and pours us each a glass. "I called in a favor from a chef friend. Told him I was having dinner with the love of my life."

My cheeks heat. "I needed this so much," I admit, sipping the rich, velvety liquid.

"I did too," he says.

From where we're sitting, we have the perfect view of London and its glittering nighttime lights. I can barely focus on anything other than how incredible it feels to be here with Asher.

"Where are you staying?" I ask.

"I have a room on another floor," he tells me. "But I thought I'd stay with you instead. If you want me to."

"Please. I was going to beg you. I don't want to be alone," I confess.

Asher reaches over and squeezes my hand. "You're never alone, princess. Not as long as my heart beats."

I blush at his words as his thumb strokes over my knuckles in a soothing motion.

"Hey, what's going through that pretty head of yours?" he asks, his voice soft.

"I'm nervous about the show and what's to come with Josh. Everything is changing so fast," I admit, scooping up mashed potatoes so creamy that they melt in my mouth.

Asher grins. "It's almost over, I promise."

"Have you figured out who hacked his site?" I ask.

"Not yet." He shakes his head, pulls his phone from his pocket, and shows me the site for Lustre Fashion.

"Less than twenty-four hours," I whisper, watching the skull and crossbones laugh. "I kinda feel bad for him."

Asher smiles. "You shouldn't. Not after how he treated you. Not after he stole your designs for years. On the flight over here, I figured out how he gained access to your designs."

I swallow the bite of chicken in my mouth, and it feels as if it's stuck in my throat. "How?"

"I can't tell you. But it was Hannah."

My nostrils flare. "My assistant? Are you sure? Asher, she's been with me since …" My words trail off.

"Since you and Josh started dating, right? She's on Lustre's payroll too," Asher replies calmly.

I inhale sharply. "Of course she is."

I pull my phone from my pocket and text Harper. She immediately replies.

HARPER

I'M FIRING HER RIGHT NOW!

I let out a heavy sigh. How could Hannah betray me like this? How long has she been spying for Josh? I lean back in my chair, realizing that was the missing piece to my puzzle. It all makes so much sense now.

"I'm so sorry. She sucks for that."

"I just can't believe it," I whisper. "All those years … she was a part of everything. Every fucking fashion show, every design meeting … Asher, she was there."

"Yeah, but something changed." His brows lift. "I found recent emails where she was panicking about feeding him information. The designs she eventually shared were so bad that Josh didn't believe they were legitimate."

I smile widely, happy I followed my gut. "I sealed our designs tight. The only people with access were me, Harper, and my directors. Nothing was to be sent digitally, except the designs we planted as fakes."

Asher grins. "So fucking smart, princess. Proud of you, Little Miss CEO."

"That means a lot to me, Ash."

We eat until we're full. I yawn, and so does Asher.

"Tomorrow is a huge day for you," he says, picking up our plates. "You should get some rest."

Just as he moves to the kitchen, there's a knock.

He opens the door to find a bellhop holding a massive bouquet of dark red roses. Asher signs for them, tips the young man, and brings the arrangement to me. A note is attached to it, and I pluck it from the top.

CAN'T WAIT TO SEE YOU AGAIN.

"What the fuck? Who sent these?" Asher asks.

My blood runs cold when I realize they didn't come from him.

"I want them out of here," I say, grabbing the flowers and entering the hallway. I set them next to the door.

Brody leans against the wall, scrolling his phone, and looks up at me. He tilts his head. "Harper was sent flowers too."

"From who?" I ask.

"Micah," he mutters. His eyes lock on me. "Do you know him?"

"No. They're probably from Josh. Dispose of them," I tell him. "Ensure nothing else is delivered to my room while I'm here."

"Okay," Brody says.

"Who knows my room number?" I ask.

Brody shakes his head. "No one other than us."

I move back inside the penthouse, where Asher is waiting for me. He grabs my hand and leads me to the bathroom, where water is already running. Candles flicker around the edge of the tub.

"I thought we could relax," he says, sliding his hands over my body.

"Yes, please," I whisper.

"Let's get you out of this," he murmurs against my lips.

The second his fingers graze the zipper of my dress, I'm already a fucking mess. My body aches for him as the fabric falls to my feet, leaving me in my lacy black bra and panties.

Asher drinks me in as his fingers trail down my spine. Sparks ignite as he unhooks my bra, letting it fall away. My breasts bounce free, and he takes his time kissing my neck as he barely tweaks one of my nipples.

Candlelight dances on the marble walls, and steam rises from the tub. Being here with him like this, with his hot breath on my skin, feels like a dream.

"Do you have any idea what you do to me?" Asher asks hoarsely, cupping my face and drawing me into another kiss.

"Yes," I say, melting against him, parting my mouth wider, allowing our tongues to dance together. I feel his cock against my stomach, hard and fucking throbbing, and I need him like he's my sustenance.

"I hoped I'd see you tonight," I confess. "I was so worried I wouldn't."

Asher lifts my chin. "I can't sleep without you next to me."

My hands slide under his T-shirt, pushing it off his body, revealing his chest. "I'm addicted to you."

I gently drop to my knees. My fingers undo his belt, and I yank his pants and boxers down in one swift motion. His cock springs free, the tip already glistening with pre-cum. I don't hesitate—I take him into my mouth, my lips wrapping around him like he was made for me.

"Princess," he growls, his voice raw, as he thrusts his fingers through my hair.

My tongue swirls around the head, and I love teasing him. I take him deep in the back of my throat, and his hips jerk forward with a groan.

I dive back down, taking him as far as I can, gagging a little as the tip hits the back of my throat. I'm working him up so damn fast that I can feel him trembling, trying not to lose it. I smirk around him, sucking harder until he's panting. I pull away before he loses himself, but I'm not done yet. I want him to unravel.

"Mine," I say, looking up at him, knowing he's the man I'll marry one day.

"Always," he tells me, his grip tightening in my hair. I focus on him and his cock, heavy in my mouth.

I worship him the way he deserves.

His moans only encourage me to keep going, to push him to the very edge. My hand works in rhythm with my mouth, and I twist and stroke him.

"So close," he whispers, his body tensing.

His eyes are hooded and full of need, and I can taste him.

I moan around him, the vibration making him curse under his

breath. I pull back, letting his cock slip out of my mouth with a pop, and look up at him through my lashes.

"How bad do you want it?" I ask, teasing.

He doesn't answer. Instead, he guides me back to him, and I take him all the way down my throat. I swallow around him, nearly suffocating on his cock as my throat muscles tighten. I suck harder, faster, my tongue working the underside of his cock as I bob my head. Asher's hips buck forward, and he groans out his release. I swallow him down, my tongue lapping at the tip to make sure I don't miss a single fucking drop.

When I finally pull away, he's breathing hard, his chest rising and falling like he just ran a marathon. He looks down at me, his eyes filled with something close to admiration, and I can't help but smirk.

"Fucking perfection," he mutters, pulling me to my feet and sliding my panties from my body. "Time to get clean, dirty girl."

Asher leads me to the tub and climbs in first, then he guides me in. I settle between his legs, my back against his chest. His hands are on my breasts, and his mouth is on my neck. I can feel his cock stirring to life again as it presses against my back.

Asher takes his time, like he's memorizing me as his fingers trail down my stomach. He continues farther down until he's between my legs, gently brushing my clit.

I gasp as I grind upward. He chuckles as he circles my sensitive bud with his thumb. His other hand slips lower, two fingers sliding into me with ease because I'm so wet for him.

"This pussy is mine," he mutters in my ear.

I can't even form words. All I can do is moan, my hips rocking against his hand as he fucks me with his fingers and rubs my clit in tight little circles. I bite my lip to keep from screaming, but it's impossible to stay quiet when it feels so damn good. The water sloshes around us as I move, splashing over the side of the tub, but I don't care. All I care about is how he's driving me closer and closer to the edge without apology.

I whimper, my nails digging into his thighs. "Please …"

"You're so damn greedy," he says, his voice dripping with satisfaction. His fingers are magic with the perfect amount of pressure.

I nod, and my breath releases in shallow gasps.

He increases his pace, thrusting into me harder and faster, and I can feel the pressure quickly building. He has my body memorized, knows exactly what I like and crave.

And as if commanded, I'm falling. Pleasure crashes over me as the orgasm takes hold. I come so hard that it nearly knocks the breath from my lungs.

My eyes slam shut, and I cry out his name. My body convulses as I lose myself, my pussy clenching around his fingers. He holds me through it, his arms strong and steady, until I stop throbbing.

I lean back on his chest, his mouth close to my ear, his arms wrapped around my stomach. A contented sigh releases from me as the candlelight casts a dreamy glow in the room.

"Thank you," I whisper, and he holds me tighter.

"For what?" he asks.

"Loving me."

It's the first time I've felt relaxed all day, and it's because of Asher.

"I'll always love you," he promises. "All I ask is that you love me in return."

I twist my body so I can meet his eyes. "I do love you, Asher. When I look at you, I feel it here." I hold my hand against my heart. "I can't imagine my life without you."

He leans forward, kissing me, and it's full of emotion and want and pure longing. This is the way it was always supposed to be, I think. He and I just like this.

His thumb brushes against my cheek. "I can't wait to leave London and spend the next two weeks with you."

"It's the only thing keeping me going. The thought is like warm sunshine after a disastrous storm," I admit.

We stay in the tub until the water is no longer warm, but we're both so comfortable that neither of us moves.

"Come on, princess," he eventually says.

I carefully stand, and so does he. Asher grabs a few towels, and we take turns carefully drying each other off. It's sensual and silent, neither of us needing words. Once we're no longer wet, he lifts me into his arms and carries me into the bedroom, which is lined with a wall of windows that overlook the city.

Asher sets me down on the mattress, and I pull the blankets down. I slide between the sheets, and he joins me, wrapping his strong arms around me. I lie on his chest as he runs his fingers through my damp hair.

"Did you read Eden's letter?" I ask him. It slipped my mind before.

"Yes. Thank you for sharing that with me," he says, and I can tell he's smiling. "She was right. As always. I can almost hear her saying *I told you so.*"

That thought brings me comfort as I drift away to dreamland with the man of my wildest fantasies.

35

ASHER

I wake up before Billie and watch her soft breaths as she sleeps quietly beside me. I inhale her sweet skin and pepper light kisses on her bare shoulder. "I'll see you at the show."

She stirs. "Are you leaving?"

"Yes, princess. I need to get dressed and take care of some business beforehand," I say, capturing her lips. "I can't wait to see what you're revealing."

She smiles behind sleepy eyes. "You inspired me."

"Love you," I whisper. "Go back to sleep. You have a few more hours before you need to be up."

"I love you. Can we leave after the show?" she asks.

"Will it make you happy?"

She nods.

"Then the answer is always yes," I tell her, stealing another kiss.

"I already miss you," she admits in a sleepy tone as I find my clothes from yesterday.

Once I'm dressed, I leave the penthouse, and when I walk into the hallway, Brody is leaning against the wall.

"Hey," I say to him, and he gives me a chin nod, then returns to his phone. "Do you ever sleep?"

"No," he says, looking me up and down. "Do you?"

"Barely." I move closer to him, unsure how to bring up this conversation. And maybe it's not the proper time to mention it. However, I also understand it will never feel right; discussions like this are inherently awkward.

"I know about you and my sister," I say, keeping my voice low. "I'm really, really fucking sorry. I can't imagine what losing her did to you."

His face slightly softens, but then returns to the same hard expression he always wears. "Not sure what you're talking about."

"Okay," I tell him, moving to the elevator.

It's clear he doesn't want to discuss it, but I don't think I would either. I press the button and wait.

As I step inside, Brody speaks up. "Who told you?"

I smile at him, remembering I found out through the letter. "My sister."

He swallows hard as the doors slide closed.

Guilt floods me. I wasn't there for him or anyone who was missing Eden. I closed myself off to the world and doubled down on making the firm the best that it could be. I wasn't living; I was surviving. That stopped the moment I kissed Billie in Weston's penthouse.

I wish I could change the past, and that my sister were still here. I think I always will.

I step off the elevator and make my way to my room, where my luggage is. Everything is exactly where I left it when I arrived. I won't sleep in this room once.

After I quickly shower, I get dressed. Just as I'm adjusting my tie, a knock taps on my door. It's almost seven in the morning. I look through the peephole, only to see Josh Lustre standing outside. I return to the bed, pulling the blankets down and roughing them up so it looks like I was here. I'm too invested in this game to fuck it up at the end.

I return to the door and open it. "Good morning."

"Morning," he says, and I can smell alcohol on his breath.

"Are you drunk?" I ask, staring him down.

"I'm ruined," he yells. "Fucking ruined!"

"Josh, lower your voice. You need to go to your suite, take a shower, and get a few hours of sleep. Then get up and get dressed for your fashion show this afternoon. Okay? Stay the course."

He leans against the doorway. "Do you know what room Billie is in?" he asks.

"No," I state. "Why? Are you planning on sending her flowers?"

"Fuck no. Why would I do that? I want to see her," he says.

Immediately, I think about the roses she was sent last night. If they didn't come from Josh, then who?

I don't fucking like how uneasy it makes me feel, knowing it was someone other than him. If he'd sent them, he'd have bragged. His ego is too large.

"Please go to your room and get some sleep. You're drunk and emotional."

"No," he says, looking over his shoulder, acting paranoid.

I step out of my room and glance down the hallway. Nothing is there.

"I'm going to find her, and you won't stop me."

Josh pushes me, and I stumble back. I catch my footing, then grab his shirt with my fist.

"You ever fucking touch me like that again, and I won't be so kind." I shove him away and slam my door shut.

It's too damn early for a brawl, and while I'd like to knock him the fuck out, it's best if I don't. I know his day is going to get a lot worse without me breaking his nose.

I know I won't be able to see Billie until Bellamore's runway show. Directly afterward is Josh's. I wonder who was responsible for that scheduling.

I place a call and order breakfast to be sent to Billie's room for her and Brody. I text Brody to let him know, considering she adamantly refused anything be delivered to her after the flowers were sent.

Brody sends me a thumbs-up emoji.

Right after, I text Weston and give him an update on everything.

> **WESTON**
> Thanks. We'll land in an hour and a half. I'll find you then.

THE BACKSTAGE AREA IS CHAOTIC. MODELS RUSH AROUND HALF-naked, makeup artists give final touches, designers frantically check seams, and voices compete over one another. Through the hecticness, my gaze narrows on Billie. I stay in the shadows, not wanting to distract her or bring attention to myself. This is her time to shine, and I love to watch her sparkle.

Regardless of the immense amount of pressure she's under, Billie calmly gives final approvals and subtle instructions as the models line up. As if she were a drill sergeant, she goes down the line, making sure every single person meets her high standards. She's glowing, determined, and I fall harder, watching her be in charge.

Right now, her hair and makeup are done, and she's wearing a smock, not the dress she'll be walking in today. It will be a surprise for everyone, a secret I can't wait for her to share.

Weston spots and approaches me.

"Is everything in place?" I ask quietly.

"Yes. Lux dropped the story thirty minutes ago. Lustre's imploding," he says.

I unlock my phone and refresh his website. The countdown has a little over an hour left, and the anticipation of what will happen when it says 0:00 has me in a choke hold. I quickly scan the headlines of Lustre Fashion's downfall that are already trending, all quoting LadyLux's article, which is full of receipts from a *whistleblower*.

"Damn," I whisper. "The *Times* already picked up the story."

"The world has." Weston smirks. "He should've never messed with my sister."

"He should've been a better person. People like him don't deserve power."

Weston turns and glances at Billie as Easton and Brody stand next to Harper. "She's handling this like a pro," Weston says.

I nod, pride swelling in my chest. "She always does. It's a Calloway trait."

He beams at her.

"Everyone got it?" Billie asks after giving her final instructions and outstretching her hand.

Her entire team squishes into the huddle.

"I just want you to know how proud I am of every single one of you. Bellamore wouldn't be where it is today without you. We're a team. You're all beautiful. Let's show the world what we're made of and how women rule this industry."

They chant together, "Bellamore, fierce and bold! Own this runway, steal the show!"

They break into applause, then scatter like leaves. Billie walks out of view, and Weston turns to me.

"I'm so fucking happy it's you," he tells me, pulling me into a brotherly hug.

"Me too." I squeeze him tight, knowing he and Easton will one day be my brothers.

Carlee walks over, grinning.

"Hi! You look great," I tell her.

"Thanks. It's Bellamore," she says, pulling me into a hug too.

"Thank you for everything," I whisper.

"I will do anything for my family. And I kinda want an exclusive from you," she says with a wink.

"Consider it done," I tell her.

"Now, shall we grab our seats?" Weston asks as Easton and Lexi approach.

Easton gives me a firm handshake. "Nice suit."

"Your sister picked it out," I tell him, adjusting the button to the suit she sent me weeks ago. The one with the light-blue lining, which matches her eyes, that she thought I trashed. Can't wait for her to see it.

I follow them to the FROW—the premium front-row seating in the venue, reserved for celebrities, influencers, fashion editors, and VIP guests. To be given one of these seats is equivalent to finding the Golden Ticket in a Willy Wonka bar.

The anticipation in the air is thrilling. The lights lower, and it feels like magic.

I catch a glimpse of Harper backstage with a clipboard and headset and give her a thumbs-up. She returns the gesture with a proud smile.

My heart races with excitement as the room dims, then pops into complete darkness for dramatic effect. Then the bass of the music drops, and the Bellamore models step out to rule the runway.

It's an *experience,* just like Billie.

From my vantage point, I see every detail—the subtle shimmer woven into the gowns, delicate lace patterns of floral sketches Billie and Harper personally created, and signature silhouettes that flow like liquid silk as the models stride by. Each design tells its own story—stories of empowerment, resilience, and even flirty romance.

Around me, there's a collective intake of breath as the models work the runway, confident and beautiful, embodying the spirit Bellamore is known for. I'm close enough to hear the whisper-soft rustle of fabric, the rhythmic click of heels echoing on beat with the music as each piece moves past me. With the spotlights above, hand-sewn crystals reflect tiny sparkles.

The diamond princess has outdone herself.

Editors, influencers, and industry insiders beside me lean in, eyes wide, fully captivated. Each look feels like Billie herself—bold, emotional, and unforgettable.

In this moment, sitting in Bellamore's coveted FROW, I don't just watch; I live it. It's more than a show; it's an experience that leaves me inspired, energized, and utterly enchanted by the woman I'm going to make my wife.

When Billie takes the runway, everything fades to a whisper. There's a noticeable shift in the room—an electric awe blankets the crowd and is immediately followed by gasps and murmurs of admiration.

Cameras snap shots of her. She steps into the spotlight, her chin raised with the kind of defiance only Billie Calloway can embody. Every step she takes radiates confidence. Her expression is vicious, but her eyes flicker with pride and a hint of vulnerability.

Her gown cascades down her thin body in waves of deep crimson, molten gold, and burning amber, seamlessly blending into each other, as if crafted from actual flames. Layers of silk chiffon and organza ripple and flow with each step, mimicking the graceful, powerful movement of phoenix wings spreading wide.

Hundreds of delicate crystals are meticulously embroidered throughout the fabric, catching the lights and shimmering like embers scattered in the wind. They gather more densely at the bodice, resembling the fiery heart of the mythical bird itself, radiating outward in shimmering lines and intricate patterns that echo feathers.

As she moves, the gown transforms into a living flame, glistening and flickering beneath the spotlight. The dramatic train billows behind her, trailing elegantly like smoke.

The gasps continue.

The gown was crafted from dreams themselves, cascading elegantly around her like waves of fire.

My breath catches in my throat. I can't tear my eyes away from her—not just because she's stunning, but because I'm so fucking proud.

Billie isn't simply wearing fashion; she is fashion. She symbolizes everything Bellamore stands for—resilience, creativity, strength, and rebirth.

Time slows as she pauses briefly at the end of the runway. Her gaze lifts, finding mine effortlessly through the sea of faces. In that heartbeat, it's like we're alone, as if this entire moment is ours. Her eyes soften, the faintest smile curving her lips, as if to say, *I did it.*

She spins, swinging her hips as she walks away like she owns the stage. Fuck, she does.

Applause erupts, pulling my attention away as my heart continues racing. The entire crowd rises, acknowledging the queen she's always been.

This isn't just a walk down a runway; it's Billie reclaiming herself, reclaiming her power, and stepping fully into who she's meant to be, who I always knew she could be. And I'm the luckiest man alive to witness it.

The stage lights lower, and then the house lights rise.

Harper moves to the edge of the stage with a microphone in her hand. "That concludes our show. The last dress is called Born from Ash and exemplifies the essence of Bellamore—unbreakable, born from the flames, triumphant and radiant—a true phoenix rising. Thank you so much for attending," Harper says, and the room cheers again.

I push my emotions down, remembering what she said to me this morning. *"You inspired me."*

It was for me as much as it was for her.

Right now, I have to see Billie. Nothing else matters.

I MOVE BACKSTAGE, FINDING HER CHATTING WITH HARPER. MY EYES lock on her, and I pull her away, crashing my lips against hers.

"I'm so fucking proud of you," I whisper between kisses, knowing I can't get enough.

"It's all because of you," she says, tears streaming down her cheeks as she meets my eyes. "Because you saw what I was capable of when no one else did."

It's just us as we lose ourselves in one another.

"Wait," she says, taking a step back. "That suit."

"My girlfriend picked it out. Like it?" I ask, raising a brow.

She rubs her hand down my sleeve, and her eyes widen when she sees the cuff links. "You?"

"I have all of your pieces, princess." I shrug. "What can I say? I'm a fan."

Her bottom lip quivers. "It's always been you?"

"In more ways than one."

"I hoped it was you. King of my heart."

We laugh against each other's mouths, and I think I hear Harper tell us to get a room.

I grab her cheeks, meeting her eyes. "Let's get out of here."

"Please," she says, and I take her hand, interlocking my fingers with hers.

"Stop!" I hear Harper scream at the top of her lungs. "No!"

I turn and look over my shoulder, alarmed by the panic in her tone.

The atmosphere shifts as Josh rushes backstage, his eyes wild and face flushed with rage. The energy crackles dangerously. Models scatter away from him, and even I recognize an approaching storm. My brows furrow, and then I notice the glint of a blade.

He has a knife.

36

BILLIE

"Josh, back the fuck up," Asher yells, tensing.

I look around him, seeing Josh's crazed eyes, and he's heaving with rage.

"It was always you," he roars.

My heart slams against my ribs as Josh's furious gaze lands directly on mine. His eyes are raw with unchecked anger, and for a moment, my entire body freezes in panic.

"What the fuck is this?" Josh's voice cuts through the air, his face twisted with disbelief and fury. His gaze flicks rapidly between Asher and me, the betrayal evident in every sharp line of his expression.

Instinctively, Asher shifts, stepping protectively in front of me, shielding me with his body. I grip the back of his jacket, my fingers trembling from adrenaline and fear. His muscles tense beneath my touch, and I can feel the tension rippling through him as he stands firm.

"Calm down," Asher warns, his voice dangerously low, but I can tell he's not fucking around.

Josh laughs bitterly, the sound harsh and cold. "Calm down? You've been playing me this whole time, haven't you, Billie?" He glares past Asher, eyes locked on to mine. "You stupid fucking bitch!"

"You should've never underestimated me," I tell him.

Seconds later, Weston and Easton rush Josh, pushing him to the ground. Brody slams his face into the concrete with a crack, then zip-ties his wrists behind his back. My cousin leans down and whispers something in his ear as the lights in the entire building shut off.

The TVs behind the stage flicker on.

A person with a Guy Fawkes mask comes on the screen. Everyone backstage grows silent and watches the screens. I hear the audience quiet down outside as the distorted and lowered voice speaks.

"Greetings, citizens of the world. We are Anonymous. Today, we bring you the truth behind the facade of Josh Lustre and Lustre Fashion. For far too long, he has exploited creativity, stolen designs, manipulated markets, and silenced voices. His actions are not just immoral; they are criminal.

"Fashion thrives on creativity, innovation, and authenticity. Yet Josh Lustre represents the opposite—corporate greed, betrayal, and dishonesty. He has built his empire on stolen ideas, fraudulent contracts, insider trading, and harassment, hidden beneath layers of lies and manipulation.

"We have watched. We have listened. We have seen the damage his actions caused—careers destroyed, artists silenced, and trust broken. Today, we say, *No more*.

"Lustre believed himself untouchable. He believed power and money would shield him from consequences. He was mistaken. Today, his secrets are exposed, his empire dismantled, and justice served.

"To those harmed by Lustre, we stand with you. Your voice matters. Your creations matter. Your truth matters.

"To Josh Lustre and those like him, your time of corruption is over.

"We are Anonymous. We are a legion. We do not forgive. We do not forget. Expect us."

No one says a word as the screens go black and the lights come on. Whispers travel through the building, and it's pure chaos as police surround us. The knife is confiscated, and I watch Josh get arrested and then pulled away by five officers.

My brothers and Brody approach me. The three of them stare at me, then glance at Asher. They don't know which of us is responsible for that and aren't brave enough to ask.

"We're getting the fuck out of here," Asher tells them, grabbing my hand and leading me down the skybridge.

He's silent, not saying a word as my heels click and echo across the floor. We step onto the elevator, and he finally turns to me.

"Did you do this?" he asks.

"No." I shake my head. "But every move is needed to win the game. Every piece is important. Someone is keeping me safe."

He pulls me into his arms, kissing me. "Bellamore didn't need me."

"Maybe not," I tell him, "But *I* did."

My heart races as we hop on the private jet, wearing casual clothes for the long flight home. Tension still hangs in the air. Josh might have been arrested, but this is far from over.

Once we're in the sky, Asher intertwines his fingers with mine. His grip makes me feel as if we're escaping it all. I just want to run away with him forever. Two weeks will have to be enough for now.

It's early morning as we touch down at East Hampton Airport, and the sun will rise soon.

The fresh ocean air hits my cheeks as soon as we arrive at Asher's beautiful beachfront home. I hear the distant sound of waves rolling to shore. Asher unlocks the door, and once we're inside, the world outside and everything that has happened disappears.

Asher leads me onto the back porch, and we watch the sun rise over the horizon. The sky bursts in pinks and yellows, casting a golden glow on everything surrounding us.

He wraps his strong arms around my waist from behind as we take it all in, and it feels like a brand-new beginning. His lips brush my ear, his warm breath melting away the last remnants of my anxiety.

"You shocked everyone. You claimed your crown," he whispers.

"I couldn't have done this without you." I turn in his arms, inhaling his familiar scent.

His hands cup my face, thumbs brushing my cheekbones as he leans in and kisses me. It's deep and full of promises as we pour ourselves into each other. I press against him, my hands slipping under his shirt to find warm skin.

"Let's go inside."

He grabs my hand and leads me through the back door. Our footsteps are quiet on the wooden floors as we take the stairs to the suite that overlooks the water. We may be jet-lagged and exhausted from the adrenaline, but nothing will stop me from having him. Right now, Asher is everything I crave and want.

The golden sun shines through the window as Asher slowly undresses me. He removes my T-shirt and undoes my jeans with ease. I stand in my bra and panties before him, and his eyes darken with lust. I gently tug his shirt, pushing it over his body, peppering kisses up his stomach and across his chest.

My eyes scan his tattoo, and I softly brush my fingers over it. "I can't wait to see it colored in."

"I want it to look like your dress," he admits. "Un-fucking-forgettable."

Emotions threaten to take over. "It's the colors I imagined."

The sun's rays spill over the horizon, lighting up the ocean in streaks of molten gold. I couldn't care less about the view because Asher is my whole world right now. His lips crash into mine like a tidal wave, full of heat and hunger, and I'm totally lost in the taste of him—minty, salty, and a little sweet.

His hands are everywhere, greedy and possessive, mapping out every curve of my body. My skin burns where he touches, and my nipples are as hard as little pebbles against the fabric of my bra. He steps even closer, his broad chest pressing into mine, and I feel his strong body as he gently but firmly guides me back onto the mattress. The fluffy comforter is cool against my bare skin as his hot mouth trails fire down to my collarbone. I moan and arch into him, my fingers getting lost in his messy hair.

"Asher." I gasp, my voice already wrecked.

He growls low in response, the sound vibrating through me like an earthquake. Carefully, his hands slide under my back, and he unhooks my bra. When my breasts are free, he dips down to swirl his tongue around one nipple while his fingers tease the other. It's electric, and it sends shots of pleasure straight to my core.

I squirm beneath him, getting so worked up and desperate for more.

"I need you," I whisper, my breath hitching as his teeth graze my skin.

His hand slides down between us, slipping under the waistband of my panties, and I can feel how turned on I am already. He smirks, giving me that cocky grin that drives me wild.

"Always so fucking eager for me," he mutters, his voice dripping with amusement as he pulls my panties down in one smooth motion.

Asher doesn't give me a second to catch my breath.

His mouth is back on my neck, nipping at my soft skin while his fingers trail down my stomach, leaving a path of fire behind. He's teasing me. His touch drives me wild as he circles my clit without actually touching it.

I whimper, my hips bucking against his hand, but he just chuckles in that incredibly sexy tone.

"Patience, princess," he purrs, his lips brushing my ear.

I don't have patience. I want him—all of him—right fucking now.

But Asher's in control, like he's always been. He's just making sure I know it.

His fingers finally dip lower, sliding through my slick folds, and I almost lose it right then and there.

"You're soaked," he whispers, and I'm desperate for more.

He gives in, slipping one finger inside me, and I clench around him, my body trembling with need.

"More," I beg, my voice breaking.

He doesn't hesitate, adding a second finger and curling them just right, hitting that spot I fucking love. My back arches off the bed, a strangled cry escaping my lips as he slowly finger-fucks me.

But it's not enough.

I need him deep inside me, claiming me completely.

"Asher." My nails lightly brush down his back.

"I love it when you say my name like that."

He kisses me, and his tongue tangles with mine. I can feel how much he wants me as his erection presses against my thigh.

With each passing second, my need for him grows more intense. His fingers dance across my skin, leaving goose bumps in their wake.

Asher fully undresses, then positions himself between my legs, waiting at my entrance. His lips are on mine, and I feel the mood shift to something else, something deeper. He pours his emotions into me as he slowly slides inside. I can barely hold back another moan as my body adjusts to every thick inch of him. He stretches me open, claiming me.

His hips thrust forward in rhythm with his thumb rubbing circles on my clit. This man is fucking me senseless, and I can feel the pleasure quickly building inside me.

"Tell me what you want," he whispers against my neck, leaving kisses along my jawline.

"I want all of you. Forever," I whisper breathlessly, arching into him even more desperately than before.

He slams into me, filling me completely, taking both our breaths away in one swift motion.

"Will that make you happy?" he asks as his movements slow.

"Yes," I whisper, knowing my future is with him.

He pulls back just enough to look at me, his golden-brown eyes almost glowing. "Consider it done."

With another thrust, he fills me so fucking perfectly that I cry out, my body clamping around him like a vise. That's all it takes before I completely fall over the edge. Guttural groans release from my throat, and Asher follows behind me.

The sun's fully up now, and we're a breathless mess. He smiles as he pushes hair out of my face. I want to be lost in this little world with him, just like this, forever.

"I love you so much," I whisper as tears of happiness prick my eyes.

"Fuck, I love you too, princess."

"Thank you for being a relentless asshole and never giving up on me," I say with a laugh.

"You wouldn't have it any other way," he tells me, playfully nibbling on my neck.

I thread my fingers through his hair, knowing he's the only man who's ever successfully been able to get under my skin. And I'm so damn thankful.

37

ASHER

ONE WEEK LATER

My pulse pounds in my ears as I carefully guide Billie along the sandy path. One hand rests on her lower back, and the other gently grips her wrists. She's blindfolded, laughing nervously but trusting me entirely as we move closer to where it all began.

"Almost there," I whisper against her ear, feeling her pulse increase under my thumb.

The ocean breeze whips her hair around, and I can taste the salt in the sea air.

"I'm trying very hard to be patient," Billie says playfully.

"Appreciate that, princess," I say softly, my voice slightly shaking from nerves.

I've rehearsed this moment countless times in my mind, yet nothing prepared me for the overwhelming rush of anticipation that fills me right now. I nearly pinch myself to make sure I'm not dreaming.

The gentle crash of waves against the shore grows louder as we step onto the soft sand. I stop, turning Billie carefully so she faces the endless ocean. This spot is exactly how it was all those years ago, under the twilight sky that paints everything in hues of lavender and gold. I kissed Billie right here, unaware that it would set off a chain of events that would define both our lives.

I swallow hard, my heart hammering against my chest, then gently untie the blindfold. Her eyes flutter, adjusting to the fading sunlight, and when she sees the blanket on the ground and the familiar stretch of beach, recognition dawns on her face.

"Ash ..." she breathes, eyes shining as she looks at me, realization hitting her. "This is ..."

"The place where *we* started," I finish, my voice rough with emotion. I take both of her hands, looking deeply into her eyes. "Billie, this spot is so fucking special to me. It's where I first felt brave enough to kiss the pretty, dark-haired girl with blue eyes who stole my heart that summer. And even after all these years, every moment spent with you feels exactly like that first kiss—full of hope, excitement, joy, and a future of possibility."

Her eyes glisten with unshed tears, a soft smile touching her lips. The wind gently lifts her hair, framing her beautiful face, and I inhale before slowly sinking to one knee on the blanket.

Her breath catches, eyes wide in disbelief. "Asher ..."

I pull the ring box from my pocket, holding it out to her with trembling fingers.

"Billie Calloway, my princess, my ice queen, you're my past, my present, and my entire future. I spent so many years trying to protect you, watching from afar, hoping you'd find true love and happiness. I never realized that happiness was us, together. Loving you is the easiest, most natural thing I've ever done."

She laughs softly through her tears, holding my gaze, her hands covering her mouth as she processes the moment.

"It feels like I've waited my entire life for this," I whisper, emotion thick in my throat. "To be yours in every possible way. You've been my biggest challenge, and you are the love of my life. Billie, will you please make me the happiest man in the world and marry me? What do you say, Ice Queen?"

She bursts into laughter as tears stream down her cheeks. "Yes, Asher Banks. A thousand times *yes*."

She drops to her knees in front of me. Her eyes shine with joy, admiration, and love that have always been reserved just for me.

Exhilaration overwhelms me, and I pull her into my arms, kissing her fiercely. She presses against me, and I know at this moment, we're exactly where we're meant to be—together, just like this.

I pull back from the kiss, breathless and grinning as I carefully slide the ring onto Billie's finger. She admires it for a moment, then looks up at me with that familiar sparkle in her ice-blue eyes that never fails to take my breath away.

"This ring," she murmurs, brushing her lips against mine again. "It's my grandmother's."

"Yes." I nod with a smile. "I spoke to your father before London."

Her brows knit together. "And?"

"He was *very* excited," I explain.

"And my brothers?" she asks.

"They know. And I got threatened with pain and murder, per usual."

She chuckles. "Harper?"

I gently kiss her. "I thought you could tell her yourself when we return to the city next week."

She wraps her arms around my neck, kisses me, then laughs. "I'm in shock."

"You're so damn pretty." I brush my thumb against her cheek, then pull her back onto the blanket with me.

We stare up at the sky.

"I remember making wishes on stars with you," she says, interlocking her fingers with mine.

I turn my head toward her, and we face one another. "I did too. And I wished that you'd be mine. Guess you're proof that wishing on stars works."

She smiles, gazing into my eyes. "I don't deserve you."

"Oh, princess, but you do. And I'm going to spend the rest of my life making sure you know that while making you happy." I pull her close again, burying my face in her neck and breathing her in.

The world around us fades away as I lose myself with the woman who's owned my heart since the first moment our eyes met.

"Thank you for choosing me," I whisper against her mouth, capturing it.

"You chose me. And now it's us against the world."

"I fucking love the sound of that," I tell her, deepening the kiss. "So damn much."

38
BILLIE

ONE WEEK LATER

I'm standing in Asher's charming little garden behind his townhouse, and the warmth of spring wraps around me. I'm excited about what I have planned, and I can't wait to share the good news with Harper. The patio is strung with lights that twinkle like stars, casting a soft glow over the table I set for our double date. I laid out a crisp white tablecloth and placed a small vase of freshly picked flowers on top of the table. Tea lights are waiting to be lit.

I promised Harper we'd get together once everything settled down. It's only been two weeks, and I've been avoiding the public and paparazzi, so tonight, we're hosting Harper and Micah in Asher's home. He cooked blackened Alaskan salmon, green beans, and garlic-roasted potatoes. The savory aroma already wafts through the air.

I can hardly contain my excitement about the evening. This isn't just about dinner; it's about sharing some big news—our engagement. I can't wait to see the surprise light up Harper's face,

The Boss Situation

her expressive eyes widening in disbelief. I've imagined it so many times.

I move into the kitchen, watching Asher comfortably move around as he works on the food.

"I'm so nervous about tonight," I confess, glancing at him.

He wipes his hand and moves closer until his lips brush against mine. A flutter of warmth spreads through me.

"Don't be. It's going to be great."

"It's this guy she's dating," I say, unable to hide my skepticism. "Something isn't right."

"Harper is smart. She'll figure it out," he replies, biting my earlobe playfully, a low growl rumbling from his throat.

"Mmm, don't do that," I protest. "This might turn into something el—"

"Billie!" Harper's voice cuts through our moment as she flings open the side gate, her energy bursting into the garden like a ray of sunshine.

I see her from the back door, that's wide open. I steal a quick kiss from Asher before meeting her outside.

Harper pulls me into a tight hug, her warmth wrapping around me like my favorite fall sweater.

"Where's your date?" I ask, glancing behind her.

Moments later, Micah strolls through, his dark hair tousled and those piercing green eyes locking on to mine. I feel a jolt in my stomach. Asher must sense it, too, because as he approaches, his hand rests firmly on my back, grounding me.

"This is Micah," Harper says, beaming as her boyfriend walks toward us, radiating a cocky confidence that's hard to ignore.

It makes the hair on the back of my neck stand up straight. I try to shake the feeling.

"Hi. I'm Billie. Harper's best friend," I introduce myself, extending my hand, my heart pounding in my chest.

He takes it, pressing his lips against my knuckles. It's unsettling.

"I'm Micah. Nice to see you again," he says.

"Again?" A nervous laughter releases from me.

Asher's grip tightens on my shirt, and I feel his unease.

"I was at the Calloway Carat Gala. We spoke there when you were with Prince Louis," Micah explains, his voice smooth. "We discussed artifacts from the *Titanic*."

"Oh, right. Of course," I reply, forcing a smile that doesn't quite reach my eyes.

"And I'm Asher. Her future husband," Asher interjects, his tone flat and serious, slicing through the chatter. "I'd appreciate it if you didn't fucking look at her like that."

Asher's words hang in the air, and he's not playing games.

"You're always making jokes," Harper says playfully to Asher.

Her laughter is light, but I catch the flicker of concern in her eyes. This is already not going how I imagined.

I think she knows Asher *wasn't* joking. It's obvious by how tightly his jaw is clenched and how his eyes don't leave Micah.

Right now, I need to walk away and get my mind right.

"Oh, please, have a seat. Would you like some wine?" I ask, trying to keep my voice light as I juggle the swirling tension.

"Honestly, I'd love some wine," Harper replies, her smile bright as Micah settles in and pulls her onto his lap, wrapping an arm around her waist possessively.

"Great. I'll be right back." I escape into the house, sucking in a deep breath.

When I'm in the kitchen, I grab a bottle of wine, and Asher enters behind me.

"What the fuck was that?" he demands, his voice furious, each word dripping with disdain. "I fucking hate this guy."

A chuckle escapes me, but it fades quickly. "I know him, but not from the gala. Somewhere else."

Asher leans close and speaks loud enough for me to hear. "If he looks at you like that again, I'm going to fuck him up."

"Stop." I laugh. "Best behavior," I remind him, removing the cork from the bottle.

The Boss Situation

I shoot my fiancé a wink, wanting to desperately change the mood as I return to the table. My heart sinks at the sight of Micah's tongue deep in Harper's mouth.

"Wine," I announce, and they break apart as I fill our glasses to the rim.

The rich red liquid swirls like my thoughts as I light the tea candles on the table. Harper sits next to me and clinks her glass against mine, her eyes sparkling with excitement, oblivious to how her date is staring at me.

"To love and friendship," Harper says, holding up her glass.

"Cheers," I tell her, my voice barely above a whisper as I clink my glass against hers and then Micah's. The sound dings in the quiet night.

Asher returns, carrying a platter of seafood-stuffed mushrooms. The aroma of garlic and herbs wafts through the air, and my mouth waters with anticipation.

"I've heard things have been going well at Bellamore since London," Micah says casually, leaning back in his chair with a relaxed grin that doesn't quite reach his eyes.

"Ah, right. We don't discuss business after five p.m.," Asher replies with an unmistakable *don't fuck with me* edge in his sharp voice.

For a moment, I'm reminded of how much of an unapologetic asshole he can be, and I'm grateful for it.

"Anything else interesting you'd like to discuss?" Asher asks.

The atmosphere shifts, and an uncomfortable silence stretches on.

Micah licks his lips with a teasing chuckle that feels forced. "It's been a very long time, Asher. How's your sister?"

"*Dead*," he snaps back, his voice dripping with disdain as the word hangs in the air. "Thanks *so* fucking much for asking."

"Oh," Harper gasps, her face turning pale as the conversation spirals out of control. She knows how Asher is. "I spoke to my brother this morning, and I told him the good news."

"Which is?" Asher asks as if he didn't just put Micah in his place.

She beams at her boyfriend, holding up her hand like a trophy. The diamond ring catches the light and sparkles brilliantly.

"We're engaged!" she squeals.

My heart sinks as I force a grin. "Oh my God, Harp. Congratulations."

In an impulsive move, I slide my ring off my finger and hand it to Asher under the table, who quickly tucks it into his pocket before they notice. The gesture feels bittersweet, but I can't steal this moment from her. I rise and wrap my arms around Harper tightly, almost suffocating her with my joy and anxiety.

"I'm so happy for you," I say as tears glisten on her cheeks, reflecting the candlelight like tiny stars. "This was your dream."

"I know," she replies, her voice full of emotion. "How lucky are we that we both found our person?"

"So lucky," I say, meeting her eyes, searching for any sign of doubt, but all I see is confirmation.

I want to support her even if my gut screams otherwise.

"Congratulations," I say to Micah, refusing to get too close to him.

Asher doesn't say anything.

My insides twist like a pretzel as I watch Harper gaze at Micah with that foolishly in love look. He leans in for another kiss that feels rehearsed and hollow. It's a performance more than a connection. It strikes me as odd, like a familiar song that's being played slightly out of tune. I see through him, but I refuse to let my mask slip in front of this man, not now, not ever.

"It was like a dream," Harper gushes as she relives the proposal. "The opera had just finished, and I was crying because it was so beautiful. Then Micah got down on one knee and proposed, right there in the middle of the crowd." She twirls a loose strand of hair around her finger.

"Wasn't that your dream proposal?" I ask, giving her a smile that feels too wide.

"Yes," she whispers, lost in the memory.

"I remember us gushing about it. Let me guess. The show was ... *La Traviata?*" I tease.

"Actually, no. It was a rendition of *Romeo and Juliet,*" she replies.

"Hmm. A tragedy," Asher interjects, unamused. He leans forward, openly judging Micah with his brows furrowed. "Why that one?"

He's onto him too. His reaction is proof that I'm not imagining this.

"My love for *her* is undying," Micah replies, his gaze sliding toward me. It's uncomfortable and unsettling, like a flame burning too close to the skin.

I quickly look away, my skin crawling under the weight of his stare, every nerve ending screaming for me to escape. I gulp down the rest of my wine and refill my glass, desperately trying to find the courage to finish this night on a positive note, but darkness falls around us.

"I have the perfect bottle of champagne to celebrate the special occasion," I say, my voice a little too cheery for my own liking. "It's your favorite, Harp."

Her eyes light up at the mention of the almond champagne I have flown in from France. It's the kind that sparkles like liquid gold. I brought a bottle for us to celebrate my engagement. It's okay though. I'll find another time to tell her when it's just us.

"I'll be right back," I say.

She practically bounces in her seat with excitement.

I slip inside the kitchen to grab it, my heart racing with anticipation and dread. I'm a roller coaster of emotions. Just as I reach for the bottle, a warm body presses against me from behind. Strong arms wrap around my waist with an intimacy that sends alarms ringing through my head.

I freeze when I realize it's not Asher.

"Now you're into it, unlike last time," Micah whispers into my ear, his breath hot and laced with a menacing undertone that makes my stomach churn. "It happened almost like this, didn't it? All those years ago?"

Panic floods my system as his hands slide down my stomach. He holds me in a suffocating grip that makes me feel trapped in my own skin, like a deer caught in headlights. Everything around me blurs as fear takes over. Suddenly, I'm thrust forward, and I hear Micah grunt behind me. My body locks up, and screams echo in my mind, but they never make it past my lips.

"What the fuck do you think you're doing?" Asher's voice cuts through the chaos.

He yanks Micah away from me with enough force to knock the breath out of him. The champagne bottle slips from my grasp. It's almost as if time slows as the bottle shatters against the floor. A cascade of glass shards scatters everywhere, glinting dangerously in the dim light of the kitchen.

Asher's fist connects with Micah's face, and a sickening crunch echoes in my ears. He punches him over and over again. Micah grins up at Asher like a deranged lunatic, unfazed by the violence. It's as if he thrives on this, feeding off it like a parasite.

"What are you doing?" Harper shrieks, her voice piercing the space as she rushes forward in a panic. She pushes Asher away from Micah, and her movements are frantic, desperate even.

"She came onto me!" Micah points at me. His expression twists, and he acts like a victim.

"No! I did not!"

His audacity rushes through me like an electric shock. I grab Harper's arm, trying to pull her away from this monster, away from this terrible man whose eyes are full of malice.

"Let me go, Billie!" she snaps, jerking away from my grasp.

She bends down, her fingers brushing against Micah's bruised face. Trust for him glimmers in her eyes. "I'm so sorry," she offers. "Let's leave, baby."

"Harp, don't go with him. *Please!*" My voice rises in desperation, a frantic plea. I reach for her again, wanting to pull her away from him forever.

"Don't touch me, Billie," she says sharply, grabbing Micah's hand with loyalty that makes my stomach turn. "He predicted you'd ruin this for us. You can never be happy for me, can you?"

"Harper, please." Tears stream down my face. "You can't be serious!"

I glance at Asher. His fury is unhinged, eyes wild with rage as they follow Harper and Micah out the door. Asher looks at Micah like a predator watching his prey escape.

And then it hits me like a freight train.

My world fragments into a million pieces, and each memory is a shard that cuts deep.

"I will destroy him," Asher vows through gritted teeth. His voice is dangerous as his promise hangs heavy in the air.

"He took my best friend." My lip quivers.

Asher pulls me into his arms, holding me tight against him while nuzzling into my hair, like he's trying to shield me from the pain, the betrayal.

"He asked me if I remembered him," I whisper.

"It happened almost like this, didn't it?"

The memory flickers like a faulty light bulb, distant yet hauntingly familiar.

My mind races through memories I buried. A fog lifts just enough for clarity to break through.

"Speak to me, princess. Please." Asher's voice is urgent yet soothing.

"I think he used to stalk me." The words tumble out before I can stop them, each syllable heavy with a weight I never wanted to carry. "There was this one time in my twenties when a man did the same thing to me, but …" My voice trails off as horror washes over me again, flooding my mind with memories I'd rather forget. "I couldn't describe him to anyone. It all happened so fast; it was like trying to catch smoke with my bare hands."

Asher holds me tighter, his arms like a fortress as sobs tear through me like glass.

"Shh. It's okay. It's fine. You're safe, my love." His voice is calm.

"Ash," I say between gasps for air, the panic clawing at my throat, "I don't think those texts were from Josh. Or the flowers in London." The realization is gut-wrenching, a sickening twist that makes my stomach churn. "I think they came from Micah."

The thought is like ice in my veins.

"And now he has Harper."

My heart races as I look into his eyes, searching for answers. "All those years ago, he threatened to steal everything I loved if I told anyone what he'd done."

The memory of his voice sends shivers down my spine.

I can see the anger bubbling beneath his surface.

"Billie, I'm so sorry. I should've protected you fro—"

"This isn't your fault," I whisper.

Asher cups my face in his hands, his touch warm, steadying me against the fear that threatens to take me under.

"You stayed in Stanford that summer while I came back to the city."

My mind races back to that time. Harper had insisted I go to the police, but how could I describe someone whose face was lost in shadows?

"My brain blocked it all out. I'd forgotten completely."

"I love you," he whispers gently, placing soft kisses on my forehead, each a tiny promise to protect me from the past that still haunts me. "It's not your fault."

"I love you," I say, crying.

"Shh." He soothes me again when fresh waves of panic hit me, the memories crashing over me like waves. "He had no right to touch you—ever."

Rage simmers in his voice as he vows between clenched teeth, "I will chop off every single one of his fucking fingers when I find him."

"We have to get Harper away from that man. I'm so worried about her," I say through ragged breaths.

Asher cracks his knuckles, eyes hardening into steel determination. His jaw is set. I haven't seen him this angry for as long as I've known him.

"He will pay for what he did to you—past and present." His words are a vow.

I shake my head. "He's going to hurt her, Ash. I can't lose Harper even if she hates me right now."

The fear of something bad happening to my best friend is almost too much for me to bear.

"Fuck!" His growl is feral, a primal sound that reverberates in the quiet room. "What has Harper gotten herself into?"

Asher turns off the oven and sets the food on top of the stove.

"Come on," he says, grabbing my hand and guiding me around the glass and spilled champagne.

"Where are we going?" I ask.

He stops and wipes the tears from my cheeks. "To find Brody."

EPILOGUE
BRODY

I slide the keys to the blacked-out Dodge Charger into my palm, feeling the cool metal against my skin. The freshly waxed paint gleams like a challenge. As an adrenaline junkie, I look forward to putting this classic muscle car through its paces.

"I'm sorry, Easton," I say, waving at the camera, knowing he doesn't have access to his phone right now, thanks to Weston. "I will take care of her."

I sink into the leather seat, holding the steering wheel tight, feeling rebellion in my grip. I crank the engine, and it roars to life. The rumble vibrates through my bones, and a smirk touches my lips because it's music to my goddamn ears.

I rev it, feeling that raw energy beneath my fingertips, allowing the engine to warm up before I take off.

Now, this is the kind of chaos I've craved. I'll have to give Harper a thank-you when I track her down.

With a swift push of the clutch, I slide it into first gear. I zoom away, the automatic garage door rises, and the street opens up. The tires scream as I peel out of the parking garage, hanging my hand out the window with a middle finger blazing. I leave rubber and smoke in my wake. My only regret is not getting to see my dear cousin's reaction when he watches the replay of that video.

I steal a glance in the rearview mirror and scan for anyone following me. In the back seat are my two duffel bags. One's crammed with clothes; the other is filled with weapons and ammo. I can never be too careful in this game.

Right now, I'm searching for trouble, and it's spelled H-A-R-P-E-R.

I can already picture her smile, that cocky little grin that says she knows more than I do.

But she doesn't. Not this time. Not when it comes to Micah. Or what she desperately needs.

Once I'm out of the city, the open road stretches before me. I grip the steering wheel a little tighter, feeling the power surge as I accelerate. The glowing lights fade away, and I drive toward darkness.

Harper can run, but she cannot hide. Not from me.

Oh, I will find her, like I always do.

Continue Brody & Harper's story in
THE BODYGUARD SITUATION
https://books2read.com/thebodyguardsituation

Need more of Asher & Billie?
Download an exclusive bonus scene featuring them here:
https://bit.ly/theboss-situation

WANT MORE OF LYRA?

The Billionaire Situation Series

The Wife Situation

The Friend Situation

The Boss Situation

The Bodyguard Situation

The Hookup Situation

The Hockey Situation

Fall I Want (connects with this world)

Valentine Texas Series

Bless Your Heart

Spill the Sweet Tea

Butter My Biscuit

Smooth as Whiskey

Fixing to be Mine

Hold Your Horses

Very Merry Series

A Very Merry Mistake

A Very Merry Nanny

A Very Merry Enemy

Every book can be read as a stand-alone, but for the full Lyra Parish experience, start at book 1 of the series because they do interconnect.

KEEP IN TOUCH

Want to stay up to date with all things Lyra Parish? Join her newsletter! You'll get special access to cover reveals, teasers, and giveaways.

lyraparish.com/newsletter

Let's be friends on social media:
TikTok 🖤 Instagram 🖤 Facebook
@lyraparish everywhere

Searching for the Lyra Parish hangout?
Join Lyra Parish's Reader Lounge on Facebook:
https://bit.ly/lyrareadergroup

ACKNOWLEDGMENTS

When I pick up a random novel, I flip to the acknowledgments first. I want to know who was so important in their journey that they felt they should always be memorialized in the pages. These words, the ones you're reading right now, will always live with this book, and I find that so special.

I am grateful to my readers who continue to show up for me no matter what. Some have a hard time describing why my books are what they love. It's a vibe. An experience. It's like taking a photograph of a cool place and showing a friend, knowing that they're not getting the whole experience unless they live it themselves. Describing it or showing someone isn't comparable. Many of you *get* my books, and I mean, REALLY get them. You feel the magic in the pages. And that makes you so special.

Thank you for being here. Thank you for reading my words. Thank you for supporting me and encouraging me to continue forward. Thank you for the kind messages, exciting emails, and tags on socials. I will never, ever, be able to thank you enough. I often have to pinch myself to make sure this is real. If it's not, I don't want to wake up.

Big thank you to my lovely assistants Erica Rogers and Kate Kelly. The two of you make my life so much easier, and I adore you! Thank you for being a part of my DREAM TEAM! Hope y'all are getting ready for our red carpet premiere.

Thank you to Bookinit! Designs (Talina & Anthony) for creating these covers for me! Thank you to my editor, Jovana Shirley, for being so kind and helpful. Thank you to my proofreader, Marla

Esposito. Super big thanks to beta bishes (Brittany, Mindy, Lakshmi, and Thorunn). I'm pretty sure Lak claimed Asher, y'all. She forced me to write this here. LOL! The four of you always make me feel much better before sending out ARCS. Thank you for loving my words. It takes a team to help me publish on this wild schedule, and I'm forever grateful for everyone's help!

Thank you so much to my ARC readers and all the bookfluencers! You are always eager to help with cover reveals and excited to spread the word even when I surprise release most books. Thank you, thank you! I hope I make this as fun for you as you make it for me. Mwah! So freaking appreciative.

And as always, a big thank you to my hubby, Will (Deepskydude). Wow, sometimes I think back to all those years ago when I was writing and didn't know if I could do this author thing. You're the only person who watched me burn to nothing and rise from the ashes. Thank you for always being here. I love you!

ABOUT LYRA PARISH

Lyra Parish is a hopeless romantic obsessed with writing spicy Hallmark-like romances. When she isn't immersed in fictional worlds, you can find her pretending to be a Vanlifer with her hubby and taking selfies with pumpkins. Lyra loves iced coffee, memes, authentic people, and living her best life. She is represented by Lesley Sabga at The Seymour Agency.

Made in United States
Cleveland, OH
28 April 2025